Subsurface

Cary Wolfe, Series Editor

67 *Subsurface*
Karen Pinkus

66 *Making Sense in Common: A Reading of Whitehead in Times of Collapse*
Isabelle Stengers

65 *Our Grateful Dead: Stories of Those Left Behind*
Vinciane Despret

64 *Prosthesis*
David Wills

63 *Molecular Capture: The Animation of Biology*
Adam Nocek

62 *Clang*
Jacques Derrida

61 *Radioactive Ghosts*
Gabriele Schwab

60 *Gaian Systems: Lynn Margulis, Neocybernetics, and the End of the Anthropocene*
Bruce Clarke

59 *The Probiotic Planet: Using Life to Manage Life*
Jamie Lorimer

58 *Individuation in Light of Notions of Form and Information Volume II: Supplemental Texts*
Gilbert Simondon

57 *Individuation in Light of Notions of Form and Information*
Gilbert Simondon

56 *Thinking Plant Animal Human: Encounters with Communities of Difference*
David Wood

55 *The Elements of Foucault*
Gregg Lambert

54 *Postcinematic Vision: The Coevolution of Moving-Image Media and the Spectator*
Roger F. Cook

53 *Bleak Joys: Aesthetics of Ecology and Impossibility*
Matthew Fuller and Olga Goriunova

52 *Variations on Media Thinking*
Siegfried Zielinski

51 *Aesthesis and Perceptronium: On the Entanglement of Sensation, Cognition, and Matter*
Alexander Wilson

(continued on page 220)

Subsurface
Karen Pinkus

posthumanities **67**

University of Minnesota Press
Minneapolis
London

Portions of chapter 2 are adapted from "Afterword: They Would Have Ended by Burning Their Own Globe," in *Ecological Form: System and Aesthetics in the Age of Empire*, ed. Nathan K. Hensley and Philip Steer, 241–48 (New York: Fordham University Press, 2018).

Copyright 2023 by the Regents of the University of Minnesota

All rights reserved. No part of this publication may be reproduced, stored in a retrieval system, or transmitted, in any form or by any means, electronic, mechanical, photocopying, recording, or otherwise, without the prior written permission of the publisher.

Published by the University of Minnesota Press
111 Third Avenue South, Suite 290
Minneapolis, MN 55401-2520
http://www.upress.umn.edu

ISBN 978-1-5179-1478-3 (hc)
ISBN 978-1-5179-1479-0 (pb)

Library of Congress record available at https://lccn.loc.gov/2022040908

The University of Minnesota is an equal-opportunity educator and employer.

Contents

Acknowledgments	vii
Introduction	1
1. Cracks	21
2. Extracting	57
3. Burial	89
4. Surface Depth	125
5. Subterranean Futures	177
Notes	189
Bibliography	207
Index	215

Acknowledgments

Work on this book was supported by a Social Science, Humanities, and Arts Residential Fellowship from Cornell University's Atkinson Center for Sustainability. My cofellows and the staff provided a perfect environment for the early stages of writing. I made significant progress on the manuscript as a Leverhulme Visiting Professor at Cambridge University, and for this and so much more I am extremely grateful to Robert Gordon and John David Rhodes, to the staff of CRASSH, and to the colleagues I met during my time in the United Kingdom. I was fortunate to present some of the material at Northwestern University (on invitation of Nasrin Qader and Domietta Torlasco), Rice University (Dominic Boyer and CENHS doctoral fellows Maureen Haver, Kevin MacDonnell, Clint Wilson, Magnús Örn Agnesar Sigurðsson), Ohio State University (Dana Renga), Cornell University (Edmundo Paz-Soldán), Temple University (Kimberly D. Williams), University of St. Andrews (Silvia Caserta), University of Lancaster (Nigel Clark, Bronislaw Szerszynski, Hazel Napier, and all the participants in the Subsurface Futures workshop), and University of Glasgow (Rhys Williams).

Thank you for feedback and pushback—Oliver Aas, Pierpaolo Antonello, Douglas Armato, Hans Baumann, Richard Block, Anna Blume, Alexander Close, Valeria Dani, Laurent Ferri, Paolo Gabrielli, Pauline Goul, Gökçe Günel, Nathan Hensley, Cymene Howe, Teresa Jordan, Robert Kaufman, Naveeda Khan, Leo Levy, Graeme Macdonald (who showed me around Aberfoyle), Natalie Mahowald, Tim Murray, Matias Oviedo, Christoph Rosol, Hilary Schor, Pascal Schwaighofer, Jason Scott-Warren, Joy Sleeman, Philip Steer, Benjamin Steininger, Allan Stoekl, Jeffrey Testor, Rochelle Tobias, Cary Wolfe, and Derek Woods. I am certain to have forgotten others, and to them I offer sincere apologies and strata upon strata of appreciation.

Introduction

The subsurface—as distinguished, perhaps, from the surface or atmosphere—has long been defined, described, or narrated as a realm of both mystery and possibility. Humans, animals (some companion, some virus-spreading, some ingestible protein), and plants (increasingly studied for their spirituality, communalism, and complexity) live on the surface (surrounded by other living and nonliving entities). The surface is the place of our dwelling, of property boundaries, of consumption of goods. It is also the place of the combustion of fossil fuels, an activity that, as we now know, led to "unintended consequences" in the atmosphere. In short, the surface is the place of "life itself" or, to paraphrase the "father of modern geology," James Hutton (1726–1797), on the surface the inert matter of the subsurface is replaced with plant, animal, and "intellectual beings" (Hutton 1795, 4). Or, as critical geographer Nigel Clark (2018, 15) puts it, "The establishment of a structural divide between molten interior and clement, sunlit crust . . . might be seen as the Earth's first and greatest binary gestures, the planet's primordial 'operational differentiation.'" The surface, we might argue, is the rightful place of the Anthropos even as we have devised considerable fantasies about life below and above us.[1] That our species attempts such mastery over the earth and sky should come as no surprise. We have messed up the planet (by which we traditionally mean the surface), so now our only hope is to store our detritus in or engineer these other realms until such time as we can get our act together and then, perhaps, we can unburden them, rewild them, or return them to their supposedly pristine states. That is one response. Perhaps this is no better than the idea of giving up and colonizing/terraforming some virgin space off-world. But we did not know, so can we really blame ourselves? And then, which portions of that broad category "Anthropos" is primarily responsible? This vexing question lies at the heart of much work in posthumanist environmental studies.[2]

Whether we experience guilt, anxiety, or no affective response whatsoever, we humans now find ourselves on one side of an ever-enlarging crevasse that is opening in the earth and dividing us from our former selves and others who existed before climate change (that is, for my purposes, before circa 2000 when the idea became broadly and widely popularized). What began as a fracture only a few decades ago has now begun to pull apart so rapidly that we are fast losing sight of the other side. In the very recent past, terms like *emergency* or *extinction* have come to be used to describe the present or near future. "Public awareness" was raised through Hollywood or independent films, documentaries, cli-fi, and events such as the COP meetings in Copenhagen ("failure"), Paris ("success"), or Glasgow ("failure" again) or through well-publicized disasters that scientists admit are made much more likely in the time of rising greenhouse gas concentrations, while preferring not to attribute direct cause to any single event. There have been hundreds of academic conferences and publications, as well as hundreds of conversations about the carbon footprint of such conferences.

There is still, even in the educated general public, muddied thinking about causes and effects. I insist on the specificity of climate change as a global and highly heterogeneous set of transformations linked to the accumulation of greenhouse gases in the atmosphere. Carbon dioxide emitted from a refinery in Texas has consequences far beyond the circumscribed radius of the flue stack. It is added to a cumulative accounting that is melting ice in Greenland and rising sea levels in the Indian Ocean, intensifying drought in the Middle East, and floods in the Far East. And so on. As might be expected, the U.S. public sphere is mostly centered on the symptoms affecting its own so-called exceptional lands and people. No doubt the fossil fuel producers are quite happy to perpetuate confused thinking about the distinction between air quality and greenhouse gases even among the educated. We still stubbornly measure greenhouse gas emissions in national terms, alongside statistics on population and economic productivity. In Paris in December 2015, almost all the nations of the world signed a nonbinding accord pledging to certain INDCs (intended *nationally* determined contributions) toward a goal of net-zero carbon emissions by a target date in midcentury. Moreover, mitigation strategies operate along decadal timescales—incompatible with the timescales of geological change and yet, now, also with the accelerated pace of tipping points and feedback loops.

Awareness is supposed to lead to action, but by whom and for what end? One might call awareness for its own sake bad faith or bad politics or naive hope. A violent rupture within ourselves and (depending on our age) with a very recent past is one of the foundations of this book. The fracture, while it is surely a metaphor, one so banal that it even makes an appearance in that graceless Hollywood product *The Day after Tomorrow* (dir. Roland Emmerich, 2004), is also a geological condition that does not obey precisely predictable conditions of linearity or temporality.[3] In August 2020, a renowned glaciologist studying crevasses in Greenland fell to his death into one—the metaphor cracking open.

Subsurface asks the reader to move between texts and proposals from the warming present and, primarily, literary narratives written in the nineteenth century, when coal was the dominant source of fuel in Europe and North America, before the so-called discovery of oil.[4] To be sure, there are few novels about oil. Since oil is sucked from the ground, it is harder to visualize its proper home. As Timothy Mitchell clarifies, the organization of labor around oil—which requires far fewer workers than mining coal—is more mechanized. Workers do not descend into the spaces of oil deposits. Coal, then, resulted in worker solidarity in ways that oil does not. Amitav Ghosh (2017, 74–75) writes that "oil is inscrutable in a way that coal never was: the energy that petrol generates is easy to aestheticize—as in images and narratives of roads and cars—but the substance itself is not. Its sources are mainly hidden from sight, veiled by technology, and its workers are hard to mythologize, being largely invisible." Or, as Michael Ziser (2011, 321) puts it in his contribution to an influential *PMLA* series on reading energy into or behind literary texts, coal opens itself to novels of labor, whereas oil "is a liquid that in the classic scenario flows to the surface almost of its own accord, gushing out in all directions and proposing an entirely different relation among labor, consumption, and the body. Once struck, oil returns so much more energy than is required to produce it that it becomes an effectively costless substitute for human and animal labor." Likewise, oil narratives tend to stress what happens on the surface to change human life rather than the subsurface, as makes perfect sense.

Recent studies address fictions or cultural productions immersed in the world of oil extraction and production, again mostly on the surface itself. These works and studies—both falling into the area of energy humanities—are of crucial interest, naturally. They have helped and will continue to help put our relations with fossil fuels into perspective. My own focus here is rather on structure and form as they might offer us glimpses into the subterranean that are shaped (distorted?) by our own desires to see and not see, to confront geology or justify our own positions. I am particularly interested, then, in moments when an author or a reader might posit a traditional narrative structure that is then undone or fractured or reveals itself to be less fruitful than one might have hoped.

Coal haunts the novels I read here, whether it drives the plot or is disavowed entirely. Case in point: the explorers who undertake a journey to the center of the earth in Jules Verne's 1864 eponymous novel are apparently in it for pure discovery. They navigate what are mostly open passageways, as if carved for them. They come upon exposed seams of coal—there, potentially, for the taking. The narrator, Axel, exclaims, "A coal mine!" His uncle replies:

"A mine without miners."
"Who knows?"
"*I* know," replied the professor firmly. "And I am certain that this tunnel cutting through the coal seams was not made by human hands. But I do not really care whether it is nature's work or not. The time for dinner has arrived. Let us therefore dine." (Verne 1992, 100–101)

So the men move on. The novel functions like a compromise formation: these characters are far too engaged in the spiritual aspect of their work to think of exploiting resources, but then, the reader supposes, someday someone else might come along and do so. That act would not have been—would not be—possible without the purely scientific impulse of the men, yet as we will see, the novel simultaneously posits the absolute uniqueness of the voyage.

If the narratives I have chosen may be fairly homogeneous in their allowance for penetration into hollowed caverns beneath the earth's crust, I still ask my readers to move between genres, periods, and affects. One might expect to learn something from a recent literary work of cli-fi that projects us into a (usually) dystopian future, in accordance, that is, with our expectations. *Subsurface* is a work of discord inasmuch as it projects the reader back (and then forward) in time. Naturally, as we are currently living in a period of transitions—energy transitions, climate thresholds, precatastrophic events, positive feedback loops, tipping points—and we should not be surprised to find *transition* in sci-fi or cli-fi marking a period in the past (from the point of view of the narration) signaling to the reader how or why things are no longer as they were in her time. For me, though, *transition* might signal an intellectual copout: it patronizes me (in the past), as if I would not have the imagination or courage to travel forward in time and experience some degree of loss there. The nineteenth century is fundamental as it represents, let us say, an opening toward the subsurface in geological knowledge and in the extraction of those fuels, formed in the earth's deep past from natural matters, that will turn out to pose a radical threat to the existence of life as we know it on the surface.

Readers and writers of the nineteenth century (and beyond) might well have suspected that industrialization or even capitalism writ large would lead to pollution and devastation of ecosystems or perhaps "the natural world," in the broadest terms. Moreover, before circa 2000, readers might have found solace in fictional narratives or escape from their own presents. They may have projected themselves into a series of social interactions, dressed in period costume, inhabiting stately homes, or riding the rough seas, or visiting the far future when the workers toil underground while the upper classes enjoy fresh air and abundant free time.[5] Or they may have measured their distance from fictional protagonists. Those readers—whatever their degree of immersion in the lifeworld of the novel—would not have been expected to think about or with the fracture, about living in a world, reading "after" climate change. Of course, one might choose to not think or pretend to not know. Yet even presumed knowledge could make one guilty or liable in certain legal narratives.

Think of a case brought by the State of New York Attorney General's office against ExxonMobil in 2017. If it could be proven, through access to company documents, for instance, that the oil giant was aware of the effects of greenhouse gas emissions, they would have a responsibility for damages beginning at the point of such awareness, lawyers argued. To be clear, this was far from the first attempt to address climate change through the courts. The New York case alleged damages to shareholders, through a "fraudulent scheme" that "in effect erected a Potemkin village to create the illusion that it had fully considered the risks of future climate change regulation and had factored those risks into its business operations."[6] The deception "exposed the company to greater risk from climate change regulation than investors were led to believe," according to the prosecutors. They worked with a lower cost of carbon, and when employees of the company pointed out this fuzzy accounting, company financial officers instructed these employees not to disclose the discrepancy. The result was that "Exxon Mobil made its assets appear significantly more secure than they really were, which had a material impact on its share price." Rather than repurpose existing environmental laws, or claim standing for present or future humans (as has been attempted in other litigation) or even for the environment itself, New York Attorney General Letitia James invoked the Martin Act, a law written in 1921 to protect investors from unscrupulous businessmen. The basis of the suit, on behalf of said shareholders, was to prove that the company had gained knowledge, that they could project into the future and imagine unimaginable disturbances to life caused by the rise in greenhouse gas emissions and global average temperatures. While they were not obliged to do anything about this under existing laws (presuming they could have done something beyond, say, shutting themselves down, which would have left them vulnerable to suits under the same act), they were obliged to clearly disclose their finances. They knew (and they acted for their own benefit), yet in the end they also won the suit that the judgment termed "hyperbolic" (*People of the State of New York v. ExxonMobil Corp.* at 3). Exxon agreed with the judge that the prosecutors did not prove they had wronged shareholders and they promised to "continue to invest in researching breakthrough technologies to reduce emissions while meeting society's growing demand for energy." The judge's findings did not "absolve ExxonMobil from responsibility for contributing to climate change through the emission of greenhouse gases," but the court felt that the state had not proven by a preponderance of the evidence that the company had misrepresented its finances (3).

Bracketing the question of evidence in this specific case, to the degree that greenhouse gases are invisible and the effects of climate change uneven, unpredictable, and nonlinear, we are dealing with forms of fiction. Of course, the subterranean has been the dominion of much speculation and fantasy from ancient myths of plutonic life to fully functioning cities to contemporary critical theory around the question of resource extraction. In many ways, the subsurface is still a frontier. Recently, for instance, scientists have discovered that the earth's core may in fact be cooling much more quickly than previously thought, with possible implications for life (millions or billions of years in the future).[7] Or perhaps the earth's barycenter, which moves in accordance with the moon's orbit and the sun's gravitational pull and is distinct from its geocenter, puts strain on the lithosphere, causing the movement of the tectonic plates.[8] In short, as one hears from time to time, we apparently know more about the moon and Mars than we do about the subsurface of our own planet.

In one sense, literary works—narrative and language—may undo geocognitive certainty. But there is a risk that this undoing could devolve into mystification or renunciation, something like a trick or a heroic gesture of decoding that would grant some grandeur to one's own reading or the object of study. The subsurface, far from being natural, might be thought as a process of conversion into what Marc Augé (1995) calls a nonplace (*non-lieu*), a place that can no longer be defined as relational, historical, or concerned with identity. From the point of view of philosophers Gilles Deleuze and

Félix Guattari (1987), such a nonplace, a place of rhizomatics or plateaus, might also be ideal for deterritorialization. Leaving the subsurface open means that it is rife for a kind of exploitation but also for a romantic notion of potentiality, both of which are problematic in their own ways. Fossil fuels reside in the subsurface, hence one of the slogans of the climate change activism movement is "Leave it [oil] in the ground!"[9] Deep time is made legible to human perception where we contemplate strata through man-made or natural cuts. Some forms of geoengineering or climate engineering involve returning carbon to underground spaces (left open by oil drilling, perhaps) or to solid formations for indefinite storage—"down there."[10] As the place of extraction and storage, the subsurface is ripe with and for exploitation but also for potential new forms of governance and new forms of commons. Historical and futuristic fantasies condition bureaucratic or technocratic management of a rapidly changing climate, as they might also productively undo a kind of certainty of the same. Roughly speaking, when we produce and consume fossil fuels, 30 percent of the emissions remain in the atmosphere, about 20 percent are taken up by the ocean, and the rest are taken up by the land. One of the biggest questions facing scientists is how much (more) the land can absorb. Biodiversity is crucial to the land as sink, whether it is to be enhanced or even sustain its current rate. For the nonscientific imagination, a sink (in French *put*, "well") implies "under" rather than "in" the ground. Out of sight, out of mind . . .

Since carbon dioxide and other (short-lived) greenhouse gases such as methane are, in the broadest sense, natural, and since the release of carbon dioxide into the atmosphere from rocks where it is trapped as they breakdown is a natural phenomenon, it is possible to conceive of climate change as primarily a temporal problem of such vastness that it cannot be grasped in the everyday languages of either scientific research or common sense. To acknowledge this, however, opens, again, a risk of fundamental abdication. Holism—or one earth or the Gaia theory—is a form of discourse that pushes us to think of interconnectedness, but this is also mystification that can make us oblivious to the local and the discontinuous. So how can we (ethically) pose the immensity of climate change's space or temporality so that thought does not turn into cavernous nihilism? This bedrock question troubles this book, erupting to the surface, often when it is least welcome. I ask how we think we know this realm, how we represent it to ourselves as a way of pointing toward the kinds of laws that we develop to govern it, and so on. There is, of course, an enormous difference between oil (mysterious, liquid, pumped up by technological means) and coal (taken out by humans from what we perceive as empty cavities, more closely tied in our imaginations to dirt, labor, and industrial history).

Literature from before climate change may grant us access to the subsurface, exposing forms of instability. Arthur Conan Doyle's *The Lost World* finds a group of Englishmen exploring a vast buried plateau. A journalist—a reluctant adventurer and unimpeachable witness—writes dispatches from the front to serve as the alibi for narration itself. The bravery of the men—led by the brilliant but unhinged Professor Challenger—allows them to explore parts of the earth that the reader, settled in an armchair in a London club, can only fantasize about. The same journalist, Malone, reappears in Doyle's story "When the World Screamed," again collaborating with Professor Challenger, who digs deeper than any man before him to force the earth's feminine, oozing core to acknowledge his presence. The reader may travel in multiple directions: in Verne's *Twenty Thousand Leagues under the Sea* to the depths of the ocean floor; in his *Mysterious Island*, colonists drill into granite with homemade dynamite and therefore have access to layers of geological history that might otherwise remain inaccessible. In Verne's 1877 *The Black Indies* (*Les Indes noires*, also translated as *The Underground City*, *The Child of the Cavern*, or *Coal City*), we descend underground and then horizontally across an astounding range of landscapes, almost as if we are fracking the rock as we read. *Journey to the Center of the Earth* is one of Jules Verne's most famous narratives, a work of literature, written not for scholars, clerics, or members of the court, not for the bourgeoisie or landed gentry, but for boys, primarily, as part of the author's collection of "extraordinary voyages." In addition to scientific works of his roughly contemporary geologists such as

Jules Férat, Coal City, illustration from Jules Verne, *The Black Indies*, 1877.

Louis Figuier, whose *The World Before the Flood* was widely known by nonspecialists, Verne was certainly influenced by both the text and illustrations of Dante's *Inferno*, as well as by the early modern geological speculations of Georgius Agricola and Athanasius Kircher, whose eleven-volume *Mundus subterraneus* (1664–1665) includes lengthy descriptions of volcanoes as well as numerous illustrations.[11] These may take the form of cutaways that allow a viewer to peer into the mountain and observe the mechanisms of the magmatic chamber and the steam valves while maintaining a safe distance. Verne draws liberally on poetry and prose books, in other words, to narrate ocular testimony of spaces and places apparently seen only once before (by a sixteenth-century alchemist) but never before recorded; never written and so never read.

Up is good, down is bad, as we know, in even the most primitive forms of human cognition. Deep ecology is more radical, apparently, then superficial attempts at sustainability. The "underland," as in the title of a creative nonfiction book by Robert Macfarlane (2019, 13), "is vital to the material structures of contemporary existence, as well as to our memories, myths and metaphors." One reads down into a work to bring truth up to the light. The narrative of descent is a key trope in Western literature: katabasis, an ancient trope, is a story of a search for knowledge, often followed by an ascent, often tinged with an element of spirituality. Orpheus, Odysseus, Aeneas, Christ—these are all figures associated with katabasis. More subtly, this is also a rhetorical term, within a short piece of writing or poem, where the movement down is compressed into a line, say, or even a few words. Put otherwise, it is a poetic term with narrative implications.

The male hero may be granted access to the subsurface in a dream or dreamlike state. He may embrace his father and learn of the fate of the fatherland. Dante does away with the dream-frame, but filial and patriarchal relations certainly structure his *Inferno*. The descent is often sanctioned by the father, or it is a gift for a son, and if the feminine is found down there, it is either purely maternal or Amazonian or monstrous. Perhaps there is nothing more to say on this topic, since we would fully expect gender to be a significant distinction in narrative forms, especially when we were confronting something so elemental as geology. And yet, it is also far too easy to forget or naturalize sexual difference when we face other cuts or other binaries.

Literary readings, then, may open up the subsurface beyond the binary of simple mastery (we can control it) or renunciation (we cannot do anything there), beyond the extremes of exploitation (what we do down there has no effect up here, so all activities are fair game) and conservation (leave it alone). Narratives and language move between the subsurface and surface, sometimes revealing unexpected cracks, drifts, and openings. Geognosy is tied to certainties (and sometimes undone by uncertainties).

Each chapter of *Subsurface* turns around one primary text from the nineteenth century, the period of the rise of fossil fuels, but also of narrative itself, in Peter Brooks's (1992, 6) terms, expressive of "an anxiety at the loss of providential plots," a time when the "sacred masterplot" no longer holds, a secularization that begins earlier and develops over time into an "obsession with questions of origin, evolution, progress, genealogy." Indeed, in defining *plot,* Brooks (11-12) turns to the *Oxford English Dictionary,* citing the four primary definitions of the term:

1. (a) A small piece of ground, generally used for a specific purpose. (b) A measured area of land: lot.
2. A ground plan, as for a building; chart; diagram.
3. The series of events consisting of an outline of the action of a narrative or drama.
4. A secret plan to accomplish a hostile or illegal purpose; scheme.

He then comments:

There may be a subterranean logic connecting these heterogeneous meanings. Common to the original sense of the word is the idea of boundedness, demarcation, the drawing of lines to mark off and order. This easily extends to the chart or diagram of the demarcated area, which in turn modulates to the outline of the literary work. From the organized space, plot becomes the organizing line, demarcating and diagramming that which was previously undifferentiated. . . . Plots are not simply organizing structures, they are also intentional structures, goal-oriented and forward-moving. (12)

In short, without making too much of *plot* as piece of land and *plot* as series of events, we can still acknowledge, with other critics, a degree of intimacy between the (under)ground and narrative. Lyric poetry might yield complementary readings. As Devin Garofalo (forthcoming) puts it, the nineteenth century is the period of "(1) the historical co-emergence of the normative lyric subject and the human species as geologic agent; and (2) the anthropomorphic genealogy of literary criticism called 'lyricization' as it dovetails with Sylvia Wynter's account of the 'over-representation' of colonial man as 'the human itself.'"[12]

In the nineteenth century, because the question of the earth was still a matter of intense debate, even scientific authors faced unique opportunities and challenges. They had to imagine life on the globe at another time. For instance, the geologist Gideon Mantell surveyed contemporary Sussex in 1827, writing in *Illustrations of the Geology of Sussex*: "What would be the nature of an estuary, formed by a mighty river flowing, in a tropical climate, over sandstone rocks and argillaceous [i.e., clayey] strata, through a country clothed with palms, arborescent ferns, and the usual vegetable productions of equinoctial regions, and inhabited by turtles, crocodiles, and other amphibious reptiles?" (quoted in Rudwick 2008, 149). This same sort of musing led Henry Thomas De La Beche to produce what is one of the most famous images of the period, *Duria Antiquior*, a more ancient Dorset, first as a watercolor and then as a series of lithographs.

Édouard Riou, who illustrated for Jules Verne and geologist Louis Figuier, was certainly influenced by this theatrical composition featuring a struggle between two giant prehistoric marine reptiles, an ichthyosaur and a plesiosaur. As in an aquarium, *Duria Antiquior* serves as a window to observe what occurs above and below the surface of the limpid water. The scene is simultaneously pure fantasy yet based on real fossils discovered in the South of England by

Henry Thomas De La Beche, *Duria Antiquior,* 1830. Watercolor.

Mary Anning, one of the few women scientists of the time. And it is this quality of contradiction or simultaneity that the reader may extract from narratives. I invoke it not as a form of enchantment that has been lost now (although that might be one mode of enjoying a work like Jules Verne's *Journey to the Center of the Earth*) but rather as a tension that exists in the plot of the novels I read here and that, ultimately, conditions their outcomes. At least if one reads them in a certain manner.

One of the principal functions that ecocriticism assigns, retroactively to literature of the past, is to describe landscapes, species, and systems now under threat. A nineteenth-century realist novel that draws us into a world with fairly predictable patterns of weather might evoke nostalgia or despair or, more recently, solastalgia. This term was coined by Glenn Albrecht (2006) to refer to the sense of loss of a place that is under attack by environmental degradation (and I would emphasize climate change above all). The philosopher describes solastalgia as a "lived experience of the loss of value of the present" that leads to a "feeling of being undermined by forces that destroy the potential for solace to be derived from the immediate and given. In brief, solastalgia is a form of homesickness one experiences when one is still at home" (35). To counter this feeling, then, we might enjoy poetry that extols the virtue of a particular bird that reappears outside our window with regularity during a certain week of the year. Readers might seek comfort in the control that literature can exercise even if or as they lament loss and recognize damage of their surroundings, and it is their position later in time that allows this kind of reading. Yet it may be that ecological writing of the sort that elicits such reading was always already a literature of loss—that is, from the very moment the pen was laid to paper in the service of description that landscape or environment was already past and mourned. One might summon various literary theorists to support this perspective, but for now I leave it open— one possible way into reading lyric or narrative from "before" climate change that will not necessarily shift when we consider what will happen "after."

What conventions—visual, linguistic, epistemological—grant us access to what lies below? This is the central question of chapter 1, titled "Cracks."

Chapter 2 deals with extraction, a word that lately seems to have taken over literary and cultural studies, whether one is trying to find it as a hidden theme in works, repositioning it as a key term to understand colonization, or actively attempting to decolonize it. Like *Anthropocene*, *extraction* is everywhere in titles of courses and books and dissertations so that one might prefer to avoid it, yet one also wants to engage with it. In considering how we take resources from the ground, it makes sense to begin with the way we represent the subsurface. Without doubt, the modes of thinking the subsurface that allow us to take resources from down there are, to a degree, violent, imperialist. The rhetoric of extraction is virile. At the same time, the removal of resources leaves hollowed-out spaces that may haunt our imagination. We are forced to question the standing of the slogan "Leave it [oil] in the ground!" Conventional narratives are haunted by a fear of resource scarcity, whereas now we are dealing with an excess of invisible gases gathering in the atmosphere. What kinds of ideological and ethical stances that govern "our" right to what lies below, where the scare quotes are clearly meant to do a lot of work, referring to settler colonialism, globalized energy markets, land grabs, and so on. How might "we" think differently, now, in the time of climate change, when we face a crisis not of scarcity of subsurface resources (as in the past) but an overabundance of invisible gases that accumulate in the atmosphere? While I am mindful of the reaches of *extractivism* as a broad synonym for *resource exploitation*, especially in regions of the poor, the colonized, or the underdeveloped, my double focus on geology and on the nineteenth century means that I do not often address the plight of forms of life specifically in such areas. In fact, it is precisely because the subsurface serves capitalism as a place to literally and figuratively take what it wants (and then bury it), or even for authors to imagine another world filled with endless resources, that it can be made to model some of the most heinous and durable forms of exploitation or to push them aside. Here I take as a point of departure Jules Verne's *The Black Indies*. This novel offers something close to a narrative of pure extraction as an idea, but one that is also completely unsullied by the dirt of coal.[13] If extraction should be allied with a story of taking out and using, in *The Black Indies* the taking is relegated to a long piece of text that seems out of place while the resource itself disappears, ephemeral and displaced, replaced, in fact, by a fable.

Burial is the subject of chapter 3. One ultimate fantasy about the subsurface is that we can store waste down there and forget about it. A growing body of recent scholarship on nuclear waste disposal considers how we might mark the surface so that future beings on Earth will leave our detritus undisturbed for long enough that it will cease to harm.[14] What about when carbon itself becomes classified as waste? It is estimated that carbon capture and sequestration (CCS or CCUS, if we add *use* to the mix) or carbon dioxide removal (CDR) could contribute significantly to holding down global temperatures. It is included in almost any scenario to avoid "catastrophic warming." But who will pay? And how much? We use terms like *oil fields* to refer to underground storage sites—that is, we deploy a comforting language that understands what is below to be a mirror of the land we know or aspire to have above.

E. T. A. Hoffmann's ([1819] 1969) story "The Mines of Falun" serves as the central point of reference here. Hoffmann's intervention is only one in a series stemming from a brief newspaper account of a real corpse buried underground that is embellished by Hoffmann (and others before and after) until the subsurface, glowing with strata of gems and minerals and creatures, becomes so much more than just a place of accidental death. The real corpse of the real miner, like others found preserved in peat bogs, for instance, or even Ötzi found in the Alps near the Italian–Austrian border, is an archaeological human remnant, a fossil that is uncannily us, but not us. As a figure, he raises a series of existential questions that are interesting in their own right. But more immediately for this project, he represents a living substance that passes time in the subsurface before being returned back to the place of ("our") life where it almost immediately perishes. Fossil fuels are also (former) life brought to the surface and then consumed. In this tale that captured the imagination of so many Romantics, in this fantasy, the subsurface appears as a realm with a separate temporality and its own laws and secrets. Common sense on the surface would push toward the idea that it is all in the head of Hoffmann's protagonist, Elis. The story leads us to think about how we might write history differently under the cloud of climate change and then to a consideration of the temporal illogics of the economics of carbon sequestration.

Chapter 4 focuses on a third way—that is, the shallow space between the surface and subsurface. On the more practical side, it has been argued that along with reduction of greenhouse gas emissions through the shift to renewable fuels and conservation, at least a partial solution to climate change is to enhance the soil as sink. Some understand the soil as dynamic and creative, even as a form of salvation. Some who push for investment in this sector would call their work biomimicry or carbon balancing. Such actions certainly sound less threatening than full-on geoengineering, but what kinds of narratives or fantasies do they imply? And do we have an ethical responsibility to undo such fantasies in order to confront climate change in good faith, beyond simply quantifying their efficacy or even their social costs? To be sure, the idea of the subsurface—

our geological past—as future is theoretically complex. Here—perversely, perhaps—I expand on a reading of Verne's *Journey to the Center of the Earth*, a story about (almost) full penetration, as I explore compromise formations that allow us to continue multiple practices and beliefs simultaneously.

In chapter 5, I speculate on possible futures for the subsurface. Dwellers might gather not to hide out after some definitive event like a nuclear explosion, not after the depletion of oil or other fossil fuels has led to anarchic violence on the surface, but as a place to be cultivated for new forms of collective life. One might speculate about thresholds beyond which the subsurface becomes terra nullius or wilderness and is thus open to grab or subject to protection. Science fiction—notably from the Victorian period—had already considered the subsurface a potential social utopia or dystopia.

It is rather easy to dismiss such work as mere fictions, but what are the consequences of thinking about the subsurface as choice, as home? Can it represent a space where we might renounce control of all resources and simply wait for the surface to return to what it was? The coming of coronavirus in 2020 and the pause it demanded suddenly made this kind of waiting scenario less implausible. What, finally, constitutes a proper relation between narrative and the subsurface?

Each chapter departs from a keyword or phrase. Weaving embedded narratives into a book with multiple perspectives can also help undo them. As long as we maintain a space below that is both colonized (we know it, we can control it) and simultaneously open (it may extend beyond our knowledge), we have hope in reserve. My aim is not to destroy this hope but to acknowledge it as such, as a space of ambivalence that deserves respect but is also symptomatic. If the voyage of the hero in a narrative of katabasis includes a return, back, as a form of redemption, I would not make such a claim for this book, its author, or its readers. My modest hope is to encourage readers to read and reread from where they stand, on the warming surface, to think differently.

To get at fantasies about what lies below the surface is also to think beyond the time of now on the surface, and this is necessary for decarbonization. The time is out of joint, because even those bodies wishing to act in good faith toward decarbonization must act within the commonsense time, Keynesianism, nonrevolutionary time, the time of compound interest and growth (perhaps, alas, with periods of recession intervening). There is no tolerance for exceeding this in the area of public policy. In the realm of narrative, almost anything is possible, and yet so many narratives bring us back to familiar territory. Perhaps escape from the tyranny of story arcs might be provided by microfractures or moments of broken logic, and these may be spaces for the emergence of new forms of life, of thought.

1
Cracks

Iceland, 1864

We are at the rim of the Snæfellsjökull or Sneffels stratovolcano, peering into the depths of the crater, about to embark on a journey to the center of the earth courtesy of Jules Verne.[1] After months of preparations, occupying at least a third of the novel, we are finally ready. How did we get here and what do we hope to accomplish? A trip to uncharted territory deep below the earth's surface will gain us fame, as it might contribute to general scientific knowledge, which in turn might be applied to industry or used for militaristic ends or to help bind together a community in peace. It might help us achieve a personal sense of satisfaction beyond the fame it will bring. Our trip might have begun as a voyage of exploration that has now evolved into an unmitigated obsession. If we return, we will be able to tell others about what we saw, advancing one or more relatively new branches of science—geophysics, stratigraphy, geognosy, or correlationism, for instance.

For Verne, who himself never made any descent down there, the earth is composed of hollowed-out spaces of various sizes. Verne's engineer—that is, his favorite sort of free-indirect-discursive alibi—imagines the following scenario in *The Black Indies*: "If, through some superhuman effort, engineers could lift up a thousand foot block from the Earth's crust, which supports all of the lakes, rivers, gulfs and waterways in the counties of Stirling, Dumbarton and Renfrew, they would find, beneath this enormous cover, a cavern so vast that the only comparison would be the famous Mammoth Cave of Kentucky" (Verne [1877] 1883a, 88). This particular geological formation, referenced elsewhere in Verne's works, serves as a felicitous model because humans can enter it, as if into a room

View of the Crater of the Great Geyser in Iceland, from Charles Lyell, *Principles of Geology,* 1830–33. Courtesy of Cornell University Library.

or forest grove. Incidentally, it is also specifically not a site of mining or excavating, so it bears no ideological baggage to intrude on a purely formal contemplation of immensity. In any case, in Verne the subsurface mirrors the surface, a trope that persists into the future, into science, and into political fictions. Below the property leased and owned by the mining companies of Scotland, families dwell, enjoying lakes and oceans, comfortable cottages, abundant food and light provided by mechanical disks, but without rain or other nuisances of the horrible climate above, including the polluting smoke from industry! However, one might also come upon seams of coal and impenetrable walls. The subsurface is both hollow and solid, navigable and impenetrable; these two contradictory geologies manage to coexist in literary writing.

Still, Verne's prose prompts a larger question: How do we know the subsurface? How can we measure, monetize, weaponize, control, or renounce the subsurface when we cannot actually go down there?

Jules Férat, *Lake Malcolm*, illustration from Jules Verne, *The Black Indies*, 1877.

The subsurface is ever more viable as a site of potential exploitation. Engineers have developed sophisticated ways of drilling wells, including the use of smaller and more precise drills fitted with digital sensors. These can send back information to data centers to allow for microadjustments by an operator off-site who never even interacts with the matter to be extracted. Fusion technology might soon allow energy companies to extract ancient heat from the core, far below the deepest hole ever drilled, the Kola Superdeep Borehole, now abandoned and topped by a rusty cap.[2]

As Jussi Parikka (2015, 14) reminds us, "our relations with the earth are mediated through technologies and techniques of visualization, sonification, calculation, mapping, prediction, simulation, and so forth: it is through and in media that we grasp earth as an object for cognitive, practical, and affective relations." And, he continues, "conversely, it is the earth that provides for media and enables it: the minerals, materials of(f) the ground, the affordances of its geophysical reality that make technical media happen. Besides the logic of ordering, we have the materiality of the uncontained, and the providing, that is constantly in tension with the operations of framing." It is hard to imagine that all this technology, along with experimental deep dives, will simply voluntarily self-annihilate or be shifted toward so-called good forms of underground surveillance.

Before confronting stories, we might contemplate images or develop an iconography or geomorphology of entrances, cracks, crevasses, and vistas. To be clear, it is completely understandable that in an attempt to achieve some sense of mastery over chaos, we may aspire to carve out clear divisions between the subsurface (the place of fossil resources to be extracted but also of sinks, of possible burial of carbon or waste), the surface (our home), and the atmosphere (the place of the accumulation of invisible greenhouse gases). An earth scientist might specialize in atmosphere, hydrosphere, lithosphere, or biosphere, but even amateurs might imagine these three primary realms with solid lines or fill them in with different colors, as in a child's drawing. Such two-dimensionality—the surface stacked on top of the subsurface—is a foundational visual trope

Lea Antonello (age 6), *Subsurface, Surface, Atmosphere*, 2020.

and it makes logical sense. We can embrace such images, simultaneously recognizing them as diagrams and as the possibility that subsurface, surface, and atmosphere interpenetrate one another, precisely, as complex systems.[3]

Put another way, Verne's *Journey* suggests the possibility of creating in words an equivalent to the cutaway or ant farm view, as in an engraving from the *Mundus subterraneus* by the German Jesuit Athanasius Kircher (1602–1680), spanning seven books and dealing with physics, oceans, water, heat, minerals, fossils, different rates of evolution, animals (dragons), machines for extraction, alchemy, and plants. The engraver manages to grant us a kind of universal access to another stratovolcano, Vesuvius. We get context and a minimal degree of perspective. The conventions of cross-hatching and realism of the terrain (land, sea, sky; flora and fauna) make it so that when the artist opens the mountain to allow us inside, while we appreciate that is not possible, we still associate the view with a high degree of scientific accuracy. To be sure, though, this image also follows a set of normalizing conventions: because the volcano

Illustration from Georgius Agricola, *De re metallica*, 1555. B669 Ag83, Rare Book and Manuscript Library, Columbia University Libraries.

protrudes upward, we are not (yet) below the surface of the earth, technically, and so what we witness is in some sense (only) a synecdoche for the larger opening(s) we would expect to find on a projected journey. The engraving represents a compromise between the empiricism demanded by science in the centuries to come and the speculations of an early modern approach to the earth, still inflected with ancient wisdom and biblical timescales, like Kircher's own prose, positing realities he himself never saw, expressed in traditional Aristotelian (Latin) rhetoric that is at once subjected to authorities of the past, tinged with imagination, and open to the future. Viewed today, this engraving appears quite aesthetically pleasing, divorced from the text itself, which is rather inaccessible.

Mount Vesuvius in Eruption, 1678, from *Mundus subterraneus*, 3rd ed. Courtesy of Cornell University Library Rare Book and Manuscript Collections.

We can imagine it framed as decor in the office of a modern volcanologist. In any case, its didactic function now is minimized, discounted, or completely forgotten. Or, in terms that make sense from the perspective of the history of science, the scientific truths Kircher's text explores have themselves become fossils, compressed under subsequent layers of information, observation, and analysis.

About a century later, James Hutton published his *Theory of the Earth* (1795) after visiting the Scottish coast. He divides the earth into three realms, but these do not correspond precisely to the arrangement—subsurface, surface, atmosphere—that I have sketched above. Rather, for him the important distinctions are between the globe, water, and air. His revolutionary text acknowledges the subsurface and deep time as simultaneously linked in scales beyond our perceptual abilities. Observation of the surface led him to speculation about the subsurface as heterogeneous and chaotic, conditioned by such variety that it could scarcely be comprehended:

> Now, if we are to take the written history of man for the rule by which we should judge of the time when the species first began, that period would be but little removed from the present state of things. The Mosaic history places this beginning of man at no great distance; and there has not been found, in natural history, any document by which a high antiquity might be attributed to the human race. But this is not the case with regard to the inferior species of animals, particularly those which inhabit the ocean and its shores. We find, in natural history, monuments which prove that those animals had long existed; and we thus procure a measure for the computation of a period of time extremely remote, though far from being precisely ascertained. (Hutton 1795, 18–19)

Hutton was accompanied to Siccar Point along the Scottish coast by his friend John Playfair, who wrote this often-cited passage concerning the revelatory nature of the visit:

> On us who saw these phenomena for the first time, the impression made will not easily be forgotten. . . . What clearer evidence could we have had of the different formation of these rocks, and of the long interval which separated their formation, had we actually seen them emerging from the bosom of the deep? We felt ourselves necessarily carried back to the time when the schistus on which we stood was yet at the bottom of the sea, and when the sandstone before us was only beginning to be deposited. . . . An epocha still more remote presented itself, when even the most ancient of these rocks, instead of standing upright in vertical beds, lay in horizontal planes at the bottom of the sea, and was not yet disturbed by that immeasurable force which has burst asunder the solid pavement of the globe. Revolutions still more remote appeared in the distance of this extraordinary perspective. The mind seemed

to grow giddy by looking so far into the abyss of time. (Playfair 1822, 4:80–81)

As these two Scotsmen attest, the subterranean opened itself to speculations for premodern authors but still left mysteries unsolved. There is a central part of the globe that we cannot/do not know. As dozens of men before and after Hutton recorded, the earth might be hollow or contain some vesicles or caverns or even be fully open after one penetrates two outer shells. It might be accessible through entrances at the poles (which are themselves not yet accessible) as in various theories of the hollow earth that persist as conspiracy or cultish myth even into the twenty-first century.

Scientists like the Englishman Humphry Davy (1778–1829), best known for the safety lamp he invented for miners to detect methane gas, had to account for the biblical flood (whether understood literally as a single event or as part of a series) and the discontinuity it must have meant between (at least) two epochs of the earth's formation. Yet they were also compelled to posit humans as the last and greatest creatures on the surface, creatures that were created by God in his image, forever. Geological progressionism stared them in the face: the oldest fossils found were those farthest down. There were no fossils of humans from the lowest strata. This could only mean that man came onto the scene later, and perhaps only after a series of destructive catastrophes. Thinking the earth's history meant making a series of cognitive compromises, preserving a certain order, and brushing over some observations that did not quite fit. Speculative or graphic images were and are important aids, but finally geology required narrative maneuvering, fiction-making.

An iconic representation of the earth's deep history, the geological column allows us to envisage the subsurface as mappable, made of up layers that we can date and know, regularized and fixed through the convenience of different colored bands, allowing the "eye to perceive in one glance . . . a synoptic summary of the inner construction of our globe," as the French geologist Louis Figuier ([1863] 1871, 11) puts it.[4] Variants of this column exist, some more simplified, some more completist, and some with more accurate senses

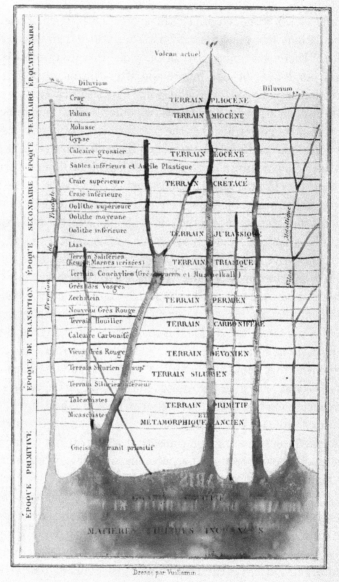

Geological column from Louis Figuier, *La terre avant le deluge,* 1871.

of scale. Some include images of exemplary flora and fauna within or adjacent to the bands. Some, like the chart of the International Commission on Stratigraphy, are so detailed that they include several different columns arranged side by side so that the eye must travel both vertically and horizontally to read history in the proper order. In any case, the form of the column develops as a vertical counter to the surface map, which is, of course, itself a two-dimensional rendering of three-dimensionality.

Some geological columns delineate epochs of varying (approximate) length by relative sizes, while others display each epoch with the same space on the page. Generally, they do not assume a viewer placed in a particular spot for optimal perspective or, put another way, the columns approach pure mathematics in a graphic form, and they are not subjective. Yet if we think about it, the geological column implies an eye or a viewer who can cut through layers of rock to see history and yet also know herself to belong to the top layer of the column, an inhabitant of the Holocene, and perhaps, very soon, of the Anthropocene, a new colored band to be added on in the very near future. The astute viewer might also realize that in order for this new band to respect the conventions of the column, and assuming it will be large enough to be visible (and perhaps large enough that, like the other epochs, its name and age could be inscribed next to it), the whole column would have to be rescaled so that it would no longer be useful in ordinary circumstances. It would not be easily reproducible in a book or as a slide for classroom use, for instance. We might indeed contemplate the paradox of the infinitesimal stratum representing our times and even acknowledge that at some point—if our current acceleration is any indication, at a point equally out of whack with the previous epochs—another colored band might take its place above ours, placed there by future beings who are enough like us to agree to carry on the representational conventions of the column.

Such contemplation in deep time is like when the narrator of Italo Calvino's ([1974] 1995, 175) story "The Petrol Pump" fills up his tank with gasoline and contemplates: "The days the Earth's crust reabsorbs the cities, this plankton sediment that was humankind will be covered by geological layers of asphalt and cement until in millions of years' time it thickens into oily deposits. On whose behalf we do not know." Calvino reminds us that the geological column represents a form of mastery where "we," the recorders of deep history, are simultaneously positioned, ontologically, at the top of the frame and yet able to see all the way down to, well, rock bottom.

Other geobiological forms existed in other colored bands beneath us as remnants of the hard parts of their bodies have been preserved. Modern science has confirmed this, building on debates that were waged, even into the nineteenth century, over the scientific and spiritual significance of fossils: as positive (animals embedded in rock) or negative (the hard and unmistakable impressions of shells, bones, leaves, and other material bodies) remnants of creatures that roamed the surface before human memory. Were fossils made by some fatty matter or *"materia pinguis,"* as the German philosopher, scientist, and alchemist Georgius Agricola suggests? Were their forms "accidental"? Were shell forms (not actual shells) made by the "tumultuous movements of terrestrial exhalations" or "heavenly bodies" (Lyell 1830, 25)? As Charles Lyell notes in his lengthy prehistory leading up to his secular view in *Principles of Geology*, those who followed Aristotelian teachings, who had learned that "a large proportion of living animals and plants were formed from the fortuitous concourse of atoms, or had sprung from the corruption of organic matter, might easily persuade themselves, that organic shapes, often imperfectly preserved in the interior of solid rocks, owed their existence to causes equally obscure and mysterious" (26).

Interestingly, and buried under stratum upon stratum of prose, Lyell (1830, 433) notes that earthquakes can certainly cause geological change. In fact, he notes, they may be credited with "the great derangement," also the title of an astounding and influential book on the limits of contemporary narrative in the face of climate change by Amitav Ghosh.[5] But even "the great derangement" of certain locales is still not enough: Lyell has to admit that only extraordinarily long periods of time can account for the vast differences one finds on the earth through observation.[6]

For us, now, the geological column offers a shorthand sense of time that is quite far from the actual way the earth has been built up and worn down in tectonic shifts, seismic events, meteoric collisions, and so on. It flattens out geographical difference. It signifies geological difference in a didactic manner, precisely by eliding detail. The colored bands of the column refer to but do not correspond with actual visible strata in the rock record and it is this mode—a mode of reference that seems graspable and yet eludes comprehension—that could cause particular discomfort, if we really think about it. Creationists today persist in using nonconformities against science.

To be clear, though, the disjunction between the regularity of a geological column and the chaos of observable reality is nothing new. For instance, Hutton (1795, 128) writes:

> The strata of the globe are actually found in every possible position: For, from horizontal, they are frequently found vertical; from continuous, they are broken and separated in every possible direction; and, from a plane, they are bent and doubled.

For Hutton, as with Lyell later on, such nonconformity is, again, proof of change over long swathes of time. Yet he cannot—one cannot—see change happen except in (science) fictions that conflate time. A widely known caricature finds Hutton confronting the rock face (that is, faces in the rock) head-on and at human scale: he can dialogue with his peers and refute their theories directly.

Lyell, who had a background in law, devised a way to question progressionism by suggesting that there was not enough evidence either way. He "split the picture in two," as geologist/historian Martin Rudwick (2008, 310–11) puts it. Rudwick argues that Lyell "claimed that 'the progressive development of organic life, from the simplest to the most complicated forms . . . though very generally received [and associated with Hutton, for instance], has no foundation in fact.' But he accepted that the human species was genuinely a recent arrival, while denying that this was 'inconsistent with the assumptions that the system of the natural world has been uniform

John Kay, *James Hutton,* caricature of James Hutton studying cartoon faces in the rock, 1789. Courtesy of Bbousman on Wikimedia Commons, made available with a Creative Commons BY-SA 4.0 license.

from the beginning.'" Fiction, even when extracted from scientific accounts and transposed to other contexts, allows for the coexistence of several different discourses. Of ambivalence. When confronting the origins of the earth, when asked to take a side for one school or another, Lyell could not very well have claimed a lack of interest, but instead, in what we might call a lawyerly manner, he shifted the terms of the debates from geology to theology, slightly misquoting Hutton, in a letter to his friend, Scrope:

> Probably there was a beginning—it is a metaphysical question, worthy of a theologian—probably there will be an end. Species as you say, have begun and ended but the analogy is faint and distant. Perhaps it is an analogy, but all I say is, there are, as Hutton said, "no signs of a beginning, no prospect of an end." . . . All I ask is, that of any given period of the past, don't stop inquiry, when puzzled, by refuge to a "beginning," which is all one with "another state of nature," as it appears to me. But there is no harm in your attacking me, provided you point out that it is the proof I deny, not the probability of a beginning. (Letter from Lyell to Scrope, June 14, 1830, quoted in Rudwick 2008, 323)

Lyell allows for both aqueous and igneous events, some violent (as had been observed in human history). This is not so different from the argument he uses to squirm out of the debate on progressionism. Yes, the organic world, and most notably plants, has been subjected to perpetual flux without any clear sense of directional change. The fact that humans are highly adaptive and yet we do not find their fossils in the deep subsurface means they have been on the earth for a relatively short time when compared with other species. But this fact also does not prove directionality. The novelty of humans is in their mental powers. With regard to their physical bodies, they are simply mammals like any other. By shifting focus, Lyell manages to keep open different narratives.

Another geological father, William Smith, author of the first geological map (of England), titled his 1817 book *A Stratigraphical System of Organized Fossils*. Previous authorities might have referred to rock formations, terrains, or mountains. Then, when scientists of the period wished to account for similarities in layers of rock across different areas of the world, they had to face the fact that such supposed correlations did not translate into easy or smooth histories but, on the contrary, implied a lack of linear universal change. To counteract such uncertainty, for instance, polymath Alexander von Humboldt (1769–1859) developed a mathematical formula to account for strata, a form of pasigraphy. This term refers to a writing system—let us say, the dream of a perfect or Adamic or Platonic language—in which each single concept (or in this case, each rock type) corresponds to a single symbol. Like mathematics, a pasigraphic system would be elegant, universal, and universally interpretable. Humboldt's dream attests to the powerful impulse to read and order strata or, better, to read and order the earth through strata.

Even such a formidable nineteenth-century writer as Karl Marx cannot seem to avoid a reference to strata. With the caveat that there are different Marxs and he is not producing a manifesto, in the chapter of *Capital*, volume 1, titled "Machinery and Modern Industry," he suggests that machines—considered as a rather homogeneous unit and not as specific modes of production—will not reduce human toil. They will only produce more surplus value: "We are only concerned here with striking and general characteristics; for epochs in the history of society are no more separated from each other by hard and fast lines of demarcation, than are geological epochs" (Marx 1967, 371). Just as Marx writes during a period when these epochs are coming to be named and dated, and just as they are rounded up to broad periods, he is not interested in exact historical events that come to define or be defined by particular tools or machines, so he resorts to the geological analogy in broad strokes.

Such views can and perhaps do coexist with the acknowledgments that strata are merely graphic indicators that flatten out difference of the type indicated by Manuel De Landa (2005) in his *A Thousand Years of Nonlinear History*—that is, sorting, settling, subsidence, and other disruptive events. In the nineteenth century, geological writing (still) tends to function geologically: that is, acknowledging, describing, and perhaps refuting earlier theories that lie beneath. Kircher may have been surpassed in many respects, for instance, but he is often invoked as part of a history that leads to any present assertions.

It is, nevertheless, a natural wish of a human in the present to see below and to fix a plaque: an epoch began here, and I, a being from the future, have been granted the vision of context to place this marker. The placement of a golden spike is a public documentary practice in contemporary geology. Technically known as a Global Boundary Stratotype Section and Point, or GSSP, the golden spike is a marker inserted into an exposed sedimentary stratum. It is literally driven into the rock face at the lowest level where a fossil characterizing a given geological period can be observed. Present to the senses when they are sharpened by knowledge, the rocky outcropping itself becomes exemplary of an epoch's fossil signature and its place in the earth's history. Yet the golden spike does not just record a singular fact or even just a complex of local or regional observations. Instead, its placement is correlated with observations across the planet, so that the periodization it exemplifies can be recognized by anyone anywhere. As one expert notes: "Before formally defining a geochronologic boundary by a GSSP, its practical value— i.e. its correlation potential—has to be thoroughly tested. In this sense, *correlation precedes definition*" (Remane 2003, 12). Within the contemporary scientific community, this activity of correlation is taken on by the International Commission on Stratigraphy, itself tied to the International Union of Geological Sciences. A subgroup of that commission continues to debate whether, how, and where to establish the boundary point at which the current geological epoch (the Anthropocene) can be distinguished from the previous one (the Holocene).

The column is in some sense an image devoid of life. Yet recent research in astrobiology has led to the discovery of new forms of extremophiles under the earth itself. Scientists have, for instance, explored gold mines in South Africa where miners had drilled small holes in the rock face and they have sometimes found small amounts of water containing microorganisms, which they analyze back on the surface. Endoliths can live inside rocks, in cracks or pores.

Chasmoendoliths can squeeze into fissures and cracks; euendoliths bore into rocks, forming tunnels that then preserve the shapes of the life forms. Cryptoendoliths are said to colonize natural cavities in porous rocks or in the tunnels left by euendoliths that move on or die. Technically, these life forms do reproduce, albeit very slowly. They are parasitic, but they may also coevolve to help coral, for instance. They have also been studied for their possible role in the extinction of dinosaurs. For now, it is enough to note their existence as a counter to the claim that no life exists down there.

When I look at the geological column, although I know otherwise, my instinct is to imagine that the band lowest down must have comprised early earth. Later it would have been crushed beneath subsequent layers, as if the core of the earth was initially small and over a few billion years sediment built on top (somehow forming a sphere). It is difficult to undo this cognitive pattern and to realize that the mass of the earth has shifted so drastically over such long periods of time that the column is an extraordinarily reductive model, but that strata are also literal. Jürgen Remane (2003) refers to psychological problems in confronting the chart. I might call them cognitive ones to distinguish them from the psychological problems confronted by characters in literary works, where the unconscious is in some way figured or positioned down there, as that which lies below—that is, the very space we are trying to map. All of this is complicated when we add to the equation the robust prose of Kathryn Yusoff (2018) in *A Billion Black Anthropocenes or None*. The subsurface is not only the place of metaphoric Blackness, she insists, although it is that. Rather, thinking about strata under the sign of race and racial violence undoes a mode of thinking the fossil and its ethos as unmarked, not just from time to time or when it might suit us, but in the most profound way, always.

The geological column allows the viewer or reader to take in deep time as some unified whole or identify the epoch that produces a particular fuel or argue about the relative safety or productivity of underground activities at a given level, for instance. We may summon the image of the geological column to give us a sense of order in the face of turbulence, fires, flooding, leakage, and so on. Early geologists recognized difference as "unconformity." Hutton writes of unconformities in his *Theory of the Earth* as "annals of a former world," a phrase taken up by John McPhee (1981) as the title of his Pulitzer Prize–winning narrative of a geological road trip across the United States. Undoing any fantasized unity and recognizing the chaotic nonlinearity of any distinctions seems crucial, facing the enormity of climate change.

Perhaps the geophilosophy of Gilles Deleuze and Félix Guattari can add an important dimension to our account of visibility and chronology. As readers will know, the two French thinkers focus a great deal of their writings on rhizomes, figures that traverse vertical and horizontal directions. They help disabuse us of our notions of borders as two-dimensional, as traced on a map that could, if large enough, be made to fit over a swath of land like a blanket. For the earth, in their thought, cannot be reduced to a flat surface but is, instead, filled with eruptions and sinks, seismic fracturing, and oozing. The rhizome might be considered a kind of map, but not one that traces existing structures. Rather, the rhizomatic map produces potential (chaotic) structures by fusing with them. *A Thousand Plateaus* is the second volume of *Capitalism and Schizophrenia*, the first being *Anti-Oedipus*. The chapters—plateaus—that make up the book are dated, but the authors do not expect them to be read in any particular order. The dates refer to a time when the concept under discussion reached its "purest incarnation," according to Brian Massumi (1987, xiv). The plateau dated 10,000 BC deals with Arthur Conan Doyle's Professor Challenger. This date, incidentally, falls slightly after the start of the Holocene, after the end of the last great glacial period, although the authors do not use these terms. They would not have because only fifty years ago there was no reason for a philosopher to consider a new geological epoch on top of the Holocene.

Plateau is, of course, fundamentally a geological term. Deleuze and Guattari (1987, 22) see *plateau* as constitutive of the rhizome. They note that anthropologist Gregory Bateson uses the word in the context of Balinese culture to "designate something very special: a continuous, self-vibrating region of intensities whose development avoids any orientation toward a culmination point or external end." They continue, "We call a 'plateau' any multiplicity connected to other multiplicities by superficial underground stems in such a way as to form or extend a rhizome." The revolutionary force of their project, then, is to literally overturn, or turn up, thought as solidified rocks that have settled into strata representing a mode of conceiving deep time as linear, set in stone, congealed consistencies—to scramble the uniformity of the geological column with its colored bands representing organized and flattened difference on a planetary scale, a project that is carried on in various affiliated works, including De Landa's idiosyncratic history.

Strata: A Geophotographic Fiction, by the American artist Robert Smithson, was published in the art journal *Aspen* (1970–71).[7] Under panoramic photographs of rock strata are lines of text that include full sentences, lists of materials, and free associations. The content of the strata in this piece do not correspond to events of the actual geological epochs listed on the left-hand side, lending Smithson's work an apparent lack of rigor in content. In *Strata*, Smithson is more interested in aggregation and form than in scientific accuracy. By virtue of its layout, *Strata* asks to be read like a narrative text, from left to right, from top to bottom, or, in geographical terms, from present to past. This mode of reading is not necessarily the same one suggested by the geological column, where one might read from bottom to top, perhaps in an attempt to grasp the scale of the Anthropocene, a term that was, again, not yet in circulation during Smithson's life, which ended in a plane crash while he was surveying his earthen ramp in Amarillo, Texas, in 1975.

To what degree are Deleuze, Guattari, and Smithson considering the strata real, lithic formations, and to what degree do they serve to clarify something else? And then, is there any point to drilling down (metaphor) to distinguish metaphor from other figures, such as analogy? Deleuze and Guattari (1987, 69) write of strata as multiple and heterogenous. "Above all," they note, "there is no lesser, no higher or lower, organization; the substratum is an integral part of the stratum, is bound up with it as the milieu in which change occurs, and not an increase in organization." They continue: "Furthermore, if we consider the plane of consistency we note that the most disparate of things and signs move upon it: a semiotic fragment rubs shoulders with a chemical interaction, an electron crashes into a language, a black hole captures a genetic message, a crystallization produces a passion, the wasp and the orchid cross a letter." They would abolish analogy and metaphor—all figures—in this case: "There is no 'like' here, we are not saying 'like an electron,' 'like an interaction,' etc. The plane of consistency is the abolition of all metaphor; all that consists is Real."

Yet metaphor is everywhere, often (mis)used to mean any figure of/in speech. It surrounds us like (analogy or simile!) a cloud, or like the environment itself, as a medium. In fact, metaphor may be, as Jacques Derrida (1974) develops most forcefully in "White Mythology," nothing less than philosophical writing, inextricable from thought in spite of the concept's pretensions to absolute, originary purity. Derrida follows Aristotle's *Poetics* in insisting that metaphor consists in giving a thing a name that belongs to something else. For Derrida, Aristotle's notion of metaphor is "a philosophical thesis on metaphor. It is also a piece of philosophical discourse the whole surface of which is worked by metaphor" (31). But even if we do not want to trace its genealogy back so far, or think beyond everyday use, we must acknowledge that metaphor is *the* trope—itself already a metaphor—of resemblance. Perhaps we should just leave it there and move on.

De Landa (2005, 28) writes that "urban infrastructure performs the same function of motion control that our bones do in relation to flesh. Adding minerals leads to explosion, increasing variety of animal and cultural designs." Notice here that De Landa signals analogy in his use of the phrase "the same function." He might have reduced this to "like" or "as." I have chosen this passage more or less at random and without implying any critique of the work. De Landa draws an analogy (interestingly, we do not say "draws a metaphor," perhaps because metaphor is, for us, more linguistic than visual). He does so in order to call attention to a parallel between the relation between the processes of mineralization of urban infrastructure and the human body—the classic macrocosm of humanism inserted into an idiosyncratic and decentered historiography. But De Landa cautions: "We must be careful when drawing these analogies, however. In particular, we must avoid the error of comparing cities to organisms, especially when the metaphor is meant to imply (as it has in the past) that both exist in a state of internal equilibrium, that is, traversed by more or less intense flows of matter-energy that provokes their unique metamorphoses" (28). The passage is confusing, to be sure. De Landa moves from analogy to metaphor without any apparent rigor or distinction. We might excuse him, since, after all, he is not precisely interested in language and certainly not in the difference of language that is literature. Rather, he simply wants to warn us about taking his comparison in a certain direction. Later in his text, he digs down to the sedimentary. He writes that "social stratum" is "clearly a metaphor involving the idea that, just as geological strata are layers of rocky materials stacked on top of each other, so classes and castes are layers—some higher, some lower—of human materials" (59). If social stratum is a metaphor, where does that leave us with regard to, say, revolutionary change? Deleuze and Guattari offer De Landa a way out of this merely tropic sphere with their concept of engineering diagrams—something not purely linguistic, yet not merely graphic. In essence, the Deleuzian diagram is itself a figure for a mode of comparing isomorphic processes. "When we say that class struggle is the motor of history," De Landa writes, "motor is a pure metaphor." And he continues: "However, when we say that 'a hurricane is a steam motor' we are *not* simply making a linguistic analogy; rather, we are saying that hurricanes embody the same diagram used by engineers to *build* steam motors" (58). The hurricane and the steam engine operate on similar thermodynamic principles. For De Landa, the link—engineered, if we like—is potentially much stronger than language, as I read it.

As one critic clarifies:

> "Geophilosophy" and the various "plateaus" of *A Thousand Plateaus* describe and prescribe the becoming-earth of philosophy and art, bearing in mind the first principle of ecology: namely, that all things assemble with other things in heterogeneous composites. To ecology's conception of life's interconnectivity and diversity, they add the "double articulation" of macro and micro (or molar and molecular) fronts, along with a flux of affects and intensities. Accordingly, earth

flows and forces give rise, on the one hand, to volatile, molecular haecceities (earthquakes, flash floods, tsunamis, stock exchange collapses, anarchic G8 demonstrations) and, on the other, to stable, molar assemblages (the Chinle formation, State flood canals and retaining sea-walls, the World Bank, the United Nations), that reterritorialize upon other, more stable assemblages (despotic infrastructure like the Three Gorges Dam, Federal Disaster Prevention and Relief Agencies, Transnational Corporations and Global Cartels), or yield to relative deterritorializations mobilized by less sedentary, more "nomadic" assemblages (portable or mobile "earth moves" architecture, anti-globalization coalitions, the Great Bear Rainforest alliance of ecological science, forest management, environmental activism, and aboriginal wisdom). (Chisholm 2007)

In such a discussion of the subsurface and forms, Doyle's Professor Challenger is a key figure, an antihero, for Deleuze and Guattari. Challenger, they suggest, understands as no other that the earth is "deterritorialized," a body without organs that is "permeated by unformed, unstable matters, by flows in all directions, by free intensities or nomadic singularities, by mad or transitory particles" (Deleuze and Guattari 1987, 40). However, at the same time, the earth is composed of strata that "consist in giving form to matters, of imprisoning intensities or locking singularities into systems of resonance and redundancy. . . . Strata are acts of capture. . . . They operate by coding and territorialization upon the earth" (40). To be sure, they are not performing a reading of a particular text. They are themselves mining a series of texts, like Smithson does in his *Strata* photo-essay, placing proper names, figures, and lines of dialogue into a great geological shifter where they may end up deformed and next to others. They are literally writing under the pressure and nonlinear chaos of deep time. So, their Challenger is not one that we could necessarily recognize from any one narrative or tie to any particular utterance or any specificity of literary language or of words uttered in a sequence as part of an analytic session where he would be caught out or cured.

Entrance to a mine. Illustration from Georgius Agricola, *De re metallica,* 1556. Courtesy of HathiTrust.

In contrast to the kind of access granted by the stratified column, we might find ourselves peering into a doorway, a threshold cut into the rock on the surface, beyond which we imagine anything we want: a gently sloping path, a hellscape, a precipitous drop, or a whole world just below the earth's crust. In an illustration from Agricola's 1556 treatise on mining, *De re metallica,* the viewer is shown a typical wooden structure for an entrance shed for a mine.[8] The miner can gain access to the riches below from level ground via a set of ladders or baskets controlled by pullies. A similar perspective is offered by the frontispiece to Jules Verne's novel *The Black Indies* where bourgeois tourists—men, women, children—are invited for an outing into a world below.

Jules Férat, frontispiece to Jules Verne, *The Black Indies,* 1877. Courtesy of Cornell University Library.

Entrance to the Onkalo facility from Michael Madsen, dir., *Into Eternity: A Film for the Future*, 2010.

And then, these images bear an uncanny resemblance to another modern one—a screen capture from the documentary on Finnish nuclear waste storage, *Into Eternity: A Film for the Future* (dir. Michael Madsen, 2010).[9] A tracking shot is made with the camera positioned on a truck entering a tunnel that begins on level ground and then slopes downward, deep into the bedrock. Once the facility has been filled with barrels of spent material nestled into salt that will expand over time, the tracking shot, one presumes, would be reversed. Then the entry door will be sealed off with concrete and the viewer/stakeholder will never think of—will never speak of—this facility again.

Perhaps there is nothing particular to be gained from pointing out a morphology of openings to the underground over several centuries, but these doorways are significant, I think, when viewed in the broader context of narrative. They represent liminal moments. First the reader is in the light, with the narrator, say, but as soon as the narrator crosses over, the reader must make some adjustments: she can no longer see, she is exposed to danger. She has entered a new realm. And the narrator or author cannot be satisfied with the representation of the doorway. Instead, the author must make a choice about what to show and which way to go, and that choice, by nature, will exclude others. This is basic narratology—nothing earth-shattering.

Columbus, Ohio, 2018

Early in the year, I visited the Byrd Polar and Climate Research Center at Ohio State University. One of the key figures there, Lonnie Thompson, is renowned for his research into melting glaciers. In the hallway, along with posters detailing various projects, hangs a world map indicating glaciers where the staff has drilled for ice cores, now stored in a vault. I noted there were no studies done in New Zealand, and my host explained that their research requires a certain type of glacial formation, one where the ice has settled vertically, essentially, and compactly. In instances when the ice settles in strata that are leaning or horizontal (or, let us say, more broadly, in a nonlinear manner), the methods for studying changes in temperature, greenhouse gases, or other chemicals in a cylindrical tube (a bit like the inside of a poster tube) over time do not function well, and this is the case in New Zealand, for instance, where I had visited an impressive glacier years ago. Similar problems face geologists who are exploring for resources. Rocks do not line up perfectly and they move and are expressed in different ways. For the methods of the paleoglaciologists to work, they seek out depth in one spot, but they also have to look in multiple directions. It is worth noting that these scientists sometimes make timescale diagrams that read from right to left. The point of their timescale diagrams, I learned, is to visualize temperature variations over one distinct period, say, the medieval warm period (c. 1100–1300). The fact that this same period is represented from left to right on other timescales (a map of human achievements, say) is not relevant to their research and, indeed, their methods may be tied to the fact that machines, such as seismographs, display the most recent data on the left. When I expressed surprise at one such poster in the hallway and wondered if it had been a mistake, my host noted that its purpose was simply to graph temperature differences and he saw nothing especially strange in the way they had represented these changes. Seeing what was, for me, a backward timeline reinforced how very entrenched modes of cognition and reading are tied to perceptions of geology, from our earliest days, and how difficult it is to think outside of narratives of progress.

Perhaps we could make an analogy between the Byrd Center timeline and forms of time travel in (science) fiction. If the point is to draw a contrast between two different moments in time or space, it may not matter how these moments are visualized. A writer can set the rules and demand that the reader accept leaps, although the best sci-fi does this organically, without didacticism. Writing in the late 1920s, so well after the time period of the key novels under consideration here but still "before" climate change, Olaf Stapledon ([1930] 2008, 13) posits a doubled narrator in *Last and First Men*:

> This book has two authors, one contemporary with its readers, the other an inhabitant of an age which they would call the distant future. The brain that conceives and writes these sentences lives in the time of Einstein. Yet I, the true inspirer of this book, I who have begotten it upon that brain, I who influence that primitive being's conception, inhabit an age which, for Einstein, lies in the very remote future.

As his writing moves forward into the far future—billions of years after the age of modern or "first" men—the author includes a number of timelines that are typeset vertically in his book with the earliest events occurring on top and the latest at the bottom. The verticality makes sense, especially for an inexpensive paperback: a horizontal timeline of any detail would be difficult to reproduce on a rectangular page and might require a foldout. But what about Stapledon's choice to ignore geology? I suspect he and his editors were thinking only of the sequence of events and did not stop to consider the cognitive effects of their reversal. Or more speculatively, the antigeological timelines are apparently the product of this second brain, one that has evolved to the point that, while it still produces prose narratives that we can read, it can signal its difference from us in a graphic form.

Bonn, Germany, Autumn 2018

The Intergovernmental Panel on Climate Change (IPCC, part of the United Nations Framework Convention on Climate Change) releases its report on 1.5°C and interest in climate change ramps up. If we have any hope of reaching net zero by 2050, if we hope to keep global average temperature rises below 2°C (keeping in mind that for various groups with more limited resources, a rise of 1.5°C already signals catastrophic change and that, at the time of this writing, we may have blown the carbon budget for both goals), we will need to do more than simply reduce greenhouse gas emissions and transition to non-fossil fuels.[10] That "more" had been called geoengineering until the very recent past, and for various constituencies this term was and still is a signal of actions considered immoral, impossible, exotic, or tied to corporate/industrial capitalism, making them insupportable as responses to the very corporate/industrial capitalism of the carbon economy.

One could critique or celebrate geoengineering (or climate intervention or negative emissions technologies, as some now prefer). It is worth noting that the broad category of "geoengineering" took and continues to take different forms along the current geophysical spectrum. One category that is less germane for this project is solar radiation management, intervention at the level of the atmosphere with cooling chemical sprays or gases to counteract the heat-trapping gases. Often grouped with solar radiation management (SRM) are technologies that might reflect the sun's harmful rays back upward (giant mirrors) or megaconstruction projects to increase the earth's albedo or the seeding of oceans to increase their ability to serve as sinks. Keep in mind that SRM—whatever its effects—is directed at mitigating temperature and precipitation (in a temporary fashion) but would not affect concentrations of greenhouse gases.[11]

A nation-state or a tech billionaire might finance the spraying of substances in the clouds to reflect the sun's heat back up or intervene at the atmospheric or tropospheric level. Some experts have recommended increasing surface albedo as mitigation. Although this action might take place, technically, on land, it is classed with other solar radiation management technologies since it involves actions to alter the amount of sunlight reaching the planet's surface. CO_2 emitted in the past and present has been and will continue to be taken up by the oceans (but the question of how much more and what kinds of collateral effects will result is up for debate—including techniques of fertilizing the ocean with iron or other nutrients) or by sinks on the land (trees, soil, and, again, the question is how much, how fast, for how long, and with what effects). We might like to think that so-called natural sinks on the surface can take care of carbon emissions, but recent reports suggest that tropical forests like the Amazon, for instance, may soon become sources of carbon. In any case, new research questions the effectiveness of forest planting as a form of offsetting. No matter what, some amount of greenhouse gases will enter the atmosphere and stay there for a relatively short time, with extreme negative effects. Some amount will stay in the atmosphere far beyond our own life spans. We may not like geoengineering in any form, but as Holly Jean Buck (2019) notes, it is not going away (although it may not go anywhere in particular). It seems rational to plan to undertake technological fixes to enhance natural sinks; as for artificial sinks, well, that is more complex. Finally, we might take carbon directly out of the atmosphere, recycle it for useful purposes, or bury it underground. It is this last form of engineering that is most pertinent for the present context.

In any case, the term *geoengineering* has gone out of favor, replaced by other, perhaps gentler, euphemisms, and the solar side of it has lost credibility even before it could develop.[12] Moreover, in its explosive 2018 report, the IPCC made clear that they are interested in the enhancing of natural sinks and in the removal of carbon dioxide emissions currently in the atmosphere. The report does not focus on capturing carbon at the site of power generation (sometimes called carbon capture and sequestration, or CCS), and, for various reasons, it does not go into detail about how the removal might work or how it might be financed. What is important to underscore is that all of the models they offer to stay under 1.5°C involve carbon dioxide removal (CDR). Some of the models call for the development of bioenergy with carbon sequestration and storage (BECSS) and removals through agriculture, forestry, or other land uses, which is to say, enhancing natural sinks for carbon. In any case, we cannot wish it away. So, if one objected to the solar radiation side because of its hypertechnology, one might well ask: Could we undertake carbon removal without digging down, without the violence of technologies of extraction, without displacing populations or causing massive and uncertain collateral damage, and without disturbing Mother Earth? A small number of treaties or experts call for governance to be developed before any form of CDR is undertaken, which essentially means waiting. But time is running out/it has run out. Others say that until a global high carbon price has been set—that is, until something has been done at the level of the surface to make carbon what I call a negative universal equivalent—nothing will be done. In any case, to the degree that carbon dioxide removal is understood as a form of geoengineering, is it seen as a last ditch measure, a set of actions to be done after we might have mitigated in other ways but did not, even if those other ways continue to be floated in the media in the context of green tech, hope, and start-ups—examples of human ingenuity, of the future.[13] Perhaps fluctuations of proposals in the policy realm in the recent past should not concern us in this present context. After all, the IPCC, like other regulatory bodies, functions within a narrow bandwidth using a technical language that communicates primarily to other experts. They make statements and then follow these up by noting the degree of certainty (low, medium, high, or very high confidence) in parentheses—a rather odd rhetorical strategy when considered from the point of view of linguistics or critical theory. They use graphs to model future scenarios. Generally speaking, such graphs are read from left to right. On the left is where we are now. The lines and arrows point to the right, toward possible futures in which we will or will not have undertaken certain actions. Some research bodies offer interactive, digital versions of their predictive charts where the user can manipulate the variables of scenarios to see how soon we will reach thresholds of extinction.

For the general public, to the degree that they are even aware of the IPCC, carbon pricing, think tanks, or start-ups working on carbon management, it may not be important to know the backstory or to follow the latest policy debates.[14] Nevertheless, I suggest that the logic remains fairly consistent: we are out of time; if we had done this only a few decades ago or even further into the past, we would not be facing the costs we now face. There really is no more time, but there is a sliver of hope if we act right now but we will not (we did not).

And yet, as I write, various experiments around carbon capture and sequestration are underway. Direct air capture methods, such as modular units developed by the Zurich-based firm Climeworks or the leaves developed by Klaus Lackner, could take up carbon anywhere on the planet—in "deserts," say, or on the outskirts of urban settlements—and even, if it were energetically economical, transported to other sites for burial or upcycling.[15] Here it is useful to recall that the Keeling Curve, the graphic representation of global atmospheric CO_2, is based on instrumentation positioned on a Hawaiian volcano with little foliage or human intervention. In theory, if enough carbon were taken up anywhere on the planet to be measurable, it would show up on Mauna Loa. However, for the most part, carbon dioxide removal is conceived of as a practice that should or would take place at the power plant itself—that is, in situ or at the flue stack. The technology has been mostly developed at coal-burning power plants and is therefore sometimes associated with the misleading term *clean coal*. Because it was (and to a great degree still is) financed by fossil fuel companies, even where such ties might be hidden until a veil is lifted by public interest or state-sponsored experimentation, it has been viewed as a cynical measure to allow them to persist rather than as a global strategy for decarbonization. Perhaps the focus shifted slightly around the time of the Paris Conference of the Parties (COP) in 2015, but most of the environmentalist-led carbon uptake projects springing up around that time seem to have petered out.

To this degree, CCS or CDR has been seen as a technology of the present that allows fossil fuel use to continue until it can be phased out at some point in the future. For some in the field, this implicit nurturing of the fossil fuel industries makes any form of capture suspect, and this is all the more the case with those forms of capture that help to push oil back up toward the surface (enhanced oil recovery) in wells that are nearly spent.

At a recent workshop at Cornell University when I brought up carbon burial, I was shot down somewhat aggressively by scientists and engineers. It is one thing to capture the carbon dioxide, they noted, but then what are you going to do with it? My colleagues appeared almost incensed that direct air capture technology is being conceived as part of model whose narrative ends with removal, whereas the real story is about transmutation of matter into monetizable and usable products. These products, not yet at scale, of course, include everything from carbonated water to artisanal vodka, from greenhouse enhancement to synthetic fuels, and, perhaps most perversely when we think of scale, rarity, and value, diamonds.[16]

In Illinois, the conglomerate Archer-Daniels-Midland is working on capturing carbon from biomass (BECSS), a technique that has aroused a great deal of hope but is also criticized as requiring too much land. Such large-scale experiments are often deemed too expensive and there are few incentives to keep them going, especially without special tariffs or carbon pricing. Moreover, many of the technologies are themselves potentially energy intensive. The few carbon sequestration projects underway often look like power plants. They are, in essence, technological eyesores on the landscape.

Of the various technologies that have been floated, those that revolve around enhancing natural carbon sinks as a third way or gentler way of engineering seem particularly attractive. But critics have raised serious questions about their viability, especially as the carbon clock ticks. In short, the field is changing rapidly, and there is a significant risk that this overview will be out of date by the time this book sees the light of day. My point here is not to survey and rank schemes but rather to consider the state of the art with the subsurface in mind.

A growing number of humanities scholars are addressing geoengineering. Philosopher Olúfẹ́mi Táíwò takes a rather pragmatic approach.[17] Rather than framing carbon capture in relation to partisanship, he proposes that we should avoid overthinking and instead focus on outcomes: "Keep it simple. Pollution: bad. Removing pollution: good." Literary theorist Frédéric Neyrat (2018) opposes all manifestations of what he calls geoconstructivism quite strongly on the grounds that these practices require a form of disavowal of humans as part of the very earth that they wish to work on, as if it were some estranged object separated from being, set there for contemplation. The geoconstructivists, Neyrat argues, are simply working in a lineage that could be traced back at least as far as Descartes and that imagines humans as masters over nature. To be clear, he also opposes a naive ecologism, guilty of reifying nature as a revered object. His critique extends to economists who see climate change as a new market opportunity but also to those scholars who are somehow enamored with the idea of the Anthropocene as a new period of study. In fact, he notes, geoengineering (let us say, of the SRM variety) requires figurative space mirrors:

> This is exactly what the young Marx, a true prototheorist of the Anthropocene, understood perfectly: Swept up by a conquering science, industry makes of the human being a "species-being" capable of "producing"—of regenerating—nature in such a way that nature "appears as his work and his reality." From then on, Marx writes in an incredibly prophetic manner, the human being, like a well-equipped god, will be able to "contemplate himself in a world he himself has created." Yes, the Anthropocene is a grand narrative, a veritable anthropo-scene, that is to say, an imaginary support structure—a scene of an industrial theatre, a gigantic mirror apparatus [*dispositif*] where the unity of the subject called "humanity" constructs and contemplates itself within the unity of the Earth object. And in this sense, climate engineering is a significant step within the process of "contemplation" described by Marx: The human species constructs a shield capable of preventing the Sun from disturbing its narcissistic contemplation. (Karl Marx, *Economic and Philosophic Manuscripts,* quoted in Neyrat 2018, 39–40)

We might think about these various forms of perspective and control by returning to Verne's explorers, on their way to the center of our shared planet. At one relatively calm moment on their journey, Professor Lidenbrock tells the narrator, Axel, that he would like to draw a vertical map of the subsurface once they have returned to the surface. Of course, he has no access to cameras that function underground or digital mapping tools. Rather, the geologist has been making careful calculations of distance and gradients, and he now estimates that they are forty miles below the surface where, according to some theories of the day, temperatures should be impossibly high.[18] Within the narrative as we have it, as Verne ultimately concludes it, and as his editor, Pierre-Jules Hetzel, ultimately published it (in two separate editions), at the end Lidenbrock will make no such map. The book itself—the narrative itself—serves to boost his fame, as it is widely read, he tells us, as if time-traveling beyond the confines of the voyage. The authenticity of the calculations Lidenbrock makes are woven into the story but never separated out as pure data. In any case, to the degree that the relationship between the uncle and nephew is Socratic, every question by Axel elicits a solution by Lidenbrock, who, finally, can call upon his predecessor, a sixteenth-century alchemist named Arne Saknussemm, who had undertaken the journey before.

But can one trust Saknussemm? As Axel explains to us, the readers, but keeps quiet from his uncle, since in the sixteenth century neither barometer nor manometer existed, how did the man know when he reached the center? On Verne's journey to the center of the earth, the men find hollowed-out spaces, enormous caves, stairs of stone that lead down along the walls, and even vast landscapes with lakes covered by clouds, beneath stone skies. There are certainly moments when the men must crawl along narrow shafts and caves, but young readers might grow up with the impression that while the subsurface presents dangers, ultimately it is a rough version (not a mirror, since it is not backward and upside down but simply a reproduction, layers down) of the surface itself. Verne was versed in the geological thought of his time. If there were unknowns down there, his scientists and mining engineers would ultimately triumph and even colonize the space.[19] He was certainly influenced, if only indirectly, by the writings and engravings of the of early modern geological thinkers like Agricola or Kircher. The literary fiction constructed by Verne predetermines responses to all kinds of questions, and it does so within a narrow structure that involves men on a quest to find truths, precisely by excluding others. This is about as far from the democratic coalitions of reader-activists that one might dream of today to confront climate change. I will suggest that Verne constructs a narrative that exceeds his own authority, in which a reader can locate scientific fact and yet avoid having to make an ultimate choice, or can make a choice but know that others are still open. He has it both ways, but he may not even be aware of the luxury of writing without a distinction. He is certainly not thinking about writing from the other side of a crack.

2
Extracting

Edinburgh, 1877[1]

Sitting in his comfortable lodgings, a retired engineer, Mr. Starr, receives a mysterious, unsigned letter summoning him to his old place of work, a coal mine in Stirling County to the northwest, where "a communication of an interesting nature will be made to him." This missive, composed in the passive voice, opens Jules Verne's *Les Indes noires* (translated as *The Black Indies* or *The Child of the Cavern* or *Coal City* or *The Underground City*), serialized in the Parisian daily *Le Temps* and printed as an illustrated, bound book soon afterward. Starr is middle-aged, sturdy, from a good family. His previous position at the productive Aberfoyle, Verne ([1877] 1883a, 2) notes, "honored that respectable group of engineers who are devouring, little by little, that carboniferous subsurface of Great Britain, from Cardiff to Newcastle to the lowlands of Scotland." (In the original: "Ses travaux honoraient la respectable corporation de ces ingénieurs qui dévourent peu à peu le sous-sol carbonifère du Royaume-Uni, aussi bien à Cardiff, à Newcastle que dans les bas comtés de l'Écosse" [Verne 1864, 2].)[2] The reader has just begun the novel and has no reason to suspect that "honored" and "respectable," referring to the work the engineer did in the past, are meant in anything but the most transparent and direct sense. But what about "devouring"? Should that be read ironically, or sideways, or with a grain of salt? Such readings are not normally warranted in Verne, except perhaps in cases of writing that are explicitly framed or signaled as parody. In another of his Scottish novels, *The Green Ray* (*Le rayon vert*), for instance, Verne introduces a possible husband for the young and pretty Helena Campbell—a scientist, and the worst sort of mansplainer, named Aristobulus Ursiclos. It is clear from the start that any man with such a name cannot be a serious contender for Helena's heart. More clues follow: Verne sets up a conflict that even the most naive reader can follow. We want this suitor out of the way. Helena will find her true love—and one worthy of her—in the Highlands.

In general, then, Verne is not a writer who asks to be read beneath his prose, only to march along through it, week by week, in many cases, in feuilleton form: to read it not for the plot, per se, but to hold out through thick description of places and people in foreign lands for the peaks of action and adventure.[3] All the rest of the prose, we might say, is there to regulate those moments. So perhaps the reader may assimilate "honored," "respectable," and "devoured" into one conglomeration summarizing the spectrum of Vernian engineers—men who combine characteristics of the heroic and the practical and appear in many of his works. In addition, we learn that Starr is a well-published amateur antiquarian, which Verne himself (we can hear his voice here—that is, as an aside, as an oral intervention) terms "one of those scientific practices that account for British prosperity" ("un de ces savants pratiques auxquels est due la prospérité de l'Angleterre" [Verne (1877) 1967, 2]). In any case, they are words penned prior to embarking on the adventure: words of the drawing room, while the reader knows adventure waits, champing at the bit, so to speak, outside.

Several hours after receiving his first letter, Starr receives a second one, unsigned, that warns him to ignore the first. He senses foul play. With this device of double letters, Verne sets up a mystery that helps propel the reader forward. It is possible that without the strange and menacing disavowal, the engineer (and, indeed, the reader) might not have been so eager to return to the mine. After all, Starr is quite comfortable and has no (more) need for money or glory, no need for any disruption to the narrative arc of his life.

Starr's housekeeper makes him a hearty meal and prepares his bags. She will no doubt keep his house in fine shape until—if—he returns. He also informs his friends at his gentlemen's club—Verne titles it nothing less than the Royal Institution—of his destination, a fact that will figure importantly into the narrative later on. But now it seems like a detail of daily life that we might expect from a subset of nineteenth-century fiction, a detail meant to give the reader some idea of the social connections between men of a certain class, brothers in honor and respect (perhaps devoured by them) and antiquarian interests. Verne begins *Around the World in Eighty Days* by introducing the reader to Phileas Fogg, a member of the London Reform Club, where he takes his meals, reads the *Times* and the *Standard,* and plays whist in front of a coal fire. It is here that the protagonist enters into a wager with fellow Reform Club members that will send him on his voyage. Incidentally, his servant, Jean Passepartout, will spend a good part of the journey fretting about the fact that he forgot to turn off the gas at home—an underlying anxiety of waste and a desire to conserve propels him toward a speedy return and toward the conclusion of the plot. Malone of Arthur Conan Doyle's *The Lost World* is an esteemed member of the Savage Club, where he will return to tell tales. The club is a significant locale for these narratives of adventure, for it is where men gather, without women, before and after the events that compose the narratives of adventure (which also take place, with few exceptions, between men). It serves as frame, alibi, and justification for telling/voyaging, and, in this regard, it is a fundamental element of such writing.

So Mr. Starr departs, first by train and then by steamboat—that is, a boat powered by coal.[4] "Steamboat" is already a displacement of fuel from the system, like "motor car" or "automobile" will be a few decades later.[5] Encountering bad weather, he (or the narrator, as they become blended at some points) finds it useful to interrupt the flow to give background on the formation of coal ("Il est convenable, pour l'intelligence de ce récit, de rappeler en quelques mots quelle est l'origine de la houille" [Verne (1877) 1967, 18]). Useful (*convenable*) for whom? What follows is not a few but thousands of words on the origins and evolution of coal through deep geological time, a didactic encyclopedic lecture including innumerable proper names, penned by Verne, of course, but with the alibi of Starr himself to verify the facts. It disrupts the momentum the novel has set up toward the revelation of the mystery: Who has called Starr and for what reason? Has the same party also sent the menacing retraction? Again, here, it is worthwhile to contrast this scene with another one, another voyage, from *The Green Ray*. Helena Campbell, accompanied by her two bachelor uncles and two servants, is traveling to the Hebrides from Glasgow. During a long steamship voyage, one of the passengers stands up and, "without being asked, but also without objection from anyone, thought it his duty to give a little historical lecture":

> In half an hour's time no one on board the Columbia, unless indeed he were deaf, need be ignorant of the fact that very probably the Romans had fortified Dumbarton; that this historical rock was transformed into a royal fortress at the beginning of the thirteenth century; that by the Act of Union it was privileged as one of the four places in Scotland to remain undismantled; that from this port in 1548, Mary Stuart, whose marriage with Francis II, was about to make her "Queen of a day," left for France; finally that Napoleon was to have been confined there in 1815, before Castlereagh had resolved to imprison him in St. Helena. (Verne 1883b, 54)

Clearly, this is the worst sort of pedantic rhetoric, and it has no value within the text except in opposition to the pure and minimalist speech of Helena's true love, Oliver Sinclair, later on.

In contrast, the completist geological excursus in *The Black Indies* corresponds to the passage of time that the reader/Starr spends on the boat trip from Edinburgh on his way to the mine. It is far longer than any single chapter in the novel. As I will discuss again with regard to *Journey to the Center of the Earth*, disproportion constitutes a significant element of Verne's narrative style, whether this is studied and cultivated or simply a result of a set of random events that might include publication schedules, editorial intervention, and so on. Certainly, this particular elucidation of coal by Starr is in line with both the pedagogical and financial aims of Pierre-Jules Hetzel, Verne's editor/father figure. It is the kind of flat, factual prose Hetzel encouraged, in general, even if he had issues with drafts of this novel in other regards. However, from a literary point of view, it is a terrible passage, almost like filler to occupy space. It does nothing for plot or characters and it could easily make the reader forget about the first and second letters that spurred Starr's initial movement toward the north of the country. While on the one hand, it is certainly true that we have no reason to make too much of such a minor issue as "over"-writing, on the other hand, if we take *The Black Indies* seriously, as literary writing, we might go in different directions. It is as if, in this passage, Verne takes over from Starr, improving on his "improving gaze" in ways that are quite predictable and well-known to scholars of imperialism. The author's description of the landscape or, better, the terrane (subsurface and surface taken together, in multiple spatiotemporal dimensions) bears an interesting relation to "overburden," which Jennifer Wenzel (2016) describes as material topping an extractable, valuable resource. It is what must be removed for the reader to get to "pay dirt," as she describes it, in an economic sense, most obviously, but also in an aesthetic sense. It is not only the toxic residues of mining but also the perfectly good landscapes that stand in the way.

As writing, Verne's interposed piece of geognosy, taken at times almost verbatim from secondary sources, is not too far removed from what a geologist might write of coal today, but with one huge exception: Verne does not know—he could not be expected to know—about the effects of accelerated historical greenhouse gas emissions on planetary warming. He therefore makes no mention of what will happen to global average temperatures or local ecosystems once carbon dioxide from the burning of coal (and then oil) crosses a certain threshold of concentration. Then again, he makes no mention of what happens to coal once it is removed from the ground either. This is not an industrial novel. Combustion is deferred, displaced to the surface and then the atmosphere, where Verne is primarily concerned with the formation of an entire city, underground, where labor is pleasant and all human wants are met without strife.

Verne did not coin the term *black indies* to refer to the coal mine. It was in circulation in his time as a way to describe a space that remained filled with anxieties and fascination of the colonial subject and the colonies. Verne might well have been aware of George Sand's *La ville noire*, published in 1861, set in a fictional town divided into a lower, black zone filled with factories and smoke (which one enters through the "hellmouth," the *Trou-d'Enfer*) and an upper zone inhabited by the corrupt bourgeoisie. Sand uses the adjective *black* throughout the novel, including in reference to the night, to men, women, and children who inhabit the quasi-subterranean hellscape, and to the thoughts of a suicidal man. In the end, though, Sand's black city is cleansed, thanks to fate and the work of a good woman who oversees a transition of the factories to more democratic, artisan, and humane conditions. The novel ends with a nuptial hymn.

For the nineteenth-century reader, *black* would connote the color that coal turns the bodies and lungs of the miners, the air in cities like Edinburgh and London, and the insides of furnaces. It may signal—on the surface of the matter—the profound connections between whiteness and geology, as well as the racial violence of extraction that is normally repressed, as Kathryn Yusoff (2018) might argue. *Indies* refers to a colonial outpost, a treasure trove of riches, but also a place of bleakness and danger. In fact, while Verne did visit his beloved Scotland several times, he never himself went below ground, there or anywhere, according to his biographers.[6] He had guidebooks, geological treatises, and literary texts (the writings of Walter Scott, above all) at his disposal. The British have named—and in Verne naming is the first act of "good colonization"—a vast subterranean realm. In *Journey to the Center of the Earth*, Professor Lidenbrock calls himself "the Columbus of these underground regions," and he means this in the very best sense—that is, he deems himself worthy of great respect (Verne 1992, 107). Like the other "good colonies" in the author's tales, in *The Black Indies* there are no dark natives to displace. While one might expect a form of racialism to be part of the work, it is notably absent from the prose of this particular text. It is as if Verne deliberately chose a title to disorient his readers, who, familiar with his other writings, might indeed expect a narrative of discovery, conquest, civilization over apparently less evolved humans. Perhaps he chose a title randomly, without thinking through coherence, as if the title made no difference for what was to come. Nevertheless, the novel does tell of a form of geological taking of a realm that is dark, but not immediately for the skin color of native peoples. This is colonization without violence to other humans: geoimperialism—another kind of fantasy.

It goes without saying that extraction (or extractivism) is everywhere these days: a key paradigm of neoliberalism, a set of real practices associated with settler colonialism, a stubborn viral metaphor. It implies operations of a large scale (so often associated with a national or multinational corporation for the taking of resources considered to belong to a nation or be traded with another). Sometimes, what is extracted is harmful to the humans who make use of it. Often the very process is harmful to the humans who undertake it. Critics who apply *extraction* to literature or culture also recall that slow violence (associated above all with Rob Nixon) or resource curses can apply just as well when the matter being brought up is not to be combusted but to be used for "good purposes" (e.g., lithium or cobalt for batteries necessary for electrification of transport, or geothermal heat). It might be thought in opposition to *excavation* to the degree that this term means, for the nineteenth century, "a modern version of the mythological quest to find truth . . . a central metaphor for intellectual inquiry in the modern age" (Williams 2008, 23). Assuming, of course, the apparent neutrality of this metaphor does not itself obfuscate forms of violence.

Extraction describes not only the physical movement of materials from the subsurface to the surface but also, at times, the hollowing-out of humanity. It is real and figurative at once. Silicon Valley, for instance, has extracted "our data, our attention, our time, our creativity, our content, our DNA, our homes, our cities, our relationships."[7] There are often devastating collateral consequences to extraction, and often for the people whose land is devastated in the process. Drilling down, open pit mining, fracking—all involve breaking rock below the surface in order to take from it the liquid or gaseous resources that have developed there over long periods of deep time. Extraction implies violence, whether today we want to conceive this in terms of a Heideggerian "rape" of the land or a form of geoengineering that, according to Frédéric

Neyrat (2018), involves mastery that is opposed to an open ecological thinking. It would be nearly impossible to read a text of mining from the nineteenth century today without these specters haunting us.

After the passage on coal characterized as *quelques mots*—perhaps a passage that Verne intended to be short but one that turned out to take up an unbalanced space in the novel as he filled pages with the information he was taking directly from books, a passage that Verne, perhaps, neglected to edit down, a passage that his readers might have found tedious depending on their level of interest in a geology lesson—Starr arrives at his appointed destination. Verne, it bears noting, deeply loved Scotland and saw it as a place of vacation and refuge from the turmoil of his life in France. Aberfoyle is a real town, at the foot of the Trossachs mountains, and is home to a slate quarry. Coal is not found there, as it was in West Fife, say, where Verne visited. But he probably chose *Aberfoyle* because he liked the sound of the word, and he may have associated the landscape with mystery (Thompson 2011, 151).

Let us sum up what has happened so far: a trigger for a trip via various means of transport, a didactic interruption, and an arrival. The rest of the novel lacks this level of detail. It is primarily set underground. The reader learns that in the past, for ten years during a very fruitful period, rather than ascending after their shifts the miners stayed underground, carving out what Verne refers to as warehouses (*magasins*) with their own hands. They lived underground in "cottages" (in English in the original). This is a significant term because it also—or primarily—refers to the places where the handloomers lived and worked before industrialization in Britain. While they inhabit the subsurface, in Verne's fantasy, the miners convert it into a homey place. Instead of a whole series of rhythms and movements of daily life of the collier that will be crucial to D. H. Lawrence, for example, in Verne we find a libidinal attachment to the subsurface. Now time has passed, and the miners have returned to the surface in search of other employment, but one family—the Fords—remain down there. Father and son continue to go out each day in search of new veins while the mother, Madge, keeps house. Along with cooking and cleaning, she marks a cross to indicate the passing of each day on a calendar, a device that helps the rescue party understand when the Fords and Starr were last at home in the cottage when they go missing later on. Why does she bother? This is the only link with the world above and serves the same sort of function as marking the days during an adventure or being lost in the wilderness or on a deserted island: a tenuous connection to the real. An acknowledgment that someday one might return. Being lost, being on the trek, is itself the stuff of the story, but for the story to be told there needs to be a reader who is projected into the future and past to frame the actions. They do not stand on their own without this, and while the same claim might be made for any novel at all, in the case of *The Black Indies,* this demand of time traveling becomes increasingly evident.

The Fords have stubbornly vowed not to abandon their own wet nurse just because her milk is now dried up ("Nous n'abandonnerons pas la mine, notre vieille nourrice, parce que son lait s'est tari!" [Verne (1887) 1967, 7]). Given that Verne wrote primarily for young boys, and given the strange quasi-colonialist allusions of the title, this image of a *ménage à quatre* is particularly disturbing, not to mention the insistence of Ford and his wife that their grown son, Harry, would have no reason to ever want to leave the subsurface for the surface—with all of its fluctuations in temperature and sociosexual vicissitudes. And as a side benefit, the family also evades the tax man. The Fords eat heartily from all the major food groups. They breathe air from some of the old shafts and light their way with both gas (no danger of firedamp now that the mine is fully evacuated) and electric lamps. Once it had been determined that the old mine was spent, the vast infrastructure was removed, extracted out from the belly of the beast and left to decay on the surface. Verne (or perhaps a combination of Verne and Starr) provides the following apt analogy: the mine is like the cadaver of a mastodon whose guts have been removed, leaving only the skeleton. On the surface since the closure of the mine, the landscape has been transformed from industrial to agricultural, and for the miners this is something to be lamented. Bear in mind this apparently upside-down trope (farming is rough and primitive, the mine is rich and ancient and yet represents the future of humans), as I will refer to it again.

So, Starr arrives and accompanies the Fords—*père et fils* and Madge, the mother—to the place where they believe they have discovered a new seam. In fact, it will turn out to be a continuation of the seam previously worked, so that it does not even merit an entirely new name. It is simply called "New Aberfoyle." As they explore, they are imprisoned in the rock by a falling boulder (an event they believe is natural but will turn out to have pernicious supernatural causes). Then Verne inserts himself with a boring-drill gaze. He notes that if the explorers had been able to pass through massive walls, they would have seen an enormous hollow space. They are so close but blocked from seeing what he can see. Finally, after many pages during which Verne turns his attention to other matters, since there is no need to morbidly dwell down there once he establishes the scene, the miners are rescued.

Three years have passed, Verne indicates, as he begins a new chapter. What happens during this time of narrative condensation? A great deal, as it turns out. An entire coal city has sprung up. We skip the labor that led to the opening of the seam. We skip any discussion of investors or industrialists who finance the operation. We skip the stages between the building of the city as we skip the science.[8] Community happens. Verne uses the term *grande famille* throughout this text to refer to the underground dwellers at Aberfoyle. As it turns out, in *The Black Indies*, la grande famille is a relatively new development. We learn of Ford's ancestors: "They labored like convicts at the work of extracting the precious combustible. It is even believed that the coal miners, like the salt-makers of that period, were actual slaves" (Verne [1877] 1883a, 49). But now the workers are happy and fully invested in the labor they do, a fantasy that seems inextricable from that of coal. Yet—and in spite of Hetzel's appeals to the author to the contrary—Verne does not include any descriptions of the labor itself.[9] The reader experiences this like one of the tourists who is invited to New Aberfoyle, entering through an inviting tunnel and enjoying a pleasant railway journey on a gentle incline to reach "Coal City" (in English in the original).

Ellipses, breaks, and chapter endings allow the novelist great control, of course. Verne is a highly selective writer, so, for instance, while he offers his readers extensive explanations of the geohistorical source of coal (in water vapors charged with carbonic acid that fed prediluvian forests) and the technologies of mining, electricity appears underground as a quasi-magical force, without any explanation of its source.[10] Coal City is lit with "electric discs; some suspended from the vaulted roofs, others hanging on the natural pillars—all, whether suns or stars in size, were fed by continuous currents produced from electro-magnetic machines" (Verne [1877] 1883a, 132). An entire society based on mining coal functions without its polluting effects. Food arrives fully cooked on the table without explanation of how it is procured. Everything is in its place and the mine works perfectly. The Fords have built a new cottage at the side of an underground lake that even contains abundant (eyeless) fish. The lake lies under a roof, a stone sky, but the reader has no need to think about overburden or overtopping in everyday life. The mine is so open, its caverns so vast, that it could even allow the miners to travel, by land and sea, all the way to America underneath the Atlantic Ocean!

Starr, who might have returned home to Edinburgh but prefers to stay among the miners, finds himself set up next to the Fords. The homes are made of brick, a natural material formed of clay that is brought (back) down to the subsurface. There is even a chapel. In many respects, then, the mine has been transformed, by labor, from a semisoft matter to a hollowed-out utopia—one invested with atavistic fears and rituals, but one where the abundance of the past still conditions the potential of the future. Perhaps this three-year-long period is not one that Verne's readers would care about. In one aspect, as we might expect, Verne creates a fantasy in which the wealth of the subsurface is yielded up to the men, the earth gives herself to them, after a slight resistance. This fantasy can only be read against the actual conditions of mining coal or other matters that fuel the Industrial Revolution. Andreas Malm (2016, 247) describes the conditions of the mines of this period:

Temperatures above 100 degrees Fahrenheit, remorseless destruction of lungs by coal dust, suffocating inhalation of the concentrated gas known as "choke-damp" (primarily carbon dioxide) and sudden ignition of "fire-damp" (primarily methane), falling roofs, fires and, of course, explosions of epic magnitudes, with hundreds of victims in single cases, made the collieries exceptionally dangerous places of work. Dwelling in the exterior interior of the landscapes, the colliers were by definition shut out from tropospheric nature, to their peril.

But the sanitizing of mining labor is not only a function of fiction. In contrast to Malm's sketch, and in one of the few works describing British coal mining as a social enterprise, J. R. Leifchild ([1856] 1968) mentions a celebration after the "winning" of a coal seam in Northern England. A "grand subterranean ball" was organized, more than thousand feet below the surface. A pit was cleaned up, seats and lighting brought down, and then men and women in fancy dress began to descend. Right out of central casting, they resemble the civilians in the frontispiece to Verne's novel. The guests begin by chipping out a piece of coal from the face, as a ritual gesture. They then proceed to dance.

> No distinction was made among the guests, and born and bred ladies joined in a general dance with born and bred pitmen's daughters. All now returned in safety, and in nice clean and well-lined baskets, to the upper regions, delighted with the amusements in which they had been engaged. . . . It was estimated that between 200–300 persons were present, and that nearly one half of them were females! It must be remembered that the pit was clean, prepared, and had not been worked; so that no smoke and dust exuded from its mouth, and every faculty was given for a comfortable, slow, and safe descent. (111)

Similarly, so far, we see that Verne's fantasy erases any tension between laborers and management, between the material to be extracted and the process of extraction. It is in this sense the antinovel to Émile Zola's *Germinal* (1894), which lingers on the material conditions and the coal as intertwined with the humans and nonhuman animals working below.[11] In Verne, the mine, which in the past had yielded up its bounty with a kind of maternal kindness, is a place in which man and nature coexist in near-perfect harmony. Verne's mine is smooth, with clear boundaries, sealed off from any leakage.

The mystery of who provided food and water for the Fords and Starr when they were trapped has not yet been solved, but it is attributed to a brownie, hobgoblin (in French, *lutin*).[12] Brownies— their name derives from Scottish Gaelic *gruagach* (a type of seaweed) or *brùnaidh*—are beings that come at night to perform household chores in exchange for a bowl of milk left on the hearth. They are important in the Scotland of Verne's story, widely held to control various unexplained phenomena around the mine, including a shipwreck that takes place on the turbulent underground lake. Indeed, a flame leads the rescue party to the Fords. For farmer Jack Ryan it is a brownie; for the man of science, it can be explained by geophysical forces.

At one point, Starr and Harry Ford converse about the wonders before them: "It's a pity that the whole planet was not made of coal," the young man remarks ("Il est à regretter que tout le globe terrestre n'ait pas été uniquement composé de charbon" [Verne (1877) 1967, 33–34]). But then the engineer reminds him of the fact that the sandstone, limestone, and granite that make up most of the planet are not flammable and therefore render life on the surface possible. "Do you mean, Mr. Starr, that humans would have finished by burning their own globe?" (Verne [1877] 1883a, 34) ("Voulez-vous dire . . . que les humaines auraient fini par brûler leur globe?" [Verne (1877) 1967, 34]). Starr responds by confirming that if all were coal, the earth would have yielded up the last bit in the forges, locomotives, steamers, and factories and thus "would have ended one fine day" (Verne [1877] 1883a, 34) ("notre monde eût fini un beau jour!" [Verne (1877) 1967, 34]). Note the strange grammar of Harry's query and Starr's response, both in the conditional past, as if the reader could position himself on a flying machine in the future and look down on the networks of energy on the earth at that moment and take in past, present, and future, imagining an alternative geological history. Compare this with the simple future deployed by engineer Cyrus Smith in Verne's 1874 *The Mysterious Island*: "one day our globe will come to an end, or rather, animal and vegetable life will no longer be possible because of an intense cooling that will take place" (Verne [1875] 2001, 231). Here Smith echoes what is a fairly common trope in the period, shifting the apocalyptic force to end everything onto the sun.[13] Perhaps there is no point, in the grand scheme of things, to make too much of verb tenses in a passage that has no particular force as far as the narrative of a long novel itself. Yet it seems almost as if Verne and Starr cannot use a constative utterance about change in the past, whereas it is easier to posit global cooling in the deep future. In the conditionality of the conversation of *The Black Indies* it is impossible to unhear a certain ambivalence about the very coal that was over-illuminated earlier.

Interestingly, Karl Marx left few words about coal or about the actual labor involved with coal mining. It was a separate sphere, apart from the factory that he studied with great care. No doubt he was aware of how the laws of capital worked in the mining industry with extreme force, and that it was necessary to the factories. Prescient as he was, he could not be expected to know about the production of excessive emissions. Although a handful of scientists in Marx's time may have discussed anthropogenic change in weather patterns (through, for example, deforestation), one can imagine that he would not have been particularly attentive to such work.[14] It was not until more than a decade after Marx's death that a Swede, Svante Arrhenius, published his findings about the burning of coal leading, someday, to the trapping of gases—later classed as "greenhouse"—in the atmosphere. In any case, Arrhenius did not gain a strong foothold in the annals of science. Marx's primary locus for exploring labor is the factory where coal has already been inserted and is invisible. Instead, workers interact with machines that are powered by coal but designed according to principles of mechanics that predate coal, as I discuss in *Fuel: A Speculative Dictionary*, where I cite this extraordinary passage:

> In the first place, in the form of machinery the implements of labour become automatic, things moving and working independent of the workman. They are thenceforth an industrial *perpetuum mobile*, that would go on producing forever, did it not meet with certain natural obstructions in the weak bodies and the strong wills of its human attendants. (Marx 1967, 272)

I cannot help but be mesmerized by the fantasy, the fantastical figure of endless energy of the machine forced to contend with the human, or, more specifically, a human qualified as worker or slave. With this in mind, it is also true that Marx maintains a strong interest in chemistry as analogy. He is unable to resist the language of chemistry when he describes the process at work, for example, in the transformation of raw material (itself far from a simple term) into value. Marx distinguishes between nature (water, soil) and raw materials, which, though in a state of relative purity, have been "filtered through previous labor." He offers as an example of "raw material" "ore already extracted and ready for washing" (178). What has been effaced here? Precisely, the labor of extracting! Marx links mining with hunting, fishing, and agriculture in that all are industrialized forms of capture of a raw material. Here it is not important for him to distinguish the subsurface from surface. Indeed, the raw materials of extraction are provided in a primary state, but the labor (rendered in English by the gerunds of the industries) disappears:

> With the exception of the extractive industries, in which the material for labour is provided immediately by Nature, such as mining, hunting, fishing, and agriculture (so far as the latter is confined to breaking up virgin soil), all branches of industry manipulate raw material, objects already filtered through labour, already products of labour. Such is seed in agriculture. Animals and plants, which we are accustomed to consider as products of Nature, are in their present form, not only products of, say last year's labour, but the result of a gradual transformation, continued through many generations, under man's superintendence, and by means of his labour. But in the great

majority of cases, instruments of labour show even to the most superficial observer, traces of the labour of past ages. (181)

There is a general evolution of intervention into raw materials suggested. Marx then goes on to specify:

> Raw material may either form the principal substance of a product, or it may enter into its formation only as an accessory. An accessory may be consumed by the instruments of labour, as coal under a boiler, oil by a wheel, hay by draft-horses, or it may be mixed with the raw material in order to produce some modification thereof, as chlorine into unbleached linen, coal with iron, dye-stuff with wool, or again, it may help to carry on the work itself, as in the case of the materials used for heating and lighting workshops. The distinction between principal substance and accessory vanishes in the true chemical industries, because there none of the raw material reappears, in its original composition, in the substance of the product. (181)

A single product may serve as raw material in different processes. "Corn, for example, is a raw material for millers, starch-manufacturers, distillers, and cattle-breeders." It is also corn, as seed, for the purpose of growing more corn. And then, Marx notes, coal, too, is at the same time the product of and a means of production in coal mining (182). This is as close as Marx ever gets to saying something like energy requires energy (or fossil fuels require fossil fuels), but the analogy with corn only goes so far, or at least it has limits. Both corn and coal require work before they can be used as raw material, and both are products of nature. But whereas corn is a matter ingested by animals in the form of energy-calories that might serve to produce further work, coal is ingested by nonliving engines to produce motion. Verne offers none of this sort of information, nor would one expect him to do so. Yet it almost seems as if the totalized system of the subterranean in his novel functions as an explicit rebuttal of such thinking.

Yes, coal subtends the Victorian novel (and with a bit of latitude, I will allow Verne to sashay into this category), perhaps invisible but powerfully embedded in language as Nathan Hensley and Philip Steer explore in most exemplary fashion.[15] It powers not only the society that produces it but also the very imperialist project that produces Britain and the various global "black indies" that also help to define it. While a small number of novels from nineteenth-century Britain may foreground coal or steam, "more common still are those that, while alluding to steam-powered travel or the products of steam-driven manufacture, regard these aspects of narrative infrastructure as entirely beneath the interests of story: they melt the socio-environmental processes of energy extraction, storage, combustion, and conversion, almost reflexively, into the category of the everyday" (Hensley and Steer 2018, 66). And they go on to suggest that precisely because it exists only slightly below the surface of all writing, it coincides with what Louis Althusser (2015, 26) termed a "defined excluded," a historical condition so basic that it goes unremarked in writing. As they note, "A society that depended entirely on coal could barely, precisely because of that dependence, become conscious of coal at all" (Hensley and Steer 2018, 67). Because Verne both is and is not a realist writer—that is, he moves in and out of the codes of realism—because he is an outsider to the British Isles, he can become conscious of coal and render it visible compared with those who live directly atop it. In Verne's *The Black Indies*, finally, coal's deep history is recounted on the very surface, almost as if to foreclose the possibility of its unconscious or, better, its subconscious effects. Verne seems to tell his readers not to worry about what goes on below, because the essential action is all happening here and now, and if there is a below it is just a mirror of the surface anyway. In his Coal City, Verne may also have absorbed elements of the tradition of thinking about the subsurface and surface as mirrors of one another. He may have metabolized the ideas in a late seventeenth-century treatise titled *Sylva subterranea*. This work has the subtitle *Or, Superb Usefulness of the Underground Forest of Mineral Coal/How the Same Is Granted and Imparted by God to the Benefit of Humans in Those Places Where Not Much Wood Grows* (*Sylva subterranea, oder Vortreffliche Nutzbarkeit des Unterirdischen Waldes der Stein-Kohlen*).[16] Coal is wood and vice versa; just flip the terrain. Topsy-turvy.

And in fact, in Verne's novella, *Topsy Turvy, or The Purchase of the North Pole*, a group of ultrawealthy Americans outbid other nations and corporations to purchase the Arctic at auction. Why? The dominant theory among the nations bidding is that the Americans, members of the Baltimore Gun Club, believe they will find coal.

After all, coal likely grows under the surface all around the globe. As Verne read in the work of Louis Figuier (and other geologists), the entire globe was once temperate or subtropical, so, based on fossil evidence, it is likely that coal grew even in certain regions that are now covered over by ice. This theory, in *Topsy Turvy*, is espoused by supposedly intelligent people and cited as the very reason behind what seems like an impulsive and bizarrely self-defeating purchase. Indeed, some of these people note:

> Very probably at the geological formation of the world, the sun was such that the difference of temperature around the equator and the poles were not appreciable. Then immense forests covered this unknown polar region a long time before mankind appeared, and when our planet was submitted to the incessant action of heat and humidity. . . . And these large forests, which disappeared with the gigantic changes of the Earth before it had taken its present form, must certainly have changed and transformed under the lapse of time and the action of internal heat and water into coal mines. (Verne 1890, 26–27)

Such a theory of a planet that was more uniformly without climates that changed, over long periods, into one with diversity seems likely, given that a variety of different kinds of stones and fossil plants, flower beds, hazel, poplar, and beech trees have been discovered in explorations of the Arctic region as far as they have progressed (which is to say, not all the way, not to the very last frontier). Vegetation on the surface signals the probability of coal beneath; it is a rather simplistic formulation to be sure. Yet if the rational reader of that novella understands the extractive impulse to conquer the poles, he may also wonder—along with representatives of nations present at the auction—why only gun men and no engineers or scientists are part of the team.

In Verne, coal is there for the taking. There is no explicit edict or taboo against it by the late nineteenth century. Still, just as mining in general developed a series of myths, demonic creatures, and practices over time, no doubt some of the anxieties of early modern Christianity infect details of writing, but also later narratives, as tropes of disavowal: mining is for extraction, yes, but it might be otherwise. One has to tread lightly.

Mining in *The Black Indies,* while not without ambivalence, is not ignoble. Surface dweller and bagpiper Jack Ryan continues to believe in magical forces down there, even though Verne offers us a real explanation for the rescue of the Fords and Starr: the good will of a foundling, Nell, and the giant subterranean-dwelling snowy owl that protects her. Verne's father-editor Hetzel begged the author to tone down what he referred to as the "Barnum" style of the novel's ending: fires, geological upheavals, the revenge of Nell's grandfather, the evil Silfax (Lucifer). First let the book have success, the editor wrote the author (in Dumas, Gondolo della Riva, and Dehs 2001, 2:144–45), then you can write a crazy epilogue. In the end, the product we have is the result of a compromise; the text was rewritten at least four times, perhaps more. Someday the new seam will be spent, but Harry and Nell will continue the line just as the subsurface will continue to offer refuge (perhaps even serving as camps for Britain's indigent classes, Verne suggests).

Nell, who speaks in old Gaelic (signaling that she belongs to a different temporality), is a subject that has never been extracted. She has no sense of the rhythms of time, days, nights, and so on. The good people of Coal City do not know how she will react when removed from her ethos, exposed to light and other stimuli of modern Scotland. Nell strikes the miners as an "antediluvian being" (Verne [1877] 1883a, 157), removed from far below, except that from a physiological point of view she is evolved like a modern human (with exceptional eyesight for the dark where she was raised). She is like one of those these exceptional creatures, a wild child, studied by modern social sciences in order to clarify the division of nature and culture. To be sure, under the nurturing care of Madge, she grows into a proper girl and a wholly appropriate bride for Harry Ford. Plans are made for the wedding. Still, the men around her come to feel that she should undertake what we may call a reverse initiation rite, a voyage to the surface of the earth, in order to see for herself what lies there and (although they do not articulate this idea) to test her in order to see if she is attracted by what she finds there before she will settle for a life underground.

Verne draws on a long tradition, in the Christian West, of fear and guilt about mining both in the taking of what God put down there and in the blasting apart of the earth. Think of Ovid's genealogy: the Iron Age begins when humans move from agriculture to mining, from a fruitful cultivation of the surface to an exploitation of what lies below. Georgius Agricola, the great early modern writer on mining and miners, while he is primarily concerned to catalog the instruments and techniques of extraction, also justifies his work with logics such as the following:

> So, let the farmers have for themselves the fruitful fields and cultivate the fertile hills for the sake of their produce; but let them leave to miners the gloomy valleys and sterile mountains, that they may draw forth from these, gems and metals which can buy, not only the crops, but all things that are sold. (Agricola [1556] 1950, 6)

Later, this kind of thinking, tempered by a more rationalist economic discourse of the law of capture based on John Locke and Adam Smith, among others, is brought in to support the idea that the riches of the subsurface belong to the one who extracts them. Such positions may lie below the writing of the nineteenth century (and so, also, now) like a bedrock.

Extraction without expenditure resounds with some of the claims and tropes of alchemy, which persist long after the beginning of modern chemistry just as atavistic cultures of mining persist long after the technologies for taking resources from the ground to the surface are ramped up to their highest state. In alchemical thought, precious mineral resources are believed to develop over time in the (feminine/maternal) earth's so-called womb, transmuting from base into noble states. The alchemist attempts to mimic these processes, but sped up, in the laboratory. It is easy to understand, then, how the miner and alchemist came together in various analogies. The miner, too, speeds up the natural processes that might, over time, bring resources to the surface by means of streams or violent disruptions to the rock. Naturally, Verne moves beyond the early modern thought around such matters, and yet one could argue that a story of transmutation subtends his writing. We can dismiss this alchemical/mining analogy as old-fashioned by Verne's time, but we can also acknowledge its persistence, even today. Doing so does not mean that we embrace a mystical relation to the earth but rather that we admit the dream of transmutation as a basic frame of reference, so stubborn as to creep into the most materialist practices. With this background, both Roland Barthes (1970) and Michel Serres (1974) offer structuralist readings of Verne that allow for the tropes of alchemy to continue.

In fact, for Serres, *The Black Indies* can be read as an allegory of alchemy where the four traditional elements—earth (the mine), water (Loch Katrin), air (the giant underground cavern), and fire (firedamp)—combine to create a microcosmic totality. The Vernian critic Jean Chesneaux (2001, 265) does not completely agree with this reading, as for him the novel is about the chemistry necessary for the Industrial Revolution. Perhaps a strictly structuralist/archetypal reading and a more evolutionary one can coincide in the sense that Verne had certainly consulted early modern works of geology, but it is not certain to what degree he had absorbed modern chemistry.

In a short text reflecting on structuralist method, Barthes (1970) imagines a student who is willing and able to enter into a given text to seek not a single result or a correct reading but to be open to plurality ("le pluriel du texte"). The work that Barthes chooses for his exercise of beginning (titled "Par où commencer?") is another novel by Verne, *The Mysterious Island*. Of course, Barthes cannot offer his readers a precise method, he can only perform it on a particular text, and in this sense he and we readers or would-be critics have to come to terms with our own distance from science. Barthes locates, in *The Mysterious Island*, a number of underlying codes (Robinsonade, Adamic/Edenic) and follows them along his reading. He calls Verne's "great work" (an alchemical term) a "Plutonian novel." This latter term refers to several elements: the men stranded on Lincoln Island use granite to build their home; in addition, Barthes suggests, Vernian Plutonism is linked to industrialization in the novelist's critique of the subterranean *Nautilus* and the destructive energy of the volcano (7). Moreover, for the critic, the novel is governed by overlapping codes of transformations: technical (materials), magical (metamorphosis), and linguistic (the generation of signs). In beginning to read, he notes, a critic must identify codes in a text and then multiply them, open them up to other, less familiar codes, and take them outside the text to one's own work and experience. Certainly, this mode of reading does not seem out of place or incorrect when brought to bear today on Verne. The structuralist analysis retains its value, or, rather, it offers an added value to a text (and if Barthes refers here to *The Mysterious Island*, the same could be said of *The Black Indies*, as well as any other number of works) that might otherwise strike the reader as pure adventure, with a plot that moves forward in a fairly linear manner. The colonists stranded on an island in the Pacific face one obstacle after another and overcome them until the final obstacle that destroys everything. After this point, they start all over again.

Barthes asks us to read Verne for the narrative (and for codes), but what if we go one step beyond and read him as literature? I mean by this not precisely narrative or ideology (although these elements might also make their appearance) but as something closer to what Giorgio Agamben (2017) describes through a parable, as an atavistic core of mystery that remains or persists, even into the modern era. In *The Fire and the Tale*, the Italian philosopher, following a rather Benjaminian trajectory, recounts the loss of an originary fire over generations of storytellers, a loss that risks being reduced to "progress" such that "the result of this progress—secularization—is the liberation of the tale from its mythical sources and the establishment of literature—now autonomous and adult—in a separate sphere—that is, culture—then that 'can be sufficient' really becomes enigmatic" (2). All literature, in this sense, marks loss over time. If so, one might well ask: Is it the role of the critic to locate and describe or name this originary loss? And conversely, may the author also be aware of it for a proper reading to function? Put another way: What relation does this loss bear to the unconscious, a term Agamben does not employ? More immediately, however, does this parable and this mode of interpretation as search for/acknowledgment of a primary loss really apply to a writer like Verne, who was and still is accused of being a nonliterary author of tales of adventure and recreation? Must a text exhibit a degree of poetic or narrative obfuscation for it to qualify for this analysis? Agamben writes that the modern novel derives from ancient forms of mystery, although traces of this may be completely absent. If modern writing is also always a working on the self, a transformation of the self, it may qualify as a modern version of ancient mysteries. Agamben gives the example of Arthur Rimbaud, whose *A Season in Hell* represents "the paradox of a literary work that claims to describe and verify a non-literary experience, whose place is the subject who, transforming himself in this way, becomes capable of writing it" (114). The link between a work and work on the self brings Agamben to the field of alchemy. He makes a rather broad statement about the *opus alchymicum,* which "implies that the transformation of metals occurs hand in hand with the transformation of the subject" (122). To be sure, Agamben's account of the opus alchymicum depends on a certain kind of (male) subject who is firmly intertwined with his own creative process, but then, one might ask: Why should the reader care? Agamben also asks a question that I ask in a longer format and in a different register in *Alchemical Mercury: A Theory of Ambivalence*: Why writing? What are we do to with the corpus of texts about alchemy, and how should we relate them to a series of practices that are hinted at but also disavowed by the writing? Agamben suggests that, following the Greeks, we think about the "care of the self" (a phrase dear to Michel Foucault) not in an aesthetic but in a moral or ethical sense. Tracing the terms through Foucault, Agamben surmises that "the care of the self necessarily passes through an opus; it inextricably implies an alchemy" (134). This might seem like a mere analogy with the transformation of metals into gold of the sort that is widespread in both critical (academic) writing and everyday speech. But—and here is where Agamben arrives at what I take to be his most original observation—it is not just the self that is transmuted but creative practice itself. "The relation with an external practice (the opus) makes possible the work on oneself only to the extent that it is constituted as a relation to a potentiality. A subject who tried to define and shape himself only through his own opus would be doomed to incessantly exchanging his life and reality with his own opus." To overcome this form of self-enclosed narcissism, the alchemical analogy must go beyond. "The real alchemist is rather the one who—in the opus and through the opus—contemplates only the potentiality that produced it" (137). In other words, by placing the focus on the potential to not be or do, on inoperativity, Agamben opens to a form-of-life that he understands as neither "life" nor "opus" but "happiness." As he finishes:

> The painter, the poet, the thinker—and, in general, anyone who practices an "art" or an "activity"—are not the appointed sovereign subjects of a creative operation and of an opus; they are rather anonymous living beings who, contemplating and making at each turn inoperative the opus of language, of vision, and of bodies, try to experience themselves and keep in relation with a potentiality, that is, to constitute their life as form-of-life. Only at this point can opus and Great Opus, metallic gold and the gold of the philosophers, be completely identified. (138)

To put this in a greater context, consider that in his famous essay "The Storyteller," Walter Benjamin (1968) cites a tale titled "An Unexpected Reunion," by Johann Peter Hebel. This story is another variant of the "miner of Falun" that will be the central subject of my next chapter. For now, let us recall that Benjamin focuses on the time that separates the death of the miner on his wedding day and the death of his bride, on the surface, after his body is exhumed:

> When Hebel, in the course of the story, was confronted with the necessity of making this long period of years graphic, he did so in the following sentences: "In the meantime the city of Lisbon was destroyed by an Earthquake, and the Seven Years'

War came and went, and Emperor Francis I died, and the Jesuit Order was abolished, and Poland was partitioned, and Empress Maria Theresa died, and Struensee was executed. America became independent, and the united French and Spanish forces were unable to capture Gibraltar. The Turks locked up General Stein in the Veterarner Cave in Hungary, and Emperor Joseph died also. King Gustavus of Sweden conquered Russian Finland, and the French Revolution and the long war began, and Emperor Leopold II went to his grave too. Napoleon captured Prussia, and the English bombarded Copenhagen, and the peasants sowed and harvested. The millers ground, the smiths hammered, and the miners dug for veins of ore in their underground workshops." (95)

Not only does Hebel place geological and human time into strange positions, but his chronology is filled with death, as Benjamin notes. Moreover, the passage is significant in that it posits the chronicle (or historiography) in relation to narrative. The historian explains events that cause other events. The chronicler has no obligation to explain why these events happen because causality or reason is governed by salvation, transformed and secularized in the modern tale. If geology, like eschatology, lifts historiographical burdens, it also creates storytelling challenges. And it is worth recalling that Benjamin makes frequent use of the alchemical analogy elsewhere in his critical writing. As Hannah Arendt (1968) notes in her introduction to the essays composing *Illuminations,* alchemy serves Benjamin to describe the process of self-transformation that we have associated with the journey or katabasis. In his discussion of critique/criticism, he offers what he calls a simile, a funeral pyre, for the work. Then, "its commentator can be likened to the chemist, its critic to the alchemist. While the former is left with wood and ashes as the sole objects of his analysis, the latter is concerned only with the enigma of the flame itself: the enigma of being alive. Thus the critic enquires about the truth whose living flame goes on burning over the heavy logs of the past and light ashes of life gone by." Arendt then comments, "The critic as an alchemist practicing the obscure art of transmuting the futile elements of the real into the shining, enduring gold of truth, or rather watching and interpreting the historical process that brings about such magical transfiguration—whatever we may think of this figure, it hardly corresponds to anything we usually have in mind when we classify a writer as a literary critic" (5).

If we cannot point to one single basic narrative of extraction, ancient variants of a voyage to the underworld followed by a redemptive return haunt our myths. Then, inasmuch as extraction is a story about knowledge that helps the hero/author transform base matter into noble through a difficult process, alchemy remains a significant referent.

As I will elaborate, the impetus for the journey in Verne comes from a text written in code by an alchemist. We might choose to simply dismiss "alchemy" as a figure of "magic" or "wizardry" or "mystery" and be on our way. But, although Verne does not mention this, there are significant literary and philosophical links between alchemy, mining, and the subsurface. In part, this is because alchemy is, in the broadest sense, the transmutation of a metal of little value into gold or, we might say, extending the figure, energy, black gold, or capital. Mining has long been infused with atavistic fears, beliefs, and superstitions. Many of these persist in mining culture to this day. As with alchemy, spiritual languages work alongside the practical. So maybe for Verne, the Icelandic alchemist is a way of preserving some mysticism about a geological realm that is being explored and demystified in his time. But more broadly, he was influenced in *Journey to the Center of the Earth* and *The Black Indies* by Athanasius Kircher's *Mundus subterraneus*, where, again, alchemy shares space with observations of types of rock, fossils, plant life, volcanoes, and other phenomena, some of which naturalists had observed in Kircher's time and others of which entered his book as legend or received knowledge from the ancients or moderns. For the *Mundus subterraneus,* one of the crucial elements of the subsurface is that exploration will yield useful substances. These can be mined and then subjected to further processes of transmutation in a variety of different vessels to yield other substances of greater value. As with Agricola, writing a few decades earlier, information on the processes belongs together in a book on the natural, the found. But unlike Agricola, whose commitment to didacticism is remarkably rigorous, in Kircher we encounter the more shadowy and speculative figure of the natural philosopher. The very structure of the world below mirrors the world above, a trope that comes directly from the alchemical *Emerald Table* and related traditions. The heat and waters that flow through the underworld, in Kircher, represent a godly form of alchemy. The combination and separation of elements in an oven on the surface is a mirror of these movements but sped up. It is important to note that such modes of thought continue on, even with a burst of activity in the geological sciences:

> To a degree even nineteenth-century texts are influenced by the ancient *Emerald Table* and its maxim: as above so below. The subsurface is a mysterious and dangerous mirror of physical and metaphysical acts on the surface, implying that careful observation of geological events could teach alchemists deep history and the perfection of their art in "shallow time." From a geologic perspective, it can also be argued that throughout the *Mundus*, Kircher used descriptions of alchemic laboratories and processes (which he actively practiced) as analogs for an interpretation of Earth and its systems. In this way, his techniques can be seen as a precursor to the use of modern analogs for interpretation of ancient Earth processes. Instead of "the present is the key to Earth's past," Kircher's interpretive maxim could be, "the modern laboratory is the key to Earth's past." The various alchemic techniques of heating, evaporating, calcining, coagulating, hardening, and fixating served as conceptual models for understanding the formation of Earth. He had ascended Vesuvius in 1638 and had himself lowered inside its crater. Escaping the wrath of Vesuvius, a few days later he witnessed the volcanic eruption from fifty miles away. His observations were interpreted within his circle of influence. He likened the volcano's heat to that of the alchemist's furnace, its smoke to that of his alchemical concoctions, and its stench to the sulfur and bitumen fumes, which he inhaled in his laboratory. (Parcell 2009, 68)

In the Kircherian globe, fire (volcanoes) and water (oceans) coexist in a hermetic relation. Oceans rush in to fill up subterranean spaces cleared by fires. There is an equilibrium of fire and water on the scale of the cosmos. These elements exist whether the scientist observes them, so what of this is carried forward to the age of Enlightenment science where alchemy has evolved into a negative analogy? James Hutton (1795) posits ocular testimony as a primary driver of the science of geology. So, he writes, critiquing a colleague:

> I am surprised to find this enlightened naturalist seeking, in the origin of this globe of our Earth, a general principle of fluidity or solution in water, like the alkahest of the alchymists, by means of which the different substances in the chemical constitution of precious stones might have been united as well as crystallised. One would have thought, that a philosopher, so conversant in the operations of subterraneous fire, would have perceived, that there is but one general principle of fluidity or dissolution, and that this is heat. (57)

There is nothing particularly surprising here. But it helps to recall how alchemy continues into modern science as a linguistic function, a rhetorical figure, and perhaps even as narrative form. It is not simply exorcised from the vocabulary. The alchemist mimics with his laboratory art what happens in the bowels of the earth, where metals gestate over periods beyond human time. God created the earth plain and coarse, we learn in the *Splendor Solis*, an important alchemical treatise, but through the influence of planets and other forces, different types of land and different degrees of moisture produce, well, geological difference. Only those who know how to read images and figures properly can reproduce these processes, hence the alchemist—and again, I use this term with the caveat that it comprises a complex set of problems—must be worthy or deemed worthy of receiving knowledge. Only a select few can learn the secrets, if we take the tradition in its broadest sense. But leaving aside a problem for historians of science who have to determine what it meant for individuals to practice forms of transmutation in laboratory spaces, I want to suggest, provocatively, that elements of alchemy, embedded in narratives and structures that persist to this day, offer a third way between technophilic extractivism and the facile conservationism of those who call for (simply) leaving resources in the ground.

After describing Coal City, Verne inserts another long chapter in which Starr, Ford, and Jack Ryan accompany Nell to the surface to make certain she would not prefer to live there. Nothing happens for pages. Verne indulges in descriptions of Edinburgh and other Scottish landscapes with the excuse that Nell is seeing them for the first time. The French author inserts a poem by Walter Scott that serves no narrative function. It simply fills up space and a certain type of reader might wish to skip it to get to the action. Just as the chapter is about to end, the party realizes that Loch Katrine, on the surface, is draining into the subsurface.

The author then abruptly leaves Nell and the men and switches time and place; he returns us below, earlier in the day. The reader has no choice but to make the same move, although if she is very nimble she might try to keep one part of her brain on the shores of the surface lake. At first, it is a day like any other. Simon Ford and Madge have finished dinner and they are relaxing when a huge explosive sound is heard. Loch Malcolm, the subsurface mirror of Loch Katrine, threatens to overflow its banks in a giant tsunami. But no worries—all will turn out well. Coal City is spared, and no miners are killed. The terrible event is traced to a rock fissure in the bed of Loch Katrine. Such a fissure might well be the result of some natural disaster, but the heroes are dubious and so, after assuring themselves that the city is safe, they return back up to Loch Katrine and confirm their suspicions that a human hand caused the flooding.

Silfax, Nell's grandfather, is a fiend of the mine, one who had risked his life in the past, before the invention of the safety lamp. He has become a malevolent protector of the space below and, the reader learns, he was the author of the second menacing letter, as well as the cause of the blockage that trapped our heroes early in the narrative. During the marriage of Nell and Harry, all of a sudden, the odor of firedamp (methane) is perceived to have entered the chapel. Once again, the city and the lives of the heroes are threatened, but Jack Ryan manages to extinguish Silfax's torch, and the old man is drowned during the pursuit. Both the flood and the gas are part manmade (so human heroism can provide a remedy) and part geological (so keeping alive the theory of catastrophism alongside gradualism or progressionism). The novel ends on a melancholic note: thanks to Jack Ryan, "the story of old Silfax and his bird will long be preserved, and handed down to future generations of the Scottish peasantry" (Verne [1877] 1883a, 246). We do not actually hear (or read) Ryan's song, however.

In the end, reading the subsurface today with extraction or extractivism lurking in the background, the steady pounding sensation that any taking of resources "forcefully" from below the surface is a form of violence (where growing/cultivation on the surface is a form of love) is difficult to escape. This notion conditions the way we might read a work of literature—as a nagging feeling that refuses to go away.

To be sure, broaching the very question of how to read Verne problematizes the subsurface, coal, and extraction in a manner not necessarily sanctioned or motivated by the text. It is reading beyond, after, climate change: coal without coal, extraction without labor, industrialization with combustion displaced. The novel will end with a marriage, a return to the work of mining, and one final, ambivalent image: the snowy owl, part savior, part jealous and unpredictable creature of the dark, forever consigned to legend and song. Starr does not return home as one might expect. Patterns or codes abound: the voyage down to personal redemption, the wild child who is brought to civilization (ironically, not on the surface but below, only inasmuch as the below is life-giving), the battle of two men to win a woman, the destruction of an evil force of nature. The novel certainly invites a structuralist reading. It also leaves in its own wake not a template for further explorations but an elegiac song (played by the bagpipes) about an animal. In this regard, it closes off the possibility of future narratives, since this is the only narrative.

The novel began with a letter, but it ends without the usual return. We do not see Starr back at the club recounting—perhaps embellishing—his adventures. Such a frame would alibi even the most preposterous elements of the story. It is as if Verne used Starr but then pushed him aside in favor of a story of a catastrophic and magical nature (above ground) while below ground the world progresses. Yes, someday the narrative of progress and growth will end, but not in the lifetime of the author or his readers. One must acknowledge it, but this becomes a theological (messianic?) gesture, pushed to the far extremes. We know it, but we do not have to deal with it. Reading today, this is no longer possible. And, as one might expect, eventually it will again bear fruit. Verne devotes a considerable amount of time and space to recounting the voyage that takes Starr up north. He also describes the period of time it takes to convince Starr to search out a new seam in the same area. What should we, careful and critical readers, make of this? Would we not expect to get this preliminary matter out of the way and spend most of our time reading about the mine itself?

Perhaps we should not simply naturalize or excuse such effusion since, after all, exploration in Verne, in Doyle, in so many authors of this period, rests upon the anchoring certitude of the feminine that waits, at home and on the surface, and whose abandonment for dark parts below could be said to constitute a kind of subdued violence. In the next chapter, we will consider narrative implications of burial of matter that will, naturally, lead us to think about repression and to consider what the subsurface can do for us as a place for (indefinite) storage of matter that we no longer want to keep with us on the surface.

3
Burial

Copenhagen, 1720

The corpse of a miner is discovered fifty years after he dies in an underground explosion. Petrified and preserved, the body is brought to the surface and recognized by his now aged fiancée. It becomes an object of scientific study. But after a short time, exposed to oxygen and bacteria, the corpse begins to disintegrate. The story of the miner, printed in newspapers, captures the imagination of writers and artists, and it reappears in a number of works of fiction as a trope about different temporalities that reign between the subsurface and surface.[1]

German Romanticist E. T. A. Hoffmann moves the story to a copper mine in Sweden and adds some of his own peculiar details. Predictably, his "The Miner of Falun" ("Die Bergwerke zu Falun," 1819) is free of all pretenses to objectivity.[2] The title character of Hoffmann's fantastical tale is a sailor, Elis Fröbom. Elis's ship comes to harbor in Gothenburg, but Elis is unwilling or unable to partake in the party that greets the sailors on their safe return. Instead, he stays on the sidelines and sulks as one of his fellow sailors taunts him, because he cannot hold his liquor (that is, he cannot participate in a ritual with the other men) or perhaps out of greed (he prefers to hoard his earnings rather than indulge himself). Either of these conditions makes him socially marginal and goes against the law of the sea, a space ruled by a set of regularized behaviors and populated with menacing trolls and sea devils (*Naeken*). These creatures are said to rain down bad luck on any ship with such a character on it. Conformity is the watchword of life on board. Elis's companions imply he is both antisocial and uninterested in the women of the town, and hence unnatural.

In the German of Hoffmann's prose, Elis works on the sea (*Auf dem Meere*). Yet he is gloomy and melancholy, and, during his shore leave, he wishes out loud that he could be buried "in the depths of the sea" ("in dem tiefsten Meeresgrunde," in the deepest sea-ground, literally [Hoffmann 2021, 10]). Later, though, he will assert that he belongs on the surface of the land, the "upper world" (Hoffmann 1969, 156; in German, the *Oberwelt* [Hoffmann 2021, 20]). Prepositions are important when we are speaking of ancient tropes and embedded relations to the earth, yet another reminder of the importance of geology for the early development of modern languages. These lamentations about the sea are overheard by a mysterious man, to whom Elis confesses (so we also hear) that his father and brother have perished, and now his mother is gone too. He is inconsolable: his greatest pleasure used to be to return home from a sea voyage and drop coins in her lap, seeing her eyes light up. According to the narrator, a voice that remains removed from the actions of the tale, without this exchange of pleasure, Elis has little motivation to live, let alone keep up his spirits during a difficult sea voyage. The reader could well suppose that the symbolism of the giving of coins in the mother's lap—as feces or sperm—is almost too obvious, too much on the surface of this strange tale. As a superficial detail, it is only one among so many others and is therefore unremarkable. Hoffmann's prose toys with the reader: read too little into this tale and you may miss what makes it truly worth reading; read too much and you risk losing your mind!

The mysterious man listens to Elis's lament. He then attempts to seduce the protagonist into leaving the profession of his father "up there" for the life of the miner "down there." The man explains this life, in precise terms, devoid of any of the supernatural elements one might expect from Hoffmann (and that will indeed come later in the story). The old miner explains, like a father, precisely what Elis could expect if he were to choose that path in life. At first Elis resists because, as a sailor, he has never had the occasion to descend into what he imagines as the "fearful depths of hell" (Hoffmann 1969, 153). The stranger replies, scolding Elis: "That sounds like the common folk who despise what they can't appreciate. Miserable pittance! As if all the fearful torment on the surface of the earth that results from trading was nobler than the miner's work, whose skill and unflagging labor unlock nature's most secret treasures" (154). Such an utterance is almost too didactic. It is what Elis needs, but we know that, so we wonder what else he needs that we do not know. That is, as readers after the invention of psychoanalysis, we cannot help but follow along on the surface of the tale and yet ask what lies beneath. Hoffmann reminds us that the directionality and morphology granted to terms like *subconscious, unconscious, latent, manifest, surface, psychical,* or even *phylogenic history* are inextricable from any apparently neutral definition we might grant them.

In his speech, a defense of the subsurface and the nobility of mining, the stranger mimics language one might expect to find in the writings, several centuries earlier, of Georgius Agricola. In book one of his *De re metallica*, Agricola ([1556] 1950, 1) defends the miner from the charge of being a wretched creature, since he must "have the greatest skill in his work, that he may know first of all what mountain or hill, what valley or plain, can be prospected most profitably, or what he should leave alone; moreover, he must understand the veins, stringers and seams in the rocks. Then he must be thoroughly familiar with the many and varied species of Earths, juices, gems, stones, marbles, rocks, metals, and compounds." As it turns out, though, Agricola's intended reader would never himself go down. He is, rather, a learned man, a supervisor, not a mere laborer. Agricola's miner must have knowledge of various fields—philosophy, medicine, law, etc.—in order to be able to effectively manage the operation. But this takes nothing—or not much—away from the rhetoric of his treatise as it is codified in later centuries and repeated by the stranger in Hoffmann's tale.

Elis hears the stranger explain that mining is not mere toil for gain but, with training in the darkness, a means to acquire the power to "recognize in the marvellous minerals the reflection of that which is hidden above the clouds" (Hoffmann 1969, 154). This father figure (actually a miner, Torbern, who had been buried by a landslide and so also belongs to a different time) manages to hypnotize the young man, who is both seduced and horrified, taken up by the thoughts of the underworld in a fantastic hallucinatory state of ambivalence. Readers of Hoffmann will be familiar with this sort of prose. The mine shaft in Falun is a hellmouth, yet Elis is fatally attracted to the glittering gems he thinks he sees. The discussion never touches on the labor of mining, only on the riches to be found under the surface. Then, briefly, Hoffmann describes the mine in very uncharacteristically straightforward terms. He begins in the present tense, as if describing a fixed locale, but then morphs into the past, as if seeing the mine at one moment, through Elis:

> As is well known, the great entrance to the mine of Falun is about twelve hundred feet long, six hundred feet wide, and one hundred and eighty feet deep. The blackish brown sidewalls at first extend down more or less vertically; about half way down, however, they are less steep because of the tremendous piles of rubble. Here and there in the banks and walls can be seen timbers of old shafts which were constructed of strong trunks laid closely together and joined at the seam in the way block houses are usually constructed. Not a tree, not a blade of grass was living in the barren, rumbled, rocky abyss. The jagged rock masses loomed up in curious shapes, sometimes like gigantic petrified animals, sometimes like human colossi. In the abyss there were stones—slag, or burned out ores—lying around in a wild jumble, and sulfurous gases rose steadily from the depths as if a hellish brew were boiling, the vapors of which were poisoning all of nature's green delights. (158)

But from this point forward the narrator (not Elis, who still stands on the surface) moves deeper into a language that is much more filled with fantasy, hyperbole, and synesthesia. Torbern appears and disappears throughout the tale, so just as the reader thinks he has gone for good, he is back to confuse the senses. The Queen of the underworld peers down at Elis, threatening to turn everything "to dreary, black stone, as occurs when Medusa's dreadful head is viewed" (Hoffmann 1969, 169). Castrated, Elis will have no choice but to go down to search for what he lacks. Fossilized, he will seek out like matter so he can feel at home. At once Hoffmann remains a distant narrator whose gaze penetrates beneath the surface, as if he were watching events through a cutaway view while he simultaneously recounts events only visible to Elis.

Hoffmann employs indirect subjective discourse so common in writings of this time that it barely deserves a mention. So, the reader may find it particularly jarring when the narrator/Hoffmann interjects: "One could believe that Dante had descended from here and seen the Inferno, with all of its wretched misery and horror" (Hoffmann 1969, 158). At this point and only briefly, Hoffmann ceases to be the author who has melded with his protagonist and at the same time with the reader. On the one hand, he throws this literary analogy out, or throws it away, with no particular care. On the other hand, it is the only literary reference in the tale, and as such it feels awkward and rather silly. One might be justified in supposing that the one who uttered it had never read Dante's text itself, as a literary text. Or rather, with this phrase he has squeezed everything out of Dante, reducing him to one image of one canto of his *Commedia*. But if we were to think more deeply, with this phrase Hoffmann is at once Virgil, the father-poet, and Elis himself, the character who is ventriloquizing this literary reference for the reader like a vapid puppet-son. He has truly taken on several different positions at once, his mobility and multiple points of view suggestively moving between the literary and the geophysical. Finally, this interjection—this nonthing, a remark tossed in that might well have been edited out without disturbing the integrity of the story—is a rather vexing shorthand. Since Hoffmann was doubtless quite familiar with Dante's poem and, more importantly, with the stratigraphic interpretations of its structure, to strip these away is akin to removing an ancient corpse from its place in the fossil record and dumping it on the surface where it will soon shrivel up. Dante does not stand on a precipice and peer down into the cone shape he imagines as if it were an open pit. He certainly does not visualize the pain of Hell until he undergoes the pilgrimage. His entrance into the experience is certainly not through a cave, and it is more physiological than geological. Dante's voyage results in a conversion, but first he must travel down in order to ascend (katabasis). In fact, the pilgrim believes he is going down when he is going up.

Perhaps the analogy is made by Elis himself, one who has not read Dante but reduced his name to a mere figure just as a poor form of psychology might reduce any word or image in a dream to a mere equivalent in the waking world. Elis is a superficial reader (perhaps through no fault of his own, but only because he was born into a working life on the sea). Hoffmann knows much more about time, depth, literary history, and reading than his character. The distance between author and character is signaled in this very moment of condescending indirect discourse of descending.

After quitting the sea for Falun, Elis meets a third father, this time a good one, the alderman Pehrson Dahlsjö. Predictably, he has a beautiful daughter, and he welcomes Elis with paternal kindness. Dahlsjö speaks, oddly, in negatives: "I cannot suppose . . . that it is mere thoughtless fickleness," and then, "nor that you have omitted to weigh maturely and consider all the difficulties and hardships of the miner's life . . . the mighty elements with which the miner has to deal, and which he controls so bravely, destroy him unless he strains with all his being to keep command of them" (Hoffmann 1969, 297). Mining is a constant battle with the earth and fire, Dahlsjö explains. But Elis is not deterred because the image of Ulla, Pehrson Dahlsjö's daughter, gives him strength during the working day. Although Elis is shy, all narrative paths seem to lead to their marriage as the rightful ending to this tale. Perhaps there should be a battle between Elis and Dahlsjö for the daughter (just as there is a missed battle with his own father for his mother). Perhaps there should be a battle with some other type of male suitor. A reader familiar with Hoffmann awaits such obstacles; even a naive reader might sense, from the prose itself, a tension between the marriage plot and the mining plot. The fact that no obstacles appear, that all seems to fit in place, is itself a readerly problem. In any case, below the surface, Elis is wildly seduced by the underground queen/mother/goddess and the glittering minerals.[3] As much as the subsurface is new to him, it also seems entirely familiar, and hence it corresponds rather neatly to the opposites of home/not home that are assimilated in the paradoxical form of Sigmund Freud's (1955, 220) *unheimlich*: "that class of the frightening which leads back to what is known of old and long familiar." Torbern, "the original miner," reappears periodically throughout the story as a reminder of the atavistic elements of mining. He battles for the soul of Elis against Pehrson Dahlsjö. They take the place of Elis's real father, who died on the sea, as they help to preserve a fantasy that there will always be fathers. Since Elis had lost his, he did not have to go through the battle to obtain his mother. He had her but without the struggle. In one sense, then, Ulla is like his mother and her father is like his. But because these paternity struggles take place on the surface of the text, does that mean they cannot mean more than what they seem to mean? Although he does return up to the town every evening, his libidinal investment is deeply entrenched below, and it is mediated through the old miner/bad father who first brought him there. The psychosexual positions are there, in Hoffmann, waiting to be filled by various characters at various moments. The subsurface is the realm of a certain kind of overwhelming feminine spirit, a mother, a lover, a queen, who triumphs over the rationality embodied in Ulla, the bright angel, the apparently correct choice who holds no particular fascination and who remains on the surface and available to the protagonist after he overcomes his timidity to woo her. Finally, on his wedding day, Elis feels himself called by the subsurface Queen. At least he tells us so, not another male voice that might be that of the father or the brother. There is no father in the story—or there are too many of them—so the reader may experience a sense of loss or feel required to take a stand, to become the father. One wants to impose order on Elis, to shake him out of his hallucinatory states and make him see what he has. Whether the reader believes in the Queen and the reality of the Queen's realm or imagines that Elis has created this entire fantasy in order to compensate for what is actually dismal work hardly matters. Hoffmann's tales dare the reader to posit a reality in contrast to that of a delusional protagonist. Go ahead and feel confident that you know what is right. Reject the subsurface in favor of a place of health and sun and you will be exposed for what you are: an average person who has sacrificed true knowledge for normalcy. These stories provoke a certain anxiety in the reader, and in this case, it is around the fact that you did not stay behind but went up hoping to find a happy ending. Elis should marry and have children so that the surface cycles can continue, but he is so taken by the temporality underground that he fails to emerge. At this point it matters whether we are talking about burial or storage, long-term, short-term, or permanent. "Storage and Burial are two variables in a continuum of operations, not fixed attributes," writes Vincent Bruyère (2018, 30) in his examination of perishability. "The distinction seems to depend less on the structure of the container itself than on what it actually contains: stored life and buried death."

When Elis's body is found many years later, it has been preserved unnaturally. It is likened to naphtha, a liquid oil that would have originally been extracted from below the surface, burning in a sheet of ice. Such a powerful image cannot but stimulate the reader's imagination. It is highly compressed, poetic. Naturally, Ulla's body undergoes the aging process on the surface. She lives an entire life unwed while Elis remains just as on the day of his wedding. In this sense, she has become his mother when he is finally found. But in addition to the psychological twists in the plot, Hoffmann seems to imply, without much subtlety, that a different temporality governs the cosmos down there, in line with the neptunists in circulation in Hoffmann's time. Because the subsurface, for a number of theorists, is formed by events of flooding and receding rather than heat, it is possible to imagine that life is sustained there, developed in its own way, at a different pace, and with different species thriving at different moments.

As I have already noted, "The Mines of Falun" is inflected with details taken from early modern writings on mining. Georgius Agricola ([1556] 1950, 159) explains that the miner must understand astronomy in order measure the orientation of ore-bearing rock. He must know the law to make claims on land, and he must develop a series of other skills beyond the physical labor of mining itself. Book six of the *De re metallica* moves from the more scientific focus of the bulk of the treatise to address the demonic creatures affiliated with certain metals that are said to live underground and play tricks on miners.[4] They may make stones glitter even when they contain no gold, silver, or lead. Such forms of intermingling of fantasy and practicality also appear in Athanasius Kircher's *Mundus subterraneus*. Like Agricola, Kircher lays bare a whole fabulous world beneath us, his panorama framed by a more modern discourse of scientific truth. With minimal observation of sedimentation, he imagines that at some points the earth is hollow and inhabited by different forms of plant and animal life. Stones grow underground, but very slowly. This is why mines were allowed to rest after a period of extraction. In any case, mines are places of minimal vitality, like deserts, where one finds life on a divergent timescale, but life nevertheless.

The newspaper story of the Danish miner became an opportunity for writers to explore formative hypotheses of the earth. For instance, doctor/geologist Gotthilf Heinrich von Schubert's fictional account of the case describes how all rock—even basalt, which appears to the eye as so apparently volcanic—derives from primeval liquids. Hoffmann, to the degree that his work is tied to prevailing theories, would appear to support the ideas of Abraham Gottlob Werner, who thought that during the early stages of the planet's formation, rocks must have formed through the chemical crystallization of liquid matter. Then, after some time, forms of rock were also deposited by flooding and subsequent recession, during what was called the Flötz, or transition period. Werner allows that the biblical flood did indeed take place, followed by other floods, which account for the multiple layers of geological difference that the eye perceives when digging underground.

Finally, in a later period of his thought, Werner acknowledges some volcanic activity might account for coal and other types of rocks and minerals in the crust. Petrified remains of animals are embedded in rock—primarily limestone, coal, basalt, chalk, or ores—from the Flötz period. Any theory of the earth's age and development had to explain the lack of any human remains in the rock record from below/before this. One explanation given was the frailty of human bones compared with those of other animals. Yet the story of the perfectly preserved corpse (which only disintegrates when brought up) might contradict this idea.

The rival theory at the time, plutonism, focused on volcanic origins of the earth (heat). Plutonism held that different types of rocks were formed in fire and that if the core of the earth was hot, this would make life far under the surface impossible. The corpse of the miner would not be expected to survive. If we read Hoffmann's variant as a tale of burial, we are essentially suggesting that if we move matter from the surface to the subsurface, it can experience a different kind of history, a different materiality. This allows the possibility of the subsurface as a space of salvation or preservation, a mode that will reappear, for instance, in Jules Verne's *Journey to the Center of the Earth*. The French author, in fact, puts forward the hypothesis that if certain flora and fauna, now extinct, are presumed to have lived before the coming of man, there is no reason they might not still exist in hollowed-out parts of the subterranean, close to the places their fossilized bones (*ossements*) are found. So, the narrator of Verne's novel, Axel, muses to himself with trepidation: if antediluvian animals lived in these underground regions, who is to say they are not still lurking down there ("si des animaux antediluviens ont vécu dans ces regions souterraines, qui nois dit que l'un de ces monstres n'erre pas encore au milieu de ces forêts sombres ou derrière ces rocs escarpés?" [Verne 1864, 144]). That time moves at a different pace down there is implicit in *Journey to the Center of the Earth*, but it is not linked to any human forms of pathology or any collective psychosis. Verne, unlike Hoffman, does not poke the reader's paranoia.

To be clear, not all versions of the Danish miner's tale focused on geology. Other variants, including Hoffmann's at points, are invested in the passions battling with each other in the subsurface and not with the matter—vital or moribund—that surrounds the human. Other authors are interested in events on the surface during the miner's absence. This is the case of Johann Peter Hebel, cited by Walter Benjamin (1968) as an example of the storyteller as chronicler, one who merely lists events without ascribing causality to them. Hebel studied natural science and botany and was a poet and prelate. Benjamin's citation from Hebel's "Unexpected Reunion" (a story beloved by Franz Kafka)—we cannot really call it a reading—is only minimally geological. Benjamin is scarcely interested in what the tale might say with regard to human time and geological time and even less so in identifying the author along a spectrum of hard-core neptunists versus plutonists.

In a lucid account of narrative and history, Hayden White (1980,

11) reproduces a fragmentary text, part of the *Annals of Saint Gall*, concerning a period, 709–734, that one human being had the opportunity to chronicle, with one entry for each year, in a vertical column, beginning with the first year and descending until the last. It is, in essence, a visual encounter with the discrepancy between the writing up that is geology and the writing down that is history. Here is the fragment White includes:

709. Hard winter. Duke Gottfried died.
710. Hard year and deficient in crops.
711.
712. Flood everywhere.
713.
714. Pippin, Mayor of the Palace, died.
715. 716. 717.
718. Charles devastated the Saxon with great destruction.
719.
720. Charles fought against the Saxons.
721. Theudo drove the Saracens out of Aquitaine.
722. Great crops.
723.
724.
725. Saracens came for the first time.
726.
727.
728.
729.
730.
731. Blessed Bede, the presbyter, died.
732. Charles fought against the Saracens at Poitiers on Saturday.
733.

For the year 709, for instance, the chronicle offers the following: "Hard winter. Duke Gottfried died." Other years remain blank (which is to say, "nothing happened") and the last entry with words, for year 732, refers to a specific day: "Charles fought against the Saracens at Poitiers on Saturday." The chronicle chosen by White, assuming it is fairly typical of its genre, engages directly with weather (and its effects on food), war, and shifts in the status of members of the nobility but not on climate (to the degree that meteorological scientists tend to define this as patterns of weather over a minimum of thirty years and possibly longer, given advanced methods of measurement and record-keeping). The genre of the historical chronicle might be said to measure a relation between (a) human life span and the anticipation of periodic hardships but not massive existential disruption. White himself wrote his essay from that other side of the crevasse, likely unaware that a general knowledge of accelerating greenhouse gas emissions and their effects might force us to read history differently, or at least to think of it as out of sync with the time of climate change. Indeed, White's main focus in this essay, and, indeed, in his broader work, concerns the very writing itself rather than its relation to measurable or provable events.

It goes without saying—to all companions in the field of environmental humanities—that the singularly most powerful piece of writing making it impossible to write history as before is Dipesh Chakrabarty's "The Climate of History: Four Theses," published in 2009 and then revised. Ian Baucom invokes a chapter, "History and Dialectic," from *The Savage Mind* in which Claude Lévi-Strauss argues that chronology (dates) are the fundamental elements of writing history, but not all dates or clusters of dates are equal in terms of scale or importance. There are times when "very little or nothing took place." Discontinuities in the timelines and "alleged historical continuity [are] secured only by dint of fraudulent outlines" (quoted in Baucom 2012, 127). In this he is arguing against a Sartrean dialectical mode of history. As Baucom puts it, Lévi-Strauss wants us to take different modes into account into one that is infrahistorical (psychology, physiology) and one that is suprahistorical, into which events related to weather or climate could be placed. Much important work on history and climate change has followed in a very compressed scholarly stratum. On this side of the crevasse.

The story of the preserved Danish miner—Hoffmann's version and perhaps others—clearly influenced George Sand. Her 1864 novel

Laura: A Voyage into the Crystal also provides material for Verne's *Journey to the Center of the Earth*.[5] As in Verne's novel, in *Laura* the protagonist/narrator, Alexis, is a young man, this time with artistic tendencies. Entering a rock shop, he accidentally breaks a geode, a spherical rock with a rough outside but a core of brilliant, colorful gems. This event spurs the merchant to pull out from his drawer the manuscript for a story he had written in his youth, also told in the first person, of a young man who works for his uncle, a famous geologist and curator of a museum of natural history in Germany. The reader will almost certainly forget the frame of the tale before she reaches the end since the anecdote of the artist who accidentally opens a geode is so short and inconsequential compared to the dazzling core of the story. The same might be true with Hoffmann's introduction to Elis Fröbom as a sailor, although this is longer and more detailed. Indeed *Laura* itself functions as a geode, with a rough and quotidian exterior covering up splendor, if only one has the time and patience to read beyond the surface. But why not just plunge right into the subsurface? Why does the frame matter to Sand? One response is that it provides a secondary set of alibis for the fictionality of the journey into the crystal or for the exaggerations of the fantastical nature of the subsurface as if—or if—these were needed. I want to suggest that the shift between "as if" (an utterance that one might make with a degree of scorn) and "if" (an utterance that serves as an insurance policy) is actually crucial for Sand's mise-en-scène. Her text fluctuates between these two utterances that serve as frame and retraction, although they are never made by her or anyone else in the text. They are assumed, as logic, although perhaps not precisely in the Kantian philosophical sense. Certainly, a brief tale would not require such framing. The reader, I want to suggest, was not aware of her need for a frame, a distance, but now she has several: the frame, the narrative itself, the embedded story of a feverish hallucination, and so on. At one point, all of these excuses for narration become like the multiple facets of the crystal itself, refracting light, coexisting but without hierarchy or order to the point that the reader risks losing a coherent sense of objective truth.

The protagonist dreams or hallucinates that his other uncle is reproaching him for not having studied coal vegetation enough. He sees Laura in a diamond while he is inside the crystal. She is willing to show him the path through the subterranean. She leads him through a garden of crystalized rocks. Finally, though, he admits that while the subsurface is marvelous, he would trade all his experiences and knowledge for life on the surface with her, even though—or perhaps precisely because—she is just a rather plain, simple bourgeoise. In this sense, *Laura* also mimics elements of not only "The Miner of Falun" but also Hoffmann's "The Sandman," where Nathaniel's lustful and bizarre fantasies take him ever further from his fiancée, Clara, who would guarantee him something like a normal life. In *Laura*, however, the fantasies move beyond the feminine body. The protagonist also hallucinates Nasias, an uncle whose sanity is in question but who is so much more interesting (like Hoffmann's seductive underground Queen who takes Elis from his bride).

Sand indulges a series of hallucinations about the subsurface until, at last, the young man and his uncle return to the light of day. In *Laura*, breaking the crystal is not only a metaphor, it is literal (Laura smashes it). Unlike Hoffmann's tale, but like Verne's *Journey*, the male narrator does marry and enjoy a normal life, never again venturing below. In all three texts, the voyage is an initiation, but given that it is a common trope, why is the actual voyage not repeatable? This is the same question I will ask in greater depth in relation to Verne's *Journey* in the next chapter. From one point of view, it is a rather silly question. After all, the novel is a unique set of words and narratives set out in a particular way and, as a literary work, it is not repeatable. Here we have content or tropes battling against the poetics of the language itself.

Sand must have also metabolized Hoffmann's more famous "The Golden Pot." In that story, a student named Anselmus hallucinates repeatedly, sometimes after drinking a potion, sometimes without diegetic motivation. He stares into a glittering gemstone set into the ring of an archivist/bibliophile/alchemist. There are so many refractions in the gem and the tale that the reader loses of any sense of what is real and what is imagined (by him or by others). There is no single rational anchoring figure, but there are two fathers who want to help Anselmus improve his station in life so he can marry their daughters. Anselmus is offered a well-paying job—to copy by hand and with perfect form some (illegible) texts in different languages that he does not know. That is, his job is to write, but write without content or originality. In fact, when he does spill ink on one of the original texts (let us call that "writing over literature," although Hoffmann does not use any similar formulation and, indeed, he seems less interested in the writing itself than in what the characters see or think they see), his punishment is to be imprisoned in a crystal bottle. Hoffmann (1992, 67) asks the reader to imagine herself "enfolded by dazzling glitter, all the objects on every side appear illuminated and surrounded by rays of light in all the colours of the rainbow—this shimmering light make everything quiver, shake, and rumble—you are floating, unable to move a muscle, in what seems like frozen ether, squeezing you so tightly that it is in vain for your spirit to issue commands to your lifeless body." But then, Anselmus might also be standing on the banks of the Elbe River. This is what he learns from other young men in crystal containers with whom he shares space on the same shelf. Eventually he is let loose from the crystal and, in what appears (at least in Hoffmann's universe) to be a happy ending, he chooses the poetic and magical bride, Serpentina, whom he saw in the facets of a gem, over Veronica, the blue-eyed but real daughter of his patron. His life will never be ordinary or bourgeois. Rather than a functionary, he becomes a poet.

Although her language and tone are quite different, Sand also describes the geode, through the voice of the uncle, as a crystal that contains within it voids and caverns ("vides et caverns"), mysterious grottos, different kinds of landscapes—in short, a microcosm of the globe, "un monde fantastique où tout serait transparence et cristallisation" (Sand [1864] 1977, 53). But there is a danger that certain men might be seduced by the crystal. In the meantime, the narrator feels a deep attraction (he himself is not sure if he should call it love) for his cousin (by marriage), Laura. There is an obstacle: she is betrothed to Alexis's best friend, Walther, whom she does not love, although she loves the idea of marriage. So Alexis plunges himself into working on his uncle's gems to forget her. Soon, however, Laura invites him to enter into a geode. To do so, the narrator must hallucinate himself in miniature. The reader, too, must make certain scale adjustments (as in the case of Hoffmann) in order to grasp the narrative progression. She must imagine herself inside a large gem with cavernous spaces—a microcosm, obviously, since the protagonist and the reader can nimbly move inside of it. And she must move fluidly between outside and inside the rock in ways that seem quite modern and cinematic, especially considering the date of Sand's composition.

The parallels with Hoffmann's miner are clear, only in Sand rather than a fantastic queen, it is the earthly (should we say banal?) object of the young man's desire who pulls him into the subterranean realm. In fact, it is only in the crystal that they find each other attractive. Otherwise, they seem to find each other quite boring. And unlike in Hoffmann, in Sand, when the protagonist is able to pull himself up/pull himself together and return to the surface, he finds the woman is no longer beautiful.

Halfway through the novel, Alexis admits to his uncle that the voyage was a hallucinatory dream, sparked by him having hit his head and being struck with a fever. He has now regained his sanity and he promises to be a good husband. But as it turns out—to the narrator's confusion—the uncle is not interested in Laura or her feelings. He demands to know what Alexis saw in the crystal. He is completely taken by what he calls a revelation. He notes that the world of the crystal—the subterranean—is the real splendor and Alexis has seen it! We know only this one thing for certain about the subsurface, the uncle notes: "That at thirty or thirty-three kilometers deep, heat is so intense that minerals can exist only in a fusible state" (Sand 1992, 109). Therefore, any man who went down there would be burned alive. But he did not actually go, as he admits it was only a hallucination, a symptom of his illness. More refractions. The reader might become disoriented so that the reference to the theory of plutonism fails to register. Sand's tale is entirely, profoundly geological, and yet it is simultaneously a marriage plot in which the geological serves as mere backdrop.

Underground burial and storage are the subject of many discussions in the time of climate change. Can the subsurface hold or neutralize toxic (nuclear detritus, say) or even so-called natural matter (CO_2, say) over time periods beyond the human?[6] Or, to put the question in terms more immediately tied to the miner's tale, can the subsurface provide an alternative temporality to the one on the surface? And if we did accept such terms—even while knowing that the physics that apply on the surface are the same that apply below it—what kinds of illogical compromises would we be forced to make? A healthy number of technologies for mitigating energy use and emissions on the surface place their hopes in the subsurface as a spatiotemporal realm for such matters to break down or regenerate. And in this technological policy realm, is it worth distinguishing between forms of capture and sequestration deep below the surface and those that take place in a more visible realm (as I will discuss in the next chapter)? The farther down, one might say, the less is known: greater risk, greater potential reward.

On the surface of it, burial of unwanted matter may seem like a viable option, given the state of things. Consider this sober statement by the National Academies (2018, 1) in a recent report on negative emissions technologies (NETs): "NETs have been part of the portfolio to achieve net emissions reductions, at least since reforestation, afforestation, and soil sequestration were brought into the United Nations Framework Convention on Climate Change, albeit as mitigation options, more than two decades ago." The term *NET*, then, does not distinguish between so-called natural sinks and manmade forms. By *mitigation,* they mean technologies that may produce energy cleanly and change geological dynamics. NETs do not mitigate in this sense, and so they figure in the category of "last resorts." If only a few years ago burial seemed to constitute a moral hazard or a technological impossibility, now forms of sequestration underground are being taken much more seriously. They could be scaled up to have a significant impact, especially as more traditional mitigation efforts to reduce emissions alone are simply not working fast enough. For a serious body like the National Academies, these new or "exotic" technologies are projected to continue into the future, alongside a transition to renewable sources of energy and a slowdown of emissions or a bending of the carbon curve.[7] The report presupposes that reductions are possible but that they are not going to stop in certain sectors, such as air travel. Naturally, the report does not suggest that stopping air travel is our only hope, so instead the report mentions "bundling" this fossil-dependent activity with a formula: setting the global average cost of carbon dioxide at a minimum of $100 per tonne could capture 2.5 kg of CO_2 per liter of fuel, which could be added to the cost of air travel in the form of a tax. Such proposals were developed before the coronavirus pandemic. Yet during the lockdowns of 2020, planes flew with skeletal crews to keep runway slots, and there were talks of allowing the airlines to avoid proposed carbon taxes once they are fully operational again. Consumers who missed the experience of air travel could pay for flights to nowhere. The industry, with variations depending on whether certain companies are nationalized or private, received significant bailout money. There were whispers about higher prices and bankruptcies and discussions about changed behaviors "on the other side of the virus."

Such maneuvers should not surprise anyone imbued with an iota of cynicism. What interests us, here and now, is the fact that capture technologies are rarely discussed on their own or as the only solution. Rather, the term *portfolio* is often used. A number of the major NETs occur, so to speak, on the surface: afforestation, reforestation, coastal blue carbon (enhancing plant life near water), and BECCS (bioenergy with carbon capture and sequestration). Others such as direct air capture and carbon mineralization involve returning CO_2 to the subsurface. In these later cases, carbon might be captured as a gas, transformed into a liquid, and transported via pipelines (perhaps, ideally, reusing existing fossil infrastructures) or in sealed containers on ships, trucks, or railroads to its final resting place.

Technologies developed for extraction (and fracking in particular) might be extended to carbon burial or, as articulated by Harold

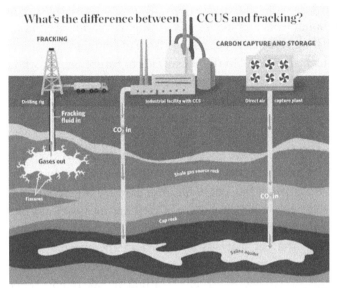

"What's the difference between CCUS and fracking?" Reprinted with permission of the Nature Conservancy.

Hamm, billionaire CEO of Continental Resources, who plans to invest in carbon capture in porous rock in North Dakota: "Horizontal drilling and hydraulic fracturing gave us the American energy renaissance. We used ingenuity to get the hydrocarbons out of the Earth. There's no reason why we can't use the same skills to put the carbon back in."[8]

The new carbon burial industry might also learn a great deal from the more established nuclear waste disposal industry. Spent radioactive matter, sealed off in containers, can be embedded in salt blocks, say, for a period of time that extends beyond what we would expect to be communicable to beings we identify with. This is the case with the Finnish Onkalo facility, subject of Michael Madsen's *Into Eternity*, mentioned in chapter 1, that considers the ethical, scientific, and temporal dimensions of waste burial. Another documentary, *Containment*, by Peter Galison and Robb Moss, addresses similar issues. Both of these works reference the earlier case of the U.S.-based WIPP (Waste Isolation Pilot Plant) project where a group of scientists found itself required to call on disciplines such as anthropology, linguistics, and the arts to think about appropriate monuments and modes of warning on the surface.[9] Important scholarship considers the strange issue of communicating that dangerous materials lie in the subsurface to future beings, who might themselves dwell down there or employ a wholly different semiotic structure or operate in a manner so distant from ours that they could not be expected to have inherited our stories, even in a distorted form.

Similar issues have not yet been widely discussed around carbon burial. Carbon itself is not intrinsically toxic; quite the contrary, it is a fundamental element of life. The industry is grappling with the possible negative consequences of (re)burying something perfectly natural that already exists in different forms in the subsurface underground but that was extracted and combusted too quickly. We do not know the timeframe or the quantity of carbon dioxide to be sequestered now. So, although carbon dioxide removal experts—some currently financed by the fossil fuel industries—exploring spent oil fields or other supposedly empty spaces below the surface have discussed appropriate linings to avoid leakage, the work is simply not far along or, at the time of this writing, innovation in this sector has been stalled. Many pilot carbon capture and sequestration (CCS) research facilities that opened in the past decade have been closed, primarily because of a lack of financial incentives. This is frustrating, of course, for those who argue that only by scaling up the process would it become more affordable. In any case, carbon leakage is meant here as a physical problem—a problem of containment. But it is worth noting that this same term also refers to the fuzzy accounting of carbon dioxide through processes such as outsourcing or moving carbon production up or down the chain of production. Nonprofits such as Buy Clean, based in California, work on closing the carbon loophole while taking into account all stages of a product or service life cycle, even in heavy industries such as cement or steel. It may be that "leakage" as the physical danger that a substance may breach its container and "leakage" as the effects of shifting blame or emissions to another entity while reporting drawdown can be considered as two sides of a coin where the wicked nexus of technology and economics reveals itself in all of its complexity.

Containment is also an issue in another version of carbon removal. Rather than being buried in seemingly hollow spaces, it can be injected into rocks and mineralized "forever." This technique is especially promising in volcanic areas of the globe such as Iceland or the Ring of Fire in the Pacific. Obviously, "carbon turned to stone" raises fascinating temporal questions, but it does not pose the same issues about markers to distinguish the surface from the subsurface in the location of its fixing, as it poses no apparent or immediate danger of being released or unexpectedly discovered.

In broader terms, in the carbon removal industries, carbon itself undergoes a shift. First, in its ancient and fossilized form, it may be extracted from the ground and inserted into machines, combusted for energy to keep things as they are on the surface. Then it is recategorized as "bad" and, at the same time, as anthropologist Gökçe Günel (2016) notes, its status shifts from commodity to waste. But before it can be sequestered, it shifts shape, again becoming a commodity (in the sense that it is acquired without distinction to its particular qualities) that could either serve in the productivity of another one (as in the case of enhanced oil recovery from older wells or as a greenhouse additive) or more directly (as a synthetic fuel or construction material, for instance). Indeed, carbon is already undergoing this shift in various experiments, but not at scale, as I have noted. Or carbon might never become this second commodity in the chain. It might simply serve no purpose, just lying there, and not necessarily underground. Obviously, this latter case is more difficult to fit within current market schemes and would require subsidies (provided by local, national, or supranational governing bodies?) to function as an accepted process.

Carbon credits differ from most other financial instruments because they are essentially granted for nonuse. The relation between carbon credits and carbon burial seems neither simple nor linear. For one thing, we could imagine that as the industry is scaled up, there might be a significant amount of labor involved, from manual to technical (automated) and financial. This labor would yield wages for workers, but rather than coming from the circulation of goods or commodities, these wages would be tied to noncirculation. With the money earned, the workers could buy another commodity that fits more readily into the traditional chain (a fossil-fuel-burning car, for instance, or a plastic toy), just as the polluter can either continue to participate at the same rate in the carbon economy, eventually producing more commodities, or invest in financial instruments that might yield wealth through the markets themselves rather than labor. In the most basic sense, carbon capture is both an economic and a physical mechanism and carbon credits are often referred to as "technologies" even if there is nothing material about them. A purchase is made of carbon by a trader who, as with most commodity trading, is set up to never have physical contact with it. This trader pays another individual to actually bury the carbon. The cycle is complex. For instance, the European Emissions Trading System, which began operating in 2005, assigns allowances to different companies. If a given company manages to reduce its emissions, they will have extra credits that they can sell to someone else for the right to produce more. On a fixed schedule, the total number of allowances should decrease (supply will be limited) so the price will rise, meaning that the incentives to not pollute will be ever stronger with time. This is not quite the opposite of a traditional market, so it cannot be understood simply by flipping it on its head.

However, there is a way in which the scheme resembles more traditional markets. Inasmuch as CO_2 is labeled in the process as a commodity (and not merely waste), it takes on a bodily form that can be sold to oil and gas companies. By its sheer bulk it helps to push viable fossil resources toward the surface of underground reservoirs, however perverse we might find this action in the grand scheme of things carbon-related. Interestingly, as Günel (2016) elaborates, the petroleum industry has responded negatively to this idea precisely because of the regulation it would require and given its ties to a series of markets and mechanisms that restrict their ability to operate autonomously. In the case of the burial of waste, it is generally the producers who pay (or the state, or a private entity). Should CCS develop as a way of allowing the coal and oil companies to continue operating (following a realist approach: we still need them, for now) or should it be primarily delinked from the fossils? In order to monetize carbon or value carbon offsets, experts in the field operate in a sphere of conditional futurity, and so in a sphere of fiction.

Günel (2016) explains that if carbon were waste, it could be buried, if not with absolute impunity, at least without massive rethinking. But once it is redefined as a commodity, then the capture system would shift. Rather than what is called the social cost of carbon (that is, the damage that emissions cause to human life where the term *social* is rather generic and suspect), the price of carbon-as-commodity would reflect its use, inasmuch as it might be employed in enhanced oil recovery or converted into fuel or other products.[10]

Let us keep in mind, that, as Andreas Malm (2016, 7) insists, in contrast, say, to an oil spill, carbon takes time to have an effect in the atmosphere. Its effects are delayed, cumulative, and last for thousands of years beyond the life of the polluter. In this regard, the geophysical traits of carbon do not fit well with other forms of industry or its accounting practices. In essence, when faced with this we are left to lament the shortsightedness of humans or of humans-as-capitalists, but then again, the nonbinding Green New Deal, proposed in the U.S. Congress in 2019, does not address this temporality either. Narratives that put different temporalities of the surface and subsurface into play seem crucial, then, not to explain behavior or account for actions but rather for how writing may posit a course and see it through to a different end or retract, undo, or thwart it.

Because carbon dioxide is not inherently toxic, discussions around carbon burial tend to focus on logistics and cost, with little of the attention paid to the traditional ethics of intergenerational fairness that circulate around other material. France Benoit's documentary *Guardians of Eternity* concerns the forever (a word repeated often throughout the film) effects of the enormous quantities of arsenic used in mining buried beneath the homeland of the Yellowknives Dene First Nation in Canada. Containment of the arsenic currently depends on freezing technologies that must be updated periodically. But what about the far future? One of the main characters, a grandmother named Mary Rose, faces the camera directly and discusses her fears about the effects of the toxic runoff on her own grandchildren, her people, and all life. She asks about communicating with the future (and in this regard her questions echo those posed by individuals in the films of Madsen and Galison/Moss), but her focus is less on written, visual, or semiotic warnings and more on the fabrication of modern, terrifying legends or stories around the burial site—a tradition deeply interwoven with her culture—that could be passed down for many generations.

Aside from scattered experiments in carbon pricing, there is no immediate cost associated with releasing carbon into the atmosphere today, whereas burial is costly. So, some argue that only a universal carbon price or tax (they are not necessarily the same thing, although the terms are often interchanged in everyday speech around this issue) would make CCS practicable.[11] Others suggest that by developing the infrastructures and means of burial we would be essentially sanctioning the practice and thus assuring the continuation of the carbon economy indefinitely into the future. Environmentalists may say that no forms of capture and sequestration should be undertaken until we have done many more studies about the potential effects on local ecosystems. Carbon sequestration in older wells, with enhanced oil recovery, is now financed by the oil and gas industries, and like these industries, it also requires governmental regulation. It is not an activity that can simply be undertaken by private actors in their own backyards or as small communities. The Bill and Melinda Gates Foundation sponsors a large prize to be awarded to researchers who manage to sequester the highest tonnage of carbon and the highest net value of the byproducts resulting from the project. To win the prize, you cannot simply take care of the first part of the equation (as in the business model of the Zurich-based direct air capture company Climeworks). You must also create a use value for the carbon you remove. But the Gates Foundation's philanthropy is not enough to sustain an entire industry indefinitely, and at the time of this writing there are few finalists left.[12] In any case, the current state of affairs is in flux, further forcing us to confront the discrepancies between deep time and the infinitesimally shallow time of policy on the surface. None of these variables takes away from the fact that carbon burial remains a compelling idea, if not a solution, whether final or temporary.

London, 1930s

In a well-known passage from his *General Theory of Employment, Interest, and Money*, John Maynard Keynes (1936, 129) writes:

> If the Treasury were to fill old bottles with banknotes, bury them at suitable depths in disused coalmines which are then filled up to the surface with town rubbish, and leave it to private enterprise on well-tried principles of *laissez-faire* to dig the notes up again (the right to do so being obtained, of course, by tendering for leases of the note-bearing territory), there need be no more unemployment and, with the help of the repercussions, the real income of the community, and its capital wealth also, would probably become a good deal greater than it actually is. It would, indeed, be more sensible to build houses and the like; but if there are political and practical difficulties in the way of this, the above would be better than nothing.[13]

A fundamental tenet of Keynesianism is that the masses should be kept employed in spite of potential costs, such as high inflation, even if—in fact, this is most often the case—the state must intervene in some manner. Keynesian obsessions with mass employment are not in preparation for a larger project of revolution in the modes of production or in the definition of work itself, of course. On the contrary, they develop in part from Keynes's calculations to bolster capitalism like a fortress against the anxiety generated after the Soviet experiments made clear the potentially disruptive power of the workers. That the workers must be taken into account in any economic scheme made Keynes appear extremely radical in the eyes of the classical economists being taught at the schools during his time. However, today Keynesianism is often invoked nostalgically against the neoliberal doctrines whose effects or, better, aftereffects structure current regimes, as a commonsense counter to those who proport to be against government invention. And we should note that the subsurface usually implies massive earth moving and grand scales, so it would be, one presumes, a highly regulated enterprise. In a sense, burial is just another variant of extractivism and certainly not its opposite or inverse.

In Keynes's time, the classical economists argued in favor of man as rational and essentially upheld the view that if men were unemployed, it was simply because they did not want to work for the wages being offered—so-called voluntary unemployment. Keynes, in contrast, argues against man's fundamental rationality. He acknowledges that demand for goods and services could also shape the level of unemployment in a given country. Therefore, at times, the state might be obliged to intervene, and public spending might be encouraged, ideally on social programs like housing or schools but, if necessary, he writes, contrary to the classical economists, "pyramid-building, Earthquakes, even wars may serve to increase wealth" (Keynes quoted in Lekachman 1966, 104).

To be clear, and compared with neoliberal doctrines of the late twentieth and early twenty-first centuries, Keynesianism does not pretend that massive infrastructure projects, whether stimulated by natural disasters or sponsored by the state, open doors for the workers to better themselves so that they can enter the private sector or climb the social ladder and eventually become capitalists themselves.

To the degree that the Green New Deal calls for new infrastructure, it sounds Keynesian, but at least one key distinction is worth making. In *The General Theory*, at least, employment is an end in itself. Full employment leads to the social stability necessary for the smooth functioning of the accumulation of wealth that will then lead to consumerism to help stabilize the markets, in turn. Wages must be kept high, even if this means intervention from the state. Without certain guarantees, workers might strike or withdraw from labor market—all ideas that broke with long-held traditions in economic thought, ideas that disrupted the traditional drama of capitalist businessmen offering going rates to workers on the stage of free market competition. As one Keynesian explains: "After all, the marginal product of unemployed men is zero. If the community puts the unemployed to work at totally useless jobs, such as the leaf-raking and ditch-digging which were the derided activities under the WPA in New Deal America, their marginal product will be zero still. But the income from this fruitless labor will be expended on food, clothing, shelter, medical care, and recreation" (Lekachman 1966, 104).

It is often said that "we are all Keynesians now," meaning that a rather diverse "we," at least in identitarian terms, with different sets of priorities, fundamentally adhere to a commonsense idea that government intervention is necessary to stave off massive disruptions, whether external or internal. The coronavirus has made such an assumption all the more powerful. Even today, investment in labor for infrastructure sounds like a middle of the road consensus-builder in political terms. In the early days of the Trump era, pundits put forward infrastructure as one area that all members of Congress could get behind, no matter how much they opposed the man, his character, or his methods. A recent *New York Times* essay, accompanied by captivating photographs, gives readers insights into a group of former coal and oil workers who have begun to find new (greener?) jobs. As one entrepreneur who grew up poor in coal country puts it, rather defensively, "It's not ideology, just math," as if to say, the transition, with subsidies, is just good common (Keynesian) sense.[14] It is not hard to read around the language of income inequality in the Green New Deal to find a kernel of the same, and this despite noise about socialism. Or maybe now socialism itself is nothing more than common sense. This resolution has little specific to say about energy transitions and nothing at all to say about carbon removal.

It might be useful to recall, as Timothy Mitchell (2011) does, that Keynes read the work of economist William Stanley Jevons, who predicted the end of coal in the 1870s. In fact, British coal peaked in 1913. As Mitchell notes, "It is indicative of the transformation in economic thinking in which Keynes played a role that the exhaustion of coal reserves no longer appeared as a crisis. The management of coal reserves could now be replaced in the mind, and in the textbooks of economics, with reserves of currency. In the era that Keynes's thinking helped to define, the supply of carbon energy was no longer a practical limit to economic possibility. What mattered was the proper circulation of banknotes" (124). Keynes ushers in a new kind of expertise. Of course, the word *economy* existed prior to 1930, but it referred to a process rather than being reified into a massive conglomerate, as we use the term today. Before the Great Depression, *economy* was a term applied to good housekeeping (home economy), or it could refer to a prudent use of resources where *political economy* referred to a "proper husbanding of goods" and the role of the sovereign in the circulation of money (126). In this regard, *economy* is also the prudent management of fossil fuels, such as the basis of civilization in Jevons.

All of this provides an important framework to Keynes's proposal to bury money, which is based on the act of burial itself as a form of labor. In contrast, for geological experts, the substances to be buried are of the utmost significance, with important distinctions to be drawn between nuclear waste, toxic byproducts, and carbon. In any case, the dream of a Keynesian system related to carbon sequestration might be this: governments would step in to fund the burial of carbon for some period of time (also providing employment for both skilled and unskilled laborers). In the future, this industry would be financed by private companies. In the meantime, fossil fuel usage would diminish to a slow drip, overtaken by other industries that would still generate enough power using non-fossil-based fuels so that in spite of economic cycles, there would be steady—if not linear—growth. To be clear, this is just a hypothetical model. In fact, the oil companies that are engaged with CCS at the time of this writing may sell the carbon they capture to other companies who burn it. The burial phase of the activity is detached from capture and there is little overall regulation.

Today the planet appears to be facing a quantitative leap forward, globally, in scale and number of such disasters, so we will have to decide whether we agree that we have crossed a threshold, beyond the nuclearized "risk society" developed after the end of Bretton Woods, into a period of acceleration such that this kind of commonsense, compound interest thinking no longer holds. In the United States, this threshold might be marked with names like Katrina, Sandy, Harvey, and Maria. In 2019, massive Australian bushfires captured global attention with images of glowing orange skies and unfathomable numbers of dead animals. The California fires of 2020 began much earlier and burned with greater intensity than the usual fires that older residents might expect to experience on a yearly basis. Extreme temperatures during the summer of 2022 have triggered calls to give future heatwaves proper names. Then again, these names or events loom large for short periods before they are eclipsed in the news cycle by other disasters, natural and unnatural.

Disasters, whatever their type or cause or intensity, were not central to Keynes's intellectual radar. Rather, his focus was on production for/toward consumption. The producers, whoever is paying them, will eventually become consumers, even if there is a time lag that may teeter on the brink of intolerability. Such extreme forms are, for his predecessors as for some today, preferable to invention in the form of state-backed loans or improvement projects. To a degree, that is, Keynes was arguing against something akin to Naomi Klein's "shock doctrine." But as his theory is not pure economics, perhaps he would think about altering it now that "we are all Keynesians," in the face of increasing monetary instability, spectral financial instruments spinning out of control, and neoliberal policies deemed responsible for the market crash of 2008, not to mention the unprecedented forms of so-called natural disasters, disruptions that are changing the insurance and reinsurance industries, the way neoliberal governments and industries will deal with adaptation to very costly storms, relocation, climate-change-related migration, and so on. Not to mention global pandemics.

The scenarios I have extracted from Keynes lead us to ask about the abstract human labor involved in the management of CO_2. Imagine that the carbon removal industry was to be scaled up very quickly—today or tomorrow. Presumably, one would place a value on the physical labor of the actual process of getting it into the ground equivalent to other forms of labor requiring a similar muscular-energetic output. It is also possible to imagine carbon dioxide removal as a form of "future job," highly automated, overseen by engineers and planners, with a small team of physical laborers— say, workers who used to be in the oil and gas industries—with limited expertise, exposed to some degree of danger, perhaps in boomtowns, but more likely in those same areas of the world where oil and gas were and are still produced. Could the industry evolve to mimic the off-grid or microgrid utility, or even small community farming, where each individual household would take care to sequester its own share of carbon? Could this form of localized responsibility lead to alternative forms of community within capitalism?

Keynes's sardonic suggestion—to remove printed money from circulation and bury it in a space linked to capture and control, to use that space as well to capture the waste of consumer culture, to encourage speculation on leases of the land by capital, and then to employ workers to dig up the money in order to give it back to capitalists—seems to warrant serious attention today, in the face of various actual practices in development around the subsurface. The Keynesian analogy functions according to a logic of employment and common wealth that, since the days of the neoliberal onslaught of the 1980s, since the financial meltdown of 2008, Trumpian nationalism, the coronavirus, and Russian military aggression, may strike us as rather quaint. It is also predicated on a fear of worker solidarity that is perhaps no longer a threat, at least in most parts of the global labor field. But perhaps what the analogy allows us to think is that the figure of the spent mine containing money suggests a rather uniform relation between two essentially uniform spaces: the surface (the space of rights obtained through leases) and the subsurface (a space of containment).

Keynes's writing is filled with figures and tropes about the subsurface as a place for burial (as well as extraction). In fact, Keynes (1936, 130) himself terms his own central figure of money burial as an analogy. He elaborates:

> The analogy between this expedient [the burying of money] and the goldmines of the real world is complete. At periods when gold is available at suitable depths experience shows that the real wealth of the world increases rapidly; and when but little of it is so available, our wealth suffers stagnation or decline. Thus gold-mines are of the greatest value and importance to

civilisation. Just as wars have been the only form of large-scale loan expenditure which statesmen have thought justifiable, so gold-mining is the only pretext for digging holes in the ground which has recommended itself to bankers as sound finance; and each of these activities has played its part in progress-failing something better.

While in the passage cited earlier Keynes imagines burying money in spent coal mines—that is, subsurface cavities in which there is no longer enough coal left to make labor profitable—he makes what first appears like a slip: for the rest of the chapter he goes on to talk about gold mining in its relation to the general wealth. In fact, coal in the previously cited passage is a hapax legomenon in *The General Theory*. Clearly, John Maynard Keynes is not lingering there himself. It is the shape and structure of the mine that interests him, not the substance that was previously buried there or what happens to it when it is removed.

So, what precisely is the analogy that Keynes owns up to? Is it, as we may have originally supposed, between the burying of money and the stimulation of the economy through more commonsense and broadly beneficial means? Or is the analogy between the burying of money (an act performed by capitalists to stimulate employment)—by chance in coal mines but any subsurface space would do—and the gold mine as a complex system that, eventually, might interweave state sponsorship, hybrid forms of labor, and global markets? If the latter, then what we have is in fact no simple analogy but a rather massive tectonic shift in registers—a shift from coal to gold, first and foremost.

Perhaps we are not justified in making too much of this question of the analogy, since for him this figure is simply a matter of common sense and therefore outside of any discussion of figuration (Lekachman 1966, 44). After all, *The General Theory* is quite long and what matters to the author are the figures of labor and control, not the substance that once occupied the mine. And yet, given the mathematical precision with which Keynes develops what Antonio Negri (1994, 49) calls a "permanent revolution" on the part of the capitalist state for its own self-preservation, and given that gold was then the standard by which the inscriptions of paper notes acquired their value, we may be more than justified in focusing on it. In Keynes, the traces of the vital matter of a fossil fuel are substituted by another substance, actually present underground, not fossil-based, and extremely rare.

It is worth recalling that both coal and gold come to be through what we might call climate change, in the broadest sense. The early modern geologists/alchemists, including Agricola and Kircher, acknowledge this. They read the subsurface as a rich landscape that mirrors the surface, filled with differentiated formations of rock resulting from epic, agonistic relations of dry and wet matters. The alchemist attempts to reproduce such activities of geological time in the laboratory, but much more quickly. To a degree, it was the speed of this geomimicry that made the alchemist a suspect figure in Christianity. Both gold and coal can be found near the surface, by small groups or individuals, but for massive quantities, extractive apparatuses are required. So the distinction between small scale use and industrial use is not only due to the equipment but to the capacity for drilling down and the recognition that some substances exist so far below (that is, are so ancient) that they will never be exploited.[15] With time, in theory, all matters inseminated by God with his special seed, as early modern authors suggest, might mature and become gold.

The labor of coal mining is complex, and it developed parallel to developments in technology—so much so that it literally founded a paradigm of collective labor under capitalism that is still dominant today in discourse if not practice. Coal miners can strike—they did so in Britain in 1926, with devastating effects, and that is precisely why, from a Keynesian perspective, it is desirable to keep them occupied. And as a side point, we should recall that when Margaret Thatcher closed down both British coal mines and Keynesianism in the wake of massive strikes in the mid-1980s, she also employed a rhetoric of environmental protection against dirty coal.

In contrast, gold miners have scant history of unionization or communalism. In the great gold boom of the American West, the rule of capture tended to reign. The same holds true for the oil rush in Pennsylvania at the end of the nineteenth century. At first, speculators from afar hired transient labor resulting in overdrilling, land abandonment, and haphazard and uncontrolled leasing. Gold was and still is mined through hydraulic means that can lead, at times, to rockslides, floods, and tremors. Indeed, Benjamin Silliman, an oil man and Yale chemist, noted that the hydraulic process itself mirrored forms of natural chaos: "Man has, in the hydraulic process, taken command of nature's agencies, employing them for his own benefit, compelling her to surrender the treasure locked in the auriferous gravel by the use of the same forces which she employed in distributing it" (quoted in McPhee 1981, 470).

The law of capture, deeply embedded in Anglo-Saxon thought, culture, and law, still dominates resources today. And as with rights to streams that flow across property lines, the courts tended to favor industrial development over the appeals of small farmers. Collective leases tend to win out over individuals. Coal—because of the large and hierarchical apparatus that surrounds it, compared with the more anarchic law of capture that characterize gold rushes—is extracted at a more predictable rate. And obviously, compared with gold, coal achieves its value only when used up, so the empty coal mine is no simple figure of storage. As I noted, Keynes was aware of Jevons and, indeed, it is precisely the slippage between coal (a limited resource) and gold (the standard for currency) tied to oil (a limited resource, but one whose price is controlled by international cartels) that makes scarcity less problematic than it might have been in the imagination of a Jules Verne or his contemporaries. Keynes's new economy based on expertise opens the way, Timothy Mitchell (2011) argues, for global oil finance. If earlier political economy means a process or a prudent use of resources or the proper husbanding of goods overseen by a sovereign, the dollar economy will depend not so much on this efficient management of fossil fuels but rather on a whole new structure of global pricing, cartels, and so on. All of this is to say that the early modern models of the subsurface may not suffice if we want to think through the full (carbon-intensive) implications of the burial of money in Keynes.

Let us keep this in mind, then, as we move on to a secondary function of Keynes's analogy of the mine: to store waste. It should not surprise us that even before a modern ecological consciousness, the subsurface was called on to serve as a garbage dump: out of sight, out of mind. Logically, green business schemes would be expected to seize upon this notion to turn disposal or burial into an opportunity under the terms of upcycling, for instance. Possibilities for both substantive and greenwashed business plans abound. For instance, landfills today are being subjected to management schemes in order to capture methane, which might otherwise escape into the atmosphere, pumped up and forced through pipelines to heat homes. As with so many supposedly eco-friendly schemes that claim or aim for total systemization, the energy-yielding landfill offers an attractive model. Environmentalists might worry that the liners of storage spaces may not contain all of the matter placed there, that toxins may seep into the soil, polluting aquifers and plants, causing local damage. Moreover, it is not clear how or if the methane produced will be regulated. Still, the idea of multi-usages, of turning waste into capital, a transmutation that is often described in alchemical terms, is a prominent figure in texts around the subsurface–surface relationship. Why a figure and not just something like a policy statement or engineering plan? After all, green design does not need tropes to function either in the open market or in nonprofit community ventures. And yet, what I want to argue is that figuration or language exceeds the containment of the landfill as closed loop not in the mode of traditional ecological language that is bothered about system failures but precisely because excess is needed to break apart the space, the zone, so that we can experience more authentically, more globally, the vastness of climate change.

Keynes wrote decades before the idea of climate change was in wide circulation. He wrote from the other side of the divide of those who do know (or should be expected to know) from those who could not be expected to know. In fact, if he had included anthropogenic climate change as a factor (distinct from natural disasters) in his writing, he would have risked being called a crackpot. His writing assumes a certain logic of accumulation that circles around the expectation of periodic crisis, war, and political change. Inasmuch as Keynesianism dominated in the period in which today's leaders were formed, it stands as a bedrock of common sense so that is very difficult to think outside of it, even for those who implicitly or explicitly oppose it by railing against Big Government or handouts (and who, it must be said, are often the first in line to take them when needed).

Jules Verne guides us through a different kind of logic where the subsurface mirrors what happens on the earth but stripped of elements of conflict. It is not (just) a place to bury waste but, in a sense, he imagines it as open, available. Hoffmann and Sand both put forward a subsurface rife with conflict but also with passion and beauty, perhaps not so much open as dynamic. Things happen down there at different paces, different rates. Put more baldly, the subsurface is one of many places in a/the romantic/Romantic imagination where difference asserts itself as such. Such difference might appear merely structural, but in the best writing, there are cracks through which flow prose that undermines the stability of the whole enterprise.

Gender difference is also an element of these narratives that could easily be dismissed as obvious, so that it does not need unburial and therefore is not worthy of remark. It seems crucial to recall it, however, if we are really to grasp the meaning of katabasis as a narrative or rhetorical term or some combination of both. It is not simply that men go down there and women stay on the surface. It is that the feminine is what spurs the masculine to go down; the gendered division of labor and access is fundamental to the literary genre but also to the geological distinction. Gender makes no difference to the rock as it forms below, but it does for literature, for writing, for thinking.

To achieve mastery over the subsurface requires a kind of violence of vision and of extraction; yet we simultaneously need to maintain the possibility of an uncolonized space that could offer resources, riches, hope, shelter. A feminist rereading of the subsurface could be vengeful/powerful, barren, transparent (this is what I am, take me as I am), or technologized. Gender difference might appear in intertextuality, borrowings, slips of the pen, or moments of aphasia. These are linguistic phenomena and should not be imagined to have any impact on the earth. They are inevitable human acts that betray weakness and serve as reminders of the power of the dream for self-mastery or self-preservation. The constellation of literary texts that circle around each other in this chapter suggests that both language and narrative aspire to exist as crystalline elements, but they flicker and move and are instable. Hoffmann's tale works with an existing narrative that could be summarized in two or three lines of prose or, as it was first transmitted, in a brief newspaper account focused only on the extraction of the miner. He then extends that core into multiple directions where it flows (like molten matter) and is then fixed forever into a text that hardens. We cannot change it; the specificity of the language cannot be undone. Elis gains a rich life underground and what is removed is his body, which shows itself to belong to that other realm. The historian might account for the difference between the aged body on the surface and the body below with a list of events or facts. This is what the human can do, and if the body had not been removed, those events would still have taken place and the body would have become something else. We need this other realm to exist, as a trope and as hope for something other, but now there is no more time. We make a great deal about the practical and unethical, but there is no more time. We cannot face the differences that separate us from these narratives, but they are profound. Hoffmann's prose toys with the reader: read too little into this tale and you are missing what makes it truly worth reading; read too much and you are losing your mind. In the next chapter, we will consider strategies to move beyond some morbid dependency on the profound, to place faith in the area slightly below the surface. Yet, ultimately, we must ask if such strategies are not simply (ultimately) forms of necessary delusion.

4

Surface Depth

Iceland, 1864

Here we are, then, at the rim of the Snæfellsjökull or Sneffels volcano, peering into the depths of the crater, about to embark on a journey to the center of the earth courtesy of Jules Verne. We are with Professor Lidenbrock (a renowned German bachelor scientist), his nephew Axel (the narrator of our adventures), and a local guide, an eider down hunter named Hans.[1] He grunts in Danish nouns that the polyglot Lidenbrock translates for Axel (and so for us, the readers) into complete thoughts (presumably in German, although we might read the novel in its original French or in English or in any of the dozens of languages in which the book was eventually released).[2] How did we get here?

Hamburg, 1863

Professor Lidenbrock has purchased a manuscript from a Jewish bookseller. His acquisition was not, apparently, motivated by any intent to trigger a plot. In fact, it is not even certain that Lidenbrock intended to read the contents of the manuscript. He simply believed that the volume, an Icelandic saga by Snorri Sturluson, would make a valuable addition to his collection.[3] Lidenbrock is leafing through when suddenly out falls a parchment bearing some runic text. The professor examines the parchment, at first without any expectation to engage in a *sortes virgilianae* or other trope of bibliomancy. Still, he cannot *not* try to read the text. It calls out to him and demands his attention. He recognizes the runes as similar to those found engraved in certain Scandinavian sites, but they do not seem to convey meaning on their own, so Lidenbrock concludes they are ciphers, most likely standing for letters. He tries to decode them on his own, but he fails, except to establish, given certain patterns, that they do not translate to Old Icelandic, the language of the manuscript. Curious, he examines the binding carefully and deduces that the volume belonged to one Arne Saknussemm, a sixteenth-century Icelandic alchemist, who must, logically, be the author of the runes.[4] Lidenbrock becomes obsessed with the idea of solving the runic puzzle. He senses that there is something important hidden therein. Several chapters of Verne's novel pass devoted to describing his fanatical behavior. It is actually Axel, the narrator, Lidenbrock's nephew and ward, who manages to crack the code. The text on the parchment gives (minimal, to be sure) instructions, translated into (backward) Latin, for the spatiotemporal point of entry by which Saknussemm, former owner of the manuscript, began a voyage to the center of the earth. The existence of this parchment, with figures written by hand several centuries prior to the novel we are reading, in a manuscript written—by hand—several centuries prior to that is confusing to say the least. Verne employs multiple displacements, perhaps to remind the reader that while the voyage to be narrated is real, it is not easily accessible. The narration is not—or, better, it does not conform to, nor will it produce—a map. On the contrary, it would discourage any rational reader from undertaking the voyage. Yet consider this strange logic: the content or message of the runes serve as the guarantee of Saknussemm's return. Two hundred or so years have passed since a brilliant man traveled to the center of the earth, returned, and hid details for another brilliant man to discover so that he too can make the trip, but in spite of technoscientific advances, no one else can reasonably hope to do so. Unless, of course, some or all the text is false: Saknussemm might never have owned the saga, he might never have made the voyage, he might never have returned, and he might never have provided an indication to only the worthiest of future geologist/explorer/bibliophiles. Indeed, the very novel you are holding may be pure fiction. Yes, on second and third thought, undoubtedly you are reading a tale of mere fantasy by Jules Verne, but just as you, a boy-reader, will lose yourself so thoroughly in the narrative that you will not pay the slightest attention to the bald truth of the work's fictionality or even to the style of writing itself, for that matter, so the men will go boldly ahead with their plans for a journey. While Axel will occasionally remind the reader of the dangers the men face and of his doubts about the sanity of the expedition, given, in part, the unverifiability of the authorship and text, his uncle will have none of that. These two positions with regard to the text are not only fully compatible but necessary, one might say, for a proper reading. Verne must keep you in suspense to keep you reading and to keep the generic conventions going, while he must also establish a minimal bedrock of plausibility so that you will learn from the geological knowledge he imparts. The Icelandic parchment is not a mere detail or even a mere analogy. Yes, Verne might have found another trick to set the men off on their way, but he found this trick and inscribed it on paper just as Saknussemm found a way (although there might be others) to the center. So that is the only way left to read. You cannot do otherwise; the text forces you into that (relatively) tight crack that is the particularity, the difference, of this work (of literature).

Aware of a very specific time that will afford them entrance into a crack in the earth, the men have a little more than a year to prepare. Uncle and nephew pack quickly, leaving behind Axel's beloved, Gräuben (Lidenbrock's ward), and the housekeeper, Martha. As in *The Black Indies*, these women will literally keep the home fires burning while we—the readers, who now carve out our difference from them—will forget about them. The men take a train, a steamship, and then another train to Copenhagen. After a brief visit around the Danish city, they take another steamship to Iceland. Details about Reykjavík, including an annotated list of necessary items to be procured for the trip such as Verne might have copied from any one of the Arctic exploration accounts, take up several more chapters. To be sure, the narrator (so also the reader) is not terribly interested in visiting Reykjavík. As Lidenbrock insists, what lies below Iceland is so much more fascinating than what appears on the surface: "Ce qui est curieux dans cette terre d'Islande n'est pas dessus, mais dessous" (Verne 1864, 47), a phrase that certainly resonates with the title of another Vernean tale of the Arctic, *Sans Dessus Dessous*, translated as *Topsy Turvy*.[5] In that work, a novella, what is up is supposed to be down. Members of the Baltimore Gun Club hope to turn the entire globe on its axis in order to green the Arctic and then exploit the coal that they assume is buried beneath the snow-covered surface. They plan to do so by launching a powerful missile that has been constructed above but buried below ground, in a silo. Their plan goes awry due to a miscalculation in the rocket's trajectory caused by the interruption of an annoying, wealthy female patron. But never mind all of that. Let us just concur that *Topsy Turvy* is a very Vernean story. It packs a lot of plot into a small projectile. It refers to other texts (by Verne and by other Arctic writers, for instance) without requiring a reader to know them intimately, only to know that they exist. It exhibits a kind of symmetry that remains elusive in *Journey to the Center of the Earth*. In any case, the reader of *Journey* is led to understand that the first third of the novel is a sort of necessary appetizer to the meat of the matter, and this is a rather strange structure, if you think about it, as I will discuss later in this chapter.

After tarrying—too long, perhaps—in the Icelandic capital city, Axel and Lidenbrock take a ferry to the Sneffels Peninsula, where they visit with locals and arrange for a caravan of horses to accompany them to the volcano's base. Although the reader knows the true purpose of the voyage to come, all the foreigners along the way to this moment assume the men are just going to the volcano for some surface exploration. Other amateur volcanologists have done the same. This is not some undiscovered territory where the men would expect to plant a flag for national pride. Even Hans, their native guide, is only made aware of Lidenbrock's true aim at the last minute, when the men arrive at the foot of the volcano. Another delay: before they can begin the real adventure, before they can receive the solar indication of their trajectory, they must ascend. Another few chapters pass, during which the narrator remarks on the growth of layered biomass, an unexploited fuel (combustible), that would suffice to heat all of Iceland for a century. This is literally a throwaway remark—a remark made sideways, while the thrust of the narrative is up (and soon, down). Of course, the narrator cares nothing for Iceland and its energy requirements. Indeed, the trope of the earth's coal on the way down reappears, again as an aside, in other works from this period. In Verne's 1877 *The Black Indies*, as we saw, everything turns around coal, but the reader scarcely notices it. And similarly, coal is—or rather, it would be—central to the enterprise mentioned in Verne's *Topsy Turvy*. It is so sought after that investors would risk throwing the entire planet out of whack to get it, but, as I noted, they fail.

In Arthur Conan Doyle's story "When the World Screamed," the narrator also passes coal deposits as he travels in a metal cage on his way down to reach the fluid, oozing core of the earth. He cannot linger, even if he would like, because the narrative, driven by the mad scientist, forces him onward. But the reader might tuck away in the back of her mind that there do exist rich deposits, to be returned to someday. In many narratives of this period, coal is posited and then withdrawn or backgrounded. Coal is often exploited as a trope of preterition. That is, one might almost say the writer of the adventure tale acknowledges its existence, then passes quickly over it because the ends of the narration themselves are not based on accumulation, and yet he subtly dares the reader to forget that he has moved the plot along, beyond the possibility of extraction. But if writing is a form of extraction, then we might say its very disavowal lies at the core of the subterranean narrative.

Sneffels Volcano, Iceland, June 23, 1864

It is more than year since the purchase of the manuscript in Hamburg. The reader has consumed more than a third of the novel. Several more chapters describe the climb up the volcano's side in cloudy weather and the tortuous wait for the sun to come out to indicate the proper fissure by which to start the descent. For several days the sky is cloudy, so Verne leaves the reader in suspense and passive with regard to the weather, as he does in *The Green Ray*. Finally, on June 28, the last possible day of the solstice period, just as the explorers are about to give up and return home with their tails between their legs, the sun breaks through the clouds and a distinctive shadow is cast, as foretold by the alchemist, Arne Saknussemm, in his runic instructions. Only in chapter 17 do the men begin their real voyage to the center of the earth—that is, the core and purpose of the narration itself. The chapter is titled, appropriately, "The Real Voyage Begins."

But before we move ahead, let us backtrack, briefly, to consider some other rhetorical-literary matters. As the men leave Reykjavík, Axel, the narrator (who is decidedly not "Jules Verne" or even Jules Verne), thanks his Icelandic host, in Latin (the language of their mutual comprehension), and notes that the host, Mr. Fridriksson, "accompanied his final goodbye to me with that line from Virgil that seemed ready-made for us, uncertain travelers on the road: *Et quacumque viam dederit fortuna sequamur*" (Verne 1992, 60). First, it is worth noting that the host speaks or recalls the verse incorrectly. In *The Aeneid* (11.128), it is actually, "et te, si qua viam dederit Fortuna, Latino [iungemus regi]," a line addressed to one person—Aeneas—and it is not meant as an envoi for a voyage (say, to the underworld, where the hero does travel earlier in the epic). Rather, it is a statement made in the hope that the goddess Fortuna will ally Aeneas to the King of the Latins, and it is uttered in gratitude because the pious hero agreed to bury the enemies' dead. None of this matters, of course. We readers are champing at the bit to get below the surface, although according to Verne's own narrative, the Icelandic host does not know this.

Still, it may be worthwhile to pause, before we take our voyage down there, to consider the logics of this moment in the novel. We already know that Axel, the narrator, is a solid Latinist because back in Hamburg he manages to crack the code of the runes. So how could this miswriting of a key line from Virgil happen in *Journey to the Center of the Earth*? Perhaps Verne made an unconscious mistake, but this is highly unlikely (and then, would his editor, Hetzel, not have corrected him)? Perhaps Verne made a conscious mistake, as if to say there is a certain pride in knowing just enough Latin without being perfect. More likely, Verne makes the Icelandic host misquote (and then neither Lidenbrock nor Axel nor "Verne" wishes to correct him, out of politeness). After all, Verne is a bit of a Montesquieuian determinist: Mr. Fridriksson lives far north, away from the center of scholarly gravity, and his brain has probably been frozen and thawed more often than is desirable. In any case, something has been knocked off-kilter, if we like, in this moment. The Virgilian line sounds like a phrase of katabasis meant for men about to descend below, but if considered in context of the ancient epic, the "via" is not physical and certainly not descending: it is a metaphorical path laid out by Fortuna for political reconciliation. What should we make of literary language if we were to strip it away from the text just as we might strip away a layer of paint? Verne seems haunted by this paradox, by the literary, we might say, even as he disavows it on the surface of his writing. The literary emerges from the subsurface, irrupting onto the surface, in his text, and at times it does so in such an obvious way that it leaves no room for reading otherwise. Having reached the peak of Sneffels, Lidenbrock cries out in joy as he has now managed to reassure himself that they are indeed on the right path. He sees a runic inscription in stone, "gnawed by time," that bears the name of Arne Saknussemm (Verne 1992, 84). Because Lidenbrock and Axel now know how to read this language, they can follow the clues. To be sure, their experience with paper has taught them. No doubt the specificity of the characters making up the name are what ground them. These are not random carvings that happen to look like letters. They are not examples of pareidolia or visions in the rocks that a believer might see and interpret as other than purely casual. They are clearly signs of a (former) human presence that has endured far beyond his lifetime because of the durability of the rock itself.

Later the reader will encounter another Virgilian phrase, this time cited correctly and in a context that makes better sense. Perhaps the reader already anticipates it, since it is such a crucial one and so famous. The men have found the proper path and have spent their first night underground. Waking, Axel feels disoriented. Lidenbrock notes that their barometer proves that so far, they have traveled on a gently sloping path that is primarily horizontal. They are still near sea level. After a hearty breakfast, Lidenbrock announces, "Now our voyage really begins." And in fact, as the men begin to "slide" downward, the author/narrator invokes the following phrase (which would have echoed in the cavernous rocks): "C'était le facilis descensus Averni de Vergile" (Verne 1864, 92)

Édouard Riou, illustration from Jules Verne, *Journey to the Center of the Earth*.

("It [the descent, the ease of movement] was, corresponded to, the *facilis descensus Averni* [the way down, to the Avernus, the underground river, or, if you like, to hell, is easy] of Virgil.")[6] There is no other way but down now: "Cette coulée de lave n'obliquait ni d'un côté ni de l'autre. Ella avait l'inflexibilité de la ligne droite" (92). Of course, the reader might also be aware of the long-standing literary tradition—most notably in Dante—that takes Virgil's line and reroutes it through a Christian or moralizing framework to mean something like: it is easier to slide down, to go to hell, than to go up, to climb toward heaven, to find redemption, and so on.

As I said, the reader might well have anticipated this line, especially after the (slightly incorrect) citation from Virgil a few chapters prior. It is almost as if Verne cannot avoid throwing this line into his novel, just as he cannot avoid referencing the trope of katabasis. Yet he must also take a certain distance from these literary precedents since he claims that his voyage is "real." And, SPOILER ALERT, the men will come very close to the center without ever reaching their absolute goal. Instead, after a series of adventures that find them, at one point, under Northern Scotland, they will be blasted upward on the top of a volcanic eruption, reemerging, at the end, at Stromboli, in Southern Italy.[7]

Verne also did not choose the famous Virgilian line that Sigmund Freud would use a few decades later for his epigraph and then again within the text of *The Interpretation of Dreams*, "Flectere si nequeo superos, Acheronta movebo." This line, spoken by Juno in *The Aeneid* (8.312) does indeed imply directionality: if I am not able to bend the will of my fellow gods of the upper realm (*superos*), I will turn to the realm below. Freud (1965, 647) refers to the line again in his text with a more directional force: "In waking life suppressed material in the mind is prevented from finding expression and is cut off from internal perception owing to the fact that the contradictions present in it are eliminated—one side being disposed of in favor of the other; but during the night, under the sway of an impetus towards the construction of compromises, this suppressed material finds methods and means of forcing its way into consciousness." Some critics suggest that Freud, who was undertaking his own analysis, was conscious that he was summoning demons through his writing. In this case, he is using the Virgilian phrase out of context rather than necessarily identifying himself with Juno (keeping in mind that elsewhere he is identified with Aeneas, a hero who has lost his father and goes to meet him in the underworld).[8]

Freud is often said to have conceived the entire work as a journey, beginning in a dark wood, an obvious Dantean reference and so, indirectly, a Virgilian one. After the line he cites, Freud suggests "there is a cavernous defile" followed by a return to high ground and a question directed to readers, "Which way do you want to go?"[9] For Freud, the interpretation of dreams (and so, the book itself) is the *via regia* to the unconscious. By definition, his method is likened to the path of the epic hero. In a chapter on infantile material, at the very end, Freud reminds his reader that dreams can have more than one meaning. And in a footnote added in 1914 he writes: "The fact that the meanings of dreams are arranged in superimposed layers is one of the most delicate, though also one of the most interesting, problems of dream-interpretation. Anyone who forgets this possibility will easily go astray and be led into making untenable assertions upon the nature of dreams. Yet it is still a fact that far too few investigations have been made into this matter. Hitherto the only thorough piece of research has been Otto Rank's into the fairly regular stratification of symbols in dreams provoked by pressure of the bladder" (Freud 1954, 219). All of these elements link strata and the voyage (downward) to knowledge.

In this context it is worthwhile noting that in *Journey to the Center of the Earth* Axel recounts a dream, or rather, a nightmare. He notes: "I was in the middle of a volcano in the depths of the Earth, I felt as if I was being thrown into interplanetary space in the form of eruptive rock" (Verne 1992, 75). The dream here is pure surface—there is nothing to read (under it) and no work of interpretation to be done! No unconscious, hence no royal road to take us there. We should keep these various factors in mind as they refer the narrative outside of itself and to other literary works, where otherwise the novel pretends to be entirely scientific and indeed functions on this tension.

To what degree, then, is *Journey to the Center of the Earth* a text to be read primarily for the plot, as a map of the journey that others might actually follow—that is, the text has something more than slight narrative value in the service of geological pedagogy—where the points along the way may bear a certain importance for the arrival? Or is the reader more likely to be captivated by suspense and so will forget or leave undigested all of the prose? Are there literary elements to excavate from below? Verne was interested in industry and the practical, not the purely theoretical. He wrote that everything for him was based in the real and possible, so where does that leave the reader? And then, what happens when the reader learns that Verne borrowed so many elements of both the plot and the prose from other sources that these simply cannot be separated out? Then, what about language itself? For the most part, Verne/Axel describe events in a fairly transparent and neutral manner.

In comparison, Lidenbrock has a tic. He has trouble pronouncing certain complex words, and this makes him angry, which in turn makes it difficult for him to exercise his pedagogical function. This could simply be a detail added by Verne offhandedly, but if we are to take this work seriously as a work of literature and not just a plot, we must pay attention to the fact that this professor trips over his words as he sometimes mishandles a rock specimen. If he has a pathology, it is precisely this: he cannot listen to another voice except his own. As Axel recounts during the early parts of the novel, and as he is first transcribing the parchment runes:

> When this work was finished, my uncle eagerly snatched up the sheet on which I had been writing, and examined it for a long time with great care.
> "What does it mean?" he kept automatically repeating.
> I swear I couldn't have told him anything. In any case he wasn't asking me and continued speaking to himself: "This is what we call a cipher, in which the meaning is hidden in letters which have deliberately been mixed up, and which, if properly laid out, would form an intelligible sentence. When I think that there is perhaps here the explanation or indication of a great discovery!"[10] (Verne 1992, 11–12)

Then again, George Sand's geologist, Professor Tungsténius, also stammers, so much, in fact, that he cannot continue to teach and is replaced by the narrator of *Laura*. So perhaps we cannot make too much of Verne's choices. Perhaps he took this speech disorder directly from Sand without hesitation.

Berkeley, California, 2009

If literary form or language matter at all to us now, these questions about how to read may bring us to the heart of a series of debates about surface versus depth. In an issue of the journal *Representations*, scholars reflect on recent trends in the field with some common vocabulary. The editors of the special issue note that contributors, influenced by a series of horrific political events happening right before their eyes, "have been drawn to modes of reading that attend to the surfaces of texts rather than plumb their depths" (Best and Marcus 2009, 2). By the way, although they write on this side of the crevasse, they do not mention climate change (nor are they obliged to do so). Various authors in the collection agree that "the way we read now" (the actual title of the journal special issue) has been influenced in the past by broad notions of "symptomatic reading," developed by Fredric Jameson: a reader should seek out what is not on the surface, we should look below to interpret. Jameson, for Best and Marcus, represents a heroic, masculine critical mode. Under his influence, literary scholars who read only the surface risk appearing weak and fearful. In comparison, critics following Marx and Freud believe that reading below a text could reveal hidden structures of power or symptoms by which one might diagnose individual or collective ills. As we know, both men utilized spatial metaphors to conceptualize this sense of *below*. Moreover, as some of the surface readers note, cognitive scientists agree that the spatial or directional mode is intrinsic to the way we read. Some of the critics who advocate for surface readings see linguistic complexity or form—appreciable without plunging down there—as crucial elements to proper reading of a literary text. In order to find value in a text (and, to be sure, the surface readers are attentive to differences of genre, style, historical period, authorship, and so on), one need not travel below. An embrace of surface reading "involves accepting texts, deferring to them instead of mastering or using them as objects, and refuses the depth model of truth, which dismisses surfaces as inessential and deceptive" (10). One need not wage "suspicious and aggressive attacks on its concealed depths" (11). There is an ethical imperative in their work, which naturally sparked some heated academic debate. It is my intention not to enter into the fray but rather to suggest that surface/depth modes cannot be thought outside of geology. They are embedded in a relation with the earth that they cannot shed: even if one tarries on the surface precisely because one believes that it offers enough, one risks losing out on what happens below.

It goes without saying that at some point in the process or journey authors must make choices that rule out other choices. When Jules Verne writes his *Journey to the Center of the Earth*, he faces a decision: he might follow a particular school or take a position with regard to questions of the core of the earth that were debated with vigor earlier in the century. He could decide for himself and ignore debates or he could find a way to acknowledge theories in his prose (and this would conform to the didactic mission of his friend and editor, Hetzel). The novel in general—and this novel in particular—does occasionally cross over into or have commerce with actual science. In *Journey*, the real Humphry Davy, an adherent of the watery core school, as I noted, is named as a friend of the fictional Lidenbrock. Essentially, Davy (and so also Lidenbrock) argues that if there were a central fire at the center of the earth, the surface would reach an unbearably high temperature. At the very least, heat should be much greater the farther one digs down in mines and wells, but Davy found no conclusive evidence of this. Granite or other rocks brought up from deep below could hardly have been formed by fire, he thought. How would such rock have been melted?

When the men are near the end of their travels. Axel, the narrator, explains:

> What did such a change mean? Until now Lidenbrock and Davy's theory had been confirmed by the evidence; until now special conditions of refracting rocks, of electricity, or of magnetism had modified the general laws of nature, making the heat stay moderate. Given that the theory of a central fire remained in my view the only correct one, the only justifiable one, were we going to return to an environment where this phenomenon held true, where the heat completely melted the

rocks? I was afraid so, and said to the professor: "If we aren't drowned or torn to pieces." (Verne 1992, 200–201)

The men take a wrong turn and come to Silurian layers dotted with trilobites, followed by layers they identify as Devonian, and then coal of the Carboniferous. They are clearly moving from older to younger and, therefore, upward rather than downward along a "reverse timeline." Axel echoes other thinkers (including René Descartes) who calculate that the earth should be 1°C warmer for every seventy feet they descend, hence 2,000,000°C at center. But Lidenbrock, appealing to Davy, argues that the earth's crust would not resist such heat and would explode. The core cannot be liquid, or else there would be tides that would cause earthquakes. Davy is correct, says Lidenbrock, in his formation theory:

> The Earth heated up through combustion on its surface, not from any other cause. The surface was composed of a great quantity of metals such as potassium and sodium, which have the property of catching fire as soon as they are in contact with air and water. These metals started to burn when the water vapour in the atmosphere fell to the ground as rain. Little by little, as the water worked its way into the cracks in the Earth's crust, it produced further fires, explosion, and eruptions. Hence the large number of volcanoes during the first days of the world. (Verne 1992, 32)

Clearly, Lidenbrock cannot deny there is heat on or close to the surface, but he refuses to believe there is heat in the core. How, then, to explain the fact that Iceland, a young landmass, is still rising? What could be pushing it up if not heat? The men are walking, downward, past a coal shaft, and Verne performs on their part a disavowal that should be familiar to readers of the present book: coal exists down there, and I recognize it, but I am not interested in taking it because my voyage is purely experiential and not tied to extraction. At this point in the novel, a new voice interrupts that is not Axel's or even, perhaps, Verne's. It is an authoritative scientific voice that explains:

Despite Professor Lidenbrock's theories [notice the voice does not refer to him as "my Uncle," so we do not think we are overhearing Axel], a violent fire smouldered in the bowels of the spheroid. Its effects were felt even in the outermost layers of the Earth's crust. The plants, shielded from the life-giving radiation of the sun, did not produce flowers or scent, but their roots drew vigorous life from the burning soils of the first days.

There were few trees, only herbaceous plants, huge grassy areas, ferns, club-mosses, and sigillarias and asterophyllites, rare families whose species were then numbered in thousands.

It was this exuberant vegetation which produced the coal. The Earth's crust, still elastic, followed the movements of the liquid mass it encased. Hence a large amount of cracking and subsiding. The plants, dragged under water, gradually built up considerable piles of matter.

Next came the action of Nature's chemistry: on the bottom of the seas, the vegetable masses became peat. Then, thanks to the effect of the gases, and in the heat from the fermentation, they underwent a complete mineralization. (102)

The following sentence, however, appears to come from a different source, one that readers might well associate with Verne himself: "These, however, will be used up by over-consumption in less than three centuries, if the industrialized nations do not take care." And immediately after this, we are back in the first person, with Axel, who takes responsibility for the preceding textbook-like prose:

These ideas passed through my mind while I looked at the coal riches accumulated in this section of the Earth's mass. Such riches will probably never be opened up. The exploitation of these faraway mines would require too much effort. What would be the point in any case, when coal is spread over the Earth's surface, so to speak, in a large number of countries? So these untouched strata I saw will probably remain exactly the same when the Earth's last hour sounds. (102)

Now to be sure, we find in this series of three (descending) selections some of Verne's key obsessions. We can also note here the submission of a boy to the absolute voice of the scientist. Axel is possessed, momentarily, by the scientific prose, but then in a semi-conscious state he takes credit for "these ideas." Such shifts should not surprise us. Indeed, we should probably not try to read beneath them. They exist, on the surface, as bits of information to be conveyed and not as reflections of characterological or ideological traits, and as such they might confirm or contradict a reader's existing biases about human behavior.

The question of choice haunts the novel. Once the men have descended into the mouth of the volcano, they come upon three different openings or chimneys. At first, they are not sure of the proper path to follow. They face, in other words, a classic dilemma of plotting or, in a shortened form, of plot.[11] Nevertheless, after a few minutes of anxiety, Lidenbrock finds a runic inscription on a rock indicating the proper way. This is the first time we realize, even if not consciously, that Saknussemm, the Icelandic author of the runes sketched on the parchment acquired by Lidenbrock, undertook his trip with the intent of signaling to future travelers, and even if he did not know if he would return or if others might follow, he had a degree of hope, so he marked (he marked himself present in) the rock for eternity. As readers of this novel, we operate under two different and contradictory logics, not unlike the compromise formation of a dream. To the degree that the reader accepts the narration as true, he knows that the men will return so that Axel can publish his narrative. However, as we are swept up into the dangerous adventure, we never know what creatures or perils await us around the next corner. Axel often tells his uncle or the reader (or both) that he fears the voyage will lead to his death, but does the reader actually believe him? And then, to what degree is this consciousness of death to be taken seriously, in the Freudian sense, as traceable or legible in relation to unconscious drives?

To be immersed in the novel's suspense, we must have doubts about the return, and these doubts require us to imagine a different kind of omniscient narrator who is putting thoughts into Axel's mind, writing with his pen, taking over his consciousness, and this would undermine his credibility. Undermining is literally a possible way to read the entire narrative. On the one hand, this voyage is so fraught that it is portrayed as an absolutely unrepeatable one that could only be taken this once . . . well, this twice . . . but now only by these extraordinary men. If it were someday going to be easy and if the journey were going to be available to masses of subsurface tourists, there would be no point in reading the book and being swept up in its narrative. On the other hand, the men cannot help but name geographical features of the subsurface after themselves (the Lidenbrock Sea, Port Gräuben, etc.), with the implication that these names confer a futurity for these places. The relation of the men to these places is not, perhaps, unlike their relation to other narratives in which a single choice is made—for instance, of a woman to marry or of a profession. Such selections may bring joy or despair, but they also foreclose others. The author of the narrative must accept such closures, and perhaps that is what it means to grow up or take on adult responsibility. To live with multiple possibilities in the balance is a more neurotic way of living. It is also a form of extending childhood or defying death. Verne manages to have it both ways or he resolves this dilemma of "the first and only time" versus "continuity and openness" at the end of his novel *The Mysterious Island*. Perhaps the deus ex machina of the volcano that utterly destroys the entire sphere of action, admired by no less a critic than Michel Butor ([1949] 1960), is a significant device not only to express a certain geological relation but also to solve narrative issues that would otherwise force Verne to make absolute decisions for or on the part of his characters.

At last the men know they are on the right way toward the earth's center. The path open before them is not a sharp vertical drop but a gentle slope in a southeasterly direction. Along the way, Axel arranges rocks so that if they were to return by the same route, they would have an easier time charting their path. After running out of water, after Axel becomes separated from his uncle and the guide, at the very brink of death he is rescued and wakes up at the shores of a vast sea, which Lidenbrock claims for himself: "The Lidenbrock Sea." There are lapping waves (tidal pulls, under the lunar influence even down there) and shores made up of sand

Édouard Riou, illustration from Jules Verne, *Journey to the Center of the Earth*.

and "dotted with those small shells that housed the first beings of creation" (Verne 1992, 137). There is also a light, described by Axel as vaguely "electrical" in nature, like an aurora borealis. The "sky" above is also filled with clouds and "the electric layers produced an astonishing play of light" (138). The space is immense, clearly, so that while Axel understands, cognitively, that he is imprisoned in a

Aeneae descensus ad inferos cum Sibylla Cumaea, 1700. Miriam and Ira D. Wallach Division of Art, Prints, and Photographs: Picture Collection, New York Public Library Digital Collections.

cavern with a ceiling and walls, he cannot actually see them. Riou's illustration, like so many visual and discursive precedents, allows viewers to understand that they are underground by the means of a sort of proscenium arch of stone. Axel is so overtaken with awe at this space that, he claims, he is without words, yet the novel continues along with no interruption, no pause for reflection. The sublime is put forward and then almost immediately withdrawn because it is in the wrong genre.

The men come upon a forest of giant versions of the same plants and trees that grow on the earth, but much larger—mushrooms, thirty to forty feet high, a veritable "hothouse of all the antediluvian plants" (Verne 1992, 142).

Axel recounts his uncle's response: "'Astonishing, magnificent, splendid!'" "'Here we have the complete flora of the Second Era of the world, the Transition Era. Here we have those humble garden plants which became trees during the first centuries of the Earth'" (Verne 1992, 142). Among these plants the men also find bones of

Édouard Riou, illustration from Jules Verne, *Journey to the Center of the Earth*. Courtesy of Bridgeman Images.

the dinosaurs, which they know only existed on the earth after the biblical flood, when sedimentary soil was formed. But Lidenbrock (via Verne's geological sources, of course) has an answer for that: the soil is sedimentary because during this period, there were upward and downward movements of the crust, and some sections of soil fell through newly opened chasms. The soil exists down there because of gravity that pulled it down. But then, is it not possible that some of the animals of that period exist down there too? Verne does not resolve these controversies here. He allows them to be spoken aloud, while the men are traveling and observing, but he leaves the response mysterious and open.

Lidenbrock maintains a kind of control over the subsurface, while Verne allows for different temporalities and subjectivities to reign there. For instance, while, as we have seen, some plants grow underground (apparently without photosynthesis), the men also find (fossilized) wood on which to build a raft. On this note, it is worth dwelling on the prose of chapter 20 in some detail. The men are walking in a natural carved-out tunnel without apparently either ascending or descending—that is, without passing any strata— but with signs they are in the Devonian era. The rocks bear impressions of fish known of that era, so compared with the day before they are "climbing up the scale of animal life, of which man forms the peak" (Verne 1992, 100). Here Verne, like various thinkers of his era, faces some apparently enormous contradictions: How to account for the biblical flood, as there is no single event to divide a before from an after in the rock record? And if there were a flood, followed by a rebuilding, then why are there no human fossils? How can one maintain the dignity of humans as the last and greatest creatures?

Verne uses the term *antediluvian* rather than *prehistoric*, which was also beginning to circulate in his time.[12] It seems he cannot help himself from planting a humanoid far down for the excitement this will bring to the narrative, even if this figure disrupts a more rigorous approach to the earth. Ultimately, although Verne does not make any grand statements, like Figuier, from whom he borrows explicitly and, at times, nearly verbatim, he leans toward a directionalist view of the earth's history and a progressionist view in the organic realm, while also nodding to catastrophism, allowing for a religious mood and leaving space for a god acting through natural causes. One might say that Lidenbrock's reasoning makes of earth science a kind of legal fiction, not so different from the argument of Charles Lyell (who "split the [geological] picture in two").[13] And then, it will turn out, as we learn only after the return, that the compass was broken, so we cannot be entirely sure of anything.

Verne's Professor Lidenbrock has the perfect opportunity to study the subsurface, without violence, fear, or anxiety about extracting the matters found there, almost as if we were staring at a geological map rather than undertaking a voyage below. He has it both ways: ocular proof and safety, suspense (there are moments of extreme threat in the novel) and security (since we are reading the narration, written from the future, we know that the explorers will, in fact, survive). At one point, for instance, the men are falling rather quickly down a long, vertical opening. Verne (and not Axel, who is too frightened to make rational arguments)—but these words come from Axel's voice, but on reflection we know they are a combination of Lidenbrock (the expert), Axel (the eyewitness), and Verne (the author)—notes three different strata: schists, gneisses, and mica schists, all resting on a bed of hard granite.

> Never had mineralogists been in such perfect circumstances for studying nature in situ. The drill, a brutal and unintelligent machine, could not bring the internal texture back to the surface of the globe—but we were going to examine it with our eyes, touch it with our hands. Through the layer of schists, coloured in wonderful green shades, there meandered metallic seams of copper and manganese, with traces of platinum and gold. I dreamed when I saw these riches hidden away in the bowels of the Earth, which human greed would never enjoy! These treasures were so deeply buried by the upheavals of the first days, that neither pick nor drill will ever be able to tear them from their tomb. (Verne 1992, 108)

Without these multiple voices, the reader would not see these marvels, these resources, ready for exploitation yet preserved forever;

see the passage of deep time yet experience it in a brief instant; see and not see; dream and yet be awake; have the kind of mastery that only literature could bring. Because there will be no further study or verification, the subsurface can remain as pure potentiality. However, there is a huge logical flaw in Verne's novel: if a professor could go down there with a ragtag band, why would exploration not be opened up in a massive way following him? Why would others—perhaps stronger, more intrepid, better trained—not be able to use his knowledge and expand on it? The very reason for writing *Journey to the Center of the Earth*—to explain how it was done—is undone, so we know the book is pure fiction, yet without some belief, we would not wish to read the book. It is a swindle of the greatest sort as it lays bare what it also tries to get us to ignore: the absolute incompatibility of its fictions with modern science, and vice versa. It is purely impure adventure.

At one point in the novel, when the men are on their way on the raft across the sea, Axel narrates, his uncle asks him to keep a ship's log, "with instructions to put down even the most trivial observations, to note interesting phenomena, the direction of the wind, our speed, the distance covered" (Verne 1992, 150). Perhaps, the reader supposes, this is because the sea voyage does not require the narrator to exert physical exertion, so there is time, and, if the group were to return by the same way they came, such observations would be quite useful. So far, so good. As Axel notes, "I will confine myself, therefore, to reproducing here those daily notes, written, as it were, at the dictation of events, in order to give a more precise account of our crossing" (150).[14] The first entry, dated Friday, August 14, indicates the wind direction and temperature, useful information to be sure. But then it goes on with the usual prose, interior monologues, and even dialogue, set off by quotation marks, as uncle and nephew discuss the characteristics of a fish they have caught. Lidenbrock insists it is like ones found fossilized from Devonian strata. "What!" exclaims the narrator, "Have we really captured live an authentic inhabitant of the primitive seas?" (151). And without any indications of the end of the log, the chapter goes on, including the recounting of a lengthy waking dream in which Axel sees before his eyes a full panorama of all of paleontology. It is not until the beginning of the next chapter, 33, that a new day is again signaled with a line that reads, "The sea retains its uniform monotony. No land in sight. The horizon seems a very long way away" (154). Yet here again, an attentive reader might well pause and ask about the kind of information that the log is supposed to convey, information perhaps not helpful in advancing the plot, not particularly exciting but necessary and important for a seafarer who might someday want to repeat this voyage. Instead, Axel's next line is "My head is still dull from the violent effects of my dream." The next entry, for Sunday, August 16, reads: "Nothing new. Same weather. The wind has a slight tendency to freshen" (155). And without any prose to set off what follows as superfluous, Axel is back to subjective impressions. The following entry contains no information about the sea, and Axel immediately plunges back into his hallucination: "Monday, 17 August. I have been trying to remember the particular instincts of the antediluvian animals from the Secondary Period, which, following on from the molluscs, the crustaceans, and the fish, emerged before the mammals appeared on the globe" (156). The rest of the chapter is taken up with the description of giant sea creatures (straight out of Louis Figuier) that fight with each other and menace the men on their raft. It could be the case that the entries are the brief introductions and all that comes after is supposed to be read separately, but there is no way to determine this. A reader might simply plow through. Finally, after a storm destroys the mast, Axel appears to write from the future, editing himself: "Here my travel notes became very incomplete. I have only found one or two fleeting observations, jotted down automatically so to speak. But even in their brevity, their incoherence, they are imprinted with the feelings which governed me and thus, better than my memory, portray my mood at the time" (167). And finally, he notes: "Here ends what I called the 'ship's log,' fortunately saved from the shipwreck. I proceed with my narrative as before" (170).

In short, the literary form of the ship's log, justified by the particular circumstances of this portion of the journey and presenting itself to the reader as spontaneous, subjective, and testimonial, should logically absolve its writer from any potential charges of plagiarism, about which I will elaborate below. Yet even the diary that interrupts the flow of prose (while it is nevertheless constituted by a flow of prose) only to peter out without fanfare into another flow of prose, a diary that should be written for the purposes of the ship's captain and crew and yet also involves direct address to a reader, may not be original to Verne. Notably, a similar writerly/readerly slippage occurs in *Robinson Crusoe*. That famous narrator explains that having completed a set of furniture for his "castle," he now finds he has enough time to write a journal, but, before offering his first entry, he warns the reader that he ran (that he will run) out of ink and the journal will stop. Some of Crusoe's entries are quite brief. Some repeat events or information that had already been conveyed to the reader in other portions of the novel. Others go on for pages so that we forget we are, in fact, reading a journal. Simultaneously, we know that Crusoe notches the passing of each day into a tree trunk so that the reader trusts Crusoe's basic accounting of the passage of time on the island.

Verne was certainly influenced by the figure of Robinson Crusoe, if not the precise arrangements of Daniel Defoe's prose. He also read another novel, a story of a sea voyage published in 1838 by a man named Arthur Gordon Pym by a man named Edgar Allan Poe.[15] That work itself, *The Narrative of Arthur Gordon Pym of Nantucket*, apparently told to Poe, then written down and delivered to the publishers by Poe, includes a preface in the first person, evidently written after the conclusion of the book, even as it narrates events leading up to the writing of the book:

> Comprising the details of a mutiny and atrocious butchery on board the American brig Grampus, on her way to the South Seas, in the month of June, 1827. With an account of the recapture of the vessel by the survivors; their shipwreck and subsequent horrible suffering from famine; their deliverance by means of the British schooner Jane Guy; the brief cruise of the latter vessel in the Antarctic ocean; her capture and the massacre of her crew among a group of Islands in the eighty-fourth parallel of Southern latitude; together with the incredible adventures and discoveries still further South to which that distressing calamity gave rise. (Poe [1838] 1999, 1)

The author explains that he had no interest in writing a book but was prodded by others to do so—a very old trope that should not be cause for any great surprise. One reason for his hesitation is purely private (and, indeed, we will never again think of it). A second reason is that "having kept no journal during a greater portion of the time in which I was absent, I feared I should not be able to write, from mere memory, a statement so minute and connected as to have the appearance of that truth it would really possess, barring only the natural and unavoidable exaggeration to which all of us are prone when detailing events which have had powerful influence in exciting the imaginative faculties" (3). The third has to do with the second, and that is the very implausibility of the events themselves. To this point, it appears as if EAP convinced AGP to allow EAP to write up the account himself "under the garb of fiction" and as a "ruse" (4). Then, we learn, after the first few installments were published under EAP's name, AGP feels sufficiently confident to affix his name to what follows. At this point, the reader might be excused for experiencing some confusion about the identity of the author, who claims it will be obvious when EAP's sections (which accurately reflect events) end and the author's begin, implying that the author is AGP. Yet there is, in fact, no clear guideline about the threshold between one and the other. The reader is bound to read the preface first, so that she may well forget it by the time she is immersed in the adventures themselves, but as the narrator of the novel actually does narrate events with great detail—indeed, with details that will strike the reader as (pleasurably) exaggerated—the preface functions like a game to throw the reader off the scent of realism. After the preface, the book begins: "My name is Arthur Gordon Pym." This is supposed to stand as a kind of guarantee, except that we know there is no such person and we assume, by convention, that the book is by EAP, and so the very story is false.

The first part of the novel concerns the young narrator and his drunken friend on his boat, the *Ariel,* and is entirely plausible. The two men are rescued by a ship called the *Penguin.* This portion of the work could function as a short story on its own. It ends.

The next chapter begins afresh, with the events of the *Ariel* fading into the background and with AGP's renewed interest in the sea and the possibility of setting out on a whaler, the *Grampus*. The narration soon becomes thick, including dialogue—that is, the sort of detail that would not be reenacted later but that seems quite specific. Because his mother is against the voyage, AGP has to stow away. The first section on the *Grampus* also forms a kind of self-enclosed short story. The next segment concerns a mutiny on board. The author—that is, we presume AGP who is speaking directly to EAP—says: "As the events of the ensuing eight days were of little importance, and had no direct bearing upon the main incidents of my narrative, I will here throw them into the form of a journal, as I do not wish to omit them altogether" (Poe [1838] 1999, 68–69). This must strike the reader as odd, since we are well into the narrative. In fact, diary entries pop up throughout the narrative for no particular reason. And for no particular reason they flow into segments of prose so long that the reader forgets them. Sometimes these entries contain information of a practical nature, as in this one from January 18, at the start of chapter 8, beginning in the morning:

> The terms morning and evening, which I have made use of to avoid confusion in my narrative, as far as possible, must not, of course, be taken in their ordinary sense. For a long time past we had had no night at all, the daylight being continual. The dates throughout are according to nautical time, and the bearings must be understood as per compass. I would also remark in this place, that I cannot, in the first portion of what is here written, pretend to strict accuracy in respect to dates, or latitudes and longitudes, having kept no regular journal until after the period of which this first portion treats. In many instances I have relied altogether upon memory. (134)

In the end, then, EAP, who is apparently fond of puns and tricks, who makes fun of his own writing and undoes its veracity, melds with AGP and his writing. These kinds of authorial maneuvers are not squarely in Verne's playbook, but there are individual elements that he plucks from Poe.[16]

Writing is ephemeral, but writing on stone has a life span far beyond that of the reader. An inscription in stone should be—if found by others—a sign of absolute authenticity.[17] Unless there is doubt as to whether it is manmade. In *Journey,* the men have no doubt that they are on the right track because Saknussemm wrote underground in the same runic language that he used on the surface. In *The Narrative of Arthur Gordon Pym,* after the narrator and his friend Peters have been buried alive in an underground cavern at the pole, the author offers to the reader several figures to show the formation of the cave, which he says he was able to draw because he had a pencil with him. These drawings are made as if from above, like Nazca Lines that cut through the surface of the earth with a radiographic gaze. These odd figures are reproduced in the published novel, presumably because they are of interest to a reader. Fine. But shortly afterward, the men find carved into the stone (soft marl or calcium carbonate) a figure that looks like a human, accompanied by what look to Peters like "alphabetical characters." This figure is also reproduced in the novel, in all its strange ambiguity. However, the narrator soon discovers flakes of marl on the cave floor that have clearly fallen off the wall. It is obvious (to him) that they are not viewing an anthropogenic occurrence but an accident of nature. So then why would AGP or EAP or Harper and Brothers (the publisher) bother to reproduce such figures—first, the ones apparently drawn by the narrator and then those found on the rock, as recalled by AGP—in the final version of the novel? This question remains in suspense as far as the story goes. Dejected, the men have to keep searching for a way out. Soon afterward, the main portion of the narrative ends with a kind of cinematic dissolve into whiteness (although there may have been some missing chapters describing what happened at the South Pole). However, in an afterword, written later, the narratorial voice (AGP?) asks the reader to reconsider the figures published in the earlier chapter, three of which are images of the chasms and one of which, he asserts, resembles alphabetical characters but is not. Still, it may be worthwhile to reconsider all of them, "especially as the facts in question have, beyond doubt, escaped the attention of Mr. Poe," we read (Poe [1838] 1999, 220). The author goes on to "redraw" the figures of the chasms in sequence and simplified form, which seems to him to correspond to an Ethiopian verbal root meaning "to be shady" or "in shadows." Moreover, reviewing the figures that AGP had dismissed as purely natural, one can now agree that some of the characters spell out an Arabic verbal root (drawn in the text) meaning "to be white," where later characters spell out an Ethiopian word meaning "the region of the south" with an indication in the proper direction. Added to this addendum to the narrative is a note, written in another voice. This voice explains:

> The circumstances connected with the late sudden and distressing death of Mr. Pym are already well known to the public through the medium of the daily press. It is feared that the few remaining chapters which were to have completed his narrative, and which were retained by him, while the above were in type, for the purpose of revision, have been irrevocably lost through the accident by which he perished himself. (179–80)

This passage apparently undoes the pretense of the foreword, if the reader remembers it, having trekked through all of the prose in between. In that text, the narrative was told orally to a man (EAP) who now casts doubt on the veracity of what has come before. Perhaps Peters might someday fill in the gaps but he "cannot be met with at the present" (180). This is odd: Is he not available? Or not to be found? Finally, then, we have the book that contains, among other sections, various diary entries that bear the pretense of being real and actual. Because they are not directed to a literary audience, they apparently represent unimpeachable prose. And yet the novel certainly presupposes readers. It cannot do otherwise. Without readers, there would be no novel. The final line of the book is one that appears to come from a source on high, or at least outside the narration itself: "I have graven it within the hills, and my vengeance upon the dust within the rock" (221). Readers might, like me, imagine this to be a biblical phrase, but they would not find it in scripture. It is purely literary. That rocks might include both natural signs to be read by geologists (fossils of animals) and natural signs or accidental signs that appear like human language is

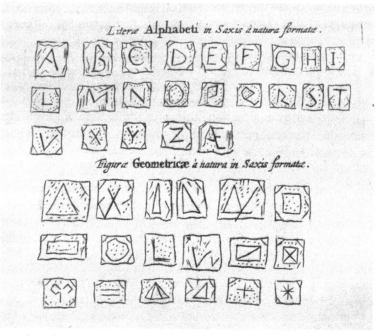

Mundus subterraneus, 3rd ed., Letters in stones, 1678. Courtesy of Cornell University Library Rare Book and Manuscript Collections.

significant. How is one to distinguish between them? Long before Poe, this question troubles Athanasius Kircher.

As noted, for Kircher there is a difference between organisms that have been fossilized—let us call these forms of life—and images that look like actual organisms. He thought the latter were not remnants of life but pictures of animals, not fundamentally different from religious images imprinted in rock like the Virgin and Child or even secular images, like cities, discovered in agate. In a short work of 1661, *Diatribe de prodigiosis crucibus,* he writes of "accidental" crosses observed on the street clothing of the people of Naples. Such images, like those of letters or cities found in rock formations, could be simultaneously natural and willed by God. They add an element of doubt to the ontological status of the subsurface and to writing itself. They are, precisely, fictions. It is natural, of

Mundus subterraneus, 3rd ed., City figured in stone, 1678. Courtesy of Cornell University Library Rare Book and Manuscript Collections.

course, to form analogies. As Verne (1992, 95) notes when the men reach a cavern:

> Sometimes a succession of arches unfolded in front of us like the aisles of a Gothic cathedral. The artists of the Middle Ages could easily have studied here all the forms of religious architecture generated by the ogive. A mile further on, we had to bow our heads under low semicircular arches in the Roman style, with thick pillars, forming part of the rock itself.

Paris, 2015

At the COP meeting held just outside the city, considerable excitement is generated by 4 X 1000, a French initiative that claims it might increase soil concentration by 0.4 percent per year to capture nearly nine gigatons of carbon. Their project allies with the thinking of some actors in the field of carbon management who have forsworn any forms of deep burial as precisely too technological, too disruptive to natural ecosystems, and perhaps too energy intensive.

Instead, these actors ask if the top layers of the soil can save us. "Soil is the second biggest reservoir of carbon on the planet, next to the oceans. It holds four times more carbon than all the plants and trees in the world," notes Jason Hickel.[18] If soil is losing its ability to serve as a sink, this is due to deforestation in some areas but also, notably, to industrial farming. Regenerative farming of crops and perhaps even pastureland would require a return to "small ag"—that is, a return to organic fertilizer, no tillage, and composting—with a notable potential for shifting soils from emitters to containers of as much as 40 percent of the CO_2 in the atmosphere, according to one—no doubt very optimistic—study, as reported by Hickel. But it will turn out that 4 X 1000 might also cost nearly as much as current agricultural subsidies worldwide (Buck 2019, 102). Even its champions have admitted recently that the predictions of 4 X 1000 may have been too optimistic. U.K. researchers found that letting land go fallow, retaining crop residues, and adding manure can increase sinks significantly, but this is not practical in many areas of the globe. Peatlands, formed of partially decomposed plant and animal life, are very important ecosystems and carbon sinks. Irish peat bogs, developed in the 1930s, provided local fuel in small scales. Although peat exists on the surface, it is like coal in that it is formed from decaying plant matter and it stores carbon. Burning it moves carbon from a storage unit on the surface into the atmosphere. Ireland (along with Scotland) is closing down mining of its bogs, but the scales will not really make a dent in global emissions. Immense peat landscapes in Canada and Congo, among other places, are crucial to the planet's carbon balance. If they are protected through regulation, then, ironically, nonuse might yield carbon credits to those who would have exploited them but do not.

Soil degradation (and hence a decline in ability to store carbon) can be linked to three principal factors, all with historical roots that have been accelerated, like everything else on the planet: overgrazing, deforestation, and agricultural mismanagement. Anthropogenic activities can lead to desertification, a term that is often thought to refer to natural shifts not directly caused by humans. As with so many ideas for climate change mitigation, soil enhancement sounds (or sounded, if we want to remain in the temporality of news cycles) wonderful, but given the significant effects on food security, it would probably be best addressed in an international treaty, and that does not seem likely to happen. As environmental engineer Peter Haff (2014) notes, our best intentions to return soil to a "picture postcard" view (another term might be "steady state"), to create a future in which soils would be those of the Holocene, "the last classical epoch in the geological pantheon of time prior to the emergence of the man- and machine-dominated Anthropocene," are simply not realistic (67).

BECCS is another technique, widely discussed, in which carbon would be captured by the very agricultural matter that is planted to use as fuel, but again, there is an enormous price to pay—namely, in the amount of land needed to achieve this, land that will not be available for the growing of food crops that are absolutely necessary to feed the world's population.[19] Still, there are new developments and new research on the horizon, as well as supposed rediscoveries of ancient matters such as biochar (the soil of Indians), which I will discuss in relation to a work of art. A 2018 headline from the *New York Times* by Moises Velasquez-Manoff asks: "Can Dirt Save the Earth?"[20] The National Academy of Sciences advocates for coastal blue carbon, a term for enhancing sinks in marshes and near shorelines.

Regenerative farming advocates espouse a rhetoric of harmony with the earth where geoengineering resonates with anthropogenic climate change itself—that is, a manipulation of earth systems on a large scale, with all sorts of possible collateral damage. As Holly Jean Buck (2019, 40) notes, fears about geoengineering get confused with entrenched false binaries such as holistic agroecology versus reductionist and mechanistic industrial ag, as if there are "biological (or natural) climate solutions, on one hand, and engineered solutions, on the other." While she recognizes that many of the forms of resistance to geoengineering are reasonable, she also urges us to think of it as not one thing but a series of different practices. Here is a characteristic response, however, from Hickel's article:

Maybe our engineers are missing the point. The problem with geo-engineering is that it proceeds from the very same logic that got us into this mess in the first place: one that treats the land as something to be subdued, dominated and consumed. But the solution to climate change won't be found in the latest schemes to bend our living planet to the will of man. Perhaps instead it lies in something much more down to Earth—an ethic of care and healing, starting with the soils on which our existence depends.

In any case, placing faith in the shallow soil also enhances recurring anxieties about the subsurface as a place that is off-limits or dangerous. Manipulating the subterranean sounds almost as unnatural as placing reflecting mirrors in space or spraying aerosols in the atmosphere. The deep subsurface is still an unknown realm, although scientists have talked of sending down sonars after blasting fissures with iron (expected to cause a massive earthquake). However, if we can intervene at the level of the pedosphere (a term developed by Haff), we might feel we are on, well, solid ground. Soil regeneration seems to imply a willful nonuse of technology. However, soil is not easily returned to an earlier state, except perhaps over very long timespans. It is not just a question of good will.

Nepal, 2019

With minimal venture capital funding, the Sacred Rivers Climate Project, financed by a start-up called HiveMind, experimented with two new so-called technologies to capture CO_2 not for transformation into useful products, not fixed in rocks or injected into the oceans or deep subsurface, but to be stored in the shallow subsurface. The first technology was proprietary, a mycelium network capable of growing in extreme climates and increasing the leafy vegetation of native trees with the Miyawaki method.[21] The specific technology here, developed by students of noted mycologist Paul Stamets, is linked to the larger idea of the wood wide web, a system of microbial organisms that connect trees by their roots.[22] It has been shown that fungi, which had long been deemed harmful to plants, actually exercise broad key symbiotic benefits. The web is composed of ectomycorrhizal fungi or arbuscular mycorrhizae that burrow directly into tree root cells: from the Greek for *fungus* (*mykós*) and *root* (*riza*). Fungi get food from trees and plants obtain nutrients such as phosphorous or nitrogen that fungi get from soil. Fungi are "the new black" of environmental humanities. Between plant and animal, they blur lines and open up new modes of thinking forms of life. As Derek Woods (2020) puts it, they suggest a "Weird Kingdom" beyond "assemblages and networks." "As fascinating as their role in plant communication and nutrition truly is, this language threatens to make fungi mediators that serve the plants, or (like the Deleuzean rhizome) simply a figure of ecosocial relationality in general." The network also allows trees to share resources and communicate, for instance, about an infestation of pests. A dying tree may even bequeath its nutriments to others. And in the case of this particular start-up, the Sacred Rivers Climate Project, the fungus technology promised that it could be developed and adapted to native plants and ecosystems on site to help increase carbon uptake capacity in measurable ways.

The second technology required for this project is financial: the company works through the mechanism of Verified Carbon Units (VCUs). In the global carbon market, each unit is equal to one ton of carbon (or carbon equivalent) removed from the atmosphere, as certified by an international registry, Verra, which also authorizes transfers between account holders. VCUs can be sold directly to oil companies or through agents, for instance.[23]

For the Sacred Rivers Climate Project to work, both the biological and financial elements must be in play, cooperating. There are, of course, many other experiments for shallow sinks underway, but I found this one intriguing because of its dual nature and clear conceptualization. Compared with carbon sequestration in the deep subsurface, Sacred Rivers seemed to require little engineering of the carbon-intensive kind. The start-up was selling a proprietary form of fungal network that experts can adapt for different climates or ecosystems, so the Sacred Rivers Climate Project, in theory, could be expanded to different parts of the developing world and function at scales small enough to bring income to local collectives.

When I first heard of the Sacred Rivers Climate Project, I was quite tempted to invest in it, and yet, as I learned only recently, it was all a hoax.[24] Meanwhile, fungi continue to attract attention. SPUN (Society for the Protection of Underground Networks) advocates for research and conservation, without making grand public claims about carbon uptake.[25]

But if we extend our view outward, it is also the case that the fungal network might offer some solutions, metaphorically, beyond the biological, as in Peter Haff's (2014, 70) notion of distributed miniature computers, to "collect and relay environmental information about the state of the soil—temperature, moisture, relative motion of near-surface particles—and to coordinate with instructions relayed back from central computing for activation and control of local actuators. . . . In other words, with sufficient computing power and development of suitable microsensors and actuators, the dynamics of the Earth's soil can be divorced from the classic forces of gravity, rain, and other environmental forces, and in turn become subject to information-based forcing by the technosphere." Smart soil, he suggests, might potentially perform valuable ecosystem services like carbon sequestration while also performing valuable aesthetic/social services, making humans feel more at peace.

Another form of shallow capture researchers are pursuing is called enhanced weathering.[26] Over long periods of time, as rain falls, moisture draws carbon from the atmosphere (as carbonic acid). As precipitation comes into contact with rocks, they break down or weather, capturing the carbon. Limestone is a prime example of carbonate rock. Some scientists have been researching ways to speed up and scale up this process so that the amount of carbon captured would be significant now, rather than in a hundred thousand years, say. This might be done by crushing some types of rocks and spreading them over considerable surface areas. Once rained upon, these crushed rocks would scale up the process, but at this moment the energy required to mine and crush the rocks is significant, not to mention the potential health hazards to humans and nonhumans who might breathe in the fine particles of dust produced during the process.[27] If only humans could find a way to bring nature up to their speed . . .

The natural transformation of matter into vital humus is likened, by one scientist, to "slow alchemy," a term that is explicitly placed in opposition to "Anthropocene."[28] Alchemy, in this context, seems to signify that soil is subject to a transhistorical and "untimely" process. In the most general sense, alchemy has often been associated with experimental commitments that take a long time (and are thus worth undertaking), so to that degree the analogy is apt. But in other respects it is not, because of the narratological implications it might bear, the elements of personal redemption and merit that are also extremely common in alchemical discourse. On the one hand, then, alchemy is invoked in popular and scientific discourse to mark slowness and to guarantee supposed naturalness. But as a transformation with tinges of the magical, on the other hand, it seems like an idea that would not really work, certainly not at a scale worthwhile for a planetary effect. It should not surprise us in the least to see alchemy called up in relation to the soteriological. Its presence in discourses around recycling, future fuels, and, as here, natural transformations is entirely predictable. It is ubiquitous, but so what? Can we do anything more with it? And, then, in what sense can we extrapolate from the promises of the mycelium network (or *panspermia rerum*, if we want to return to early modern versions of this paradigm) for the kind of thinking that literature allows?

New York, 1979

Artist Robert Morris gives a lecture on land art as reclamation, later published in the journal *October*. He is not the only artist of his generation interested in such matters, of course. In the years prior to his death, for instance, Robert Smithson had proposed a giant platform, a "reclamation project," in the pit of the Bingham Canyon Mine in Utah. Like Smithson, Morris responds to environmental degradation and mentions both deep and shallow (strip or pit) mining, the latter cheaper but more damaging to the land. "Given the present energy policies of the nation," he notes, "there can be no doubt that surface mining to produce coal—and hydrocarbon-based energy sources will continue to accelerate" (Morris 1980, 88). In the early 1970s, the U.S. government discussed projects to restore the mined lands as they also discussed synthetic fuel projects. In any case, Morris repeats passages about local (yet profound) effects of pollution, and for this reason the federal government put reclamation into the hands of states. He squeezes in a very brief account of the genealogy of ecological thinking, from the coining of the term in nineteenth-century Germany to accelerating demand for resources by modern industry. Morris critiques the new crash program to produce synthetic fuels within ten years because it takes no responsibility to address "the consequences of lowering the water table in the process or of leading to a CO_2 greenhouse effect" (93). One issue here is the depletion of nonrenewable resources. Another is "pollution of the Earth," a broad category that Morris takes from an essay by German writer Hans Magnus Enzensberger, which he quotes at length:

> Poisoning caused by harmful substances—physiological damage from pesticides, radioactive isotopes, detergents, pharmaceutical preparations, food additives, artificial manures, trace quantities of lead and mercury, fluoride, carcinogens, gene mutants, and a vast quantity of other substances are only another facet of the same question. The changes in the atmosphere and in the sources of land and water traceable to metabolic issues such as production of smog, changes in climate, irreversible changes to rivers and lakes, and oceanographic changes must also be taken into account. (Enzensberger quoted in Morris 1980, 94)

Another factor is what Morris calls "psychic pollution." The artist's essay reads as rather naive, frankly, but to say we have now gone far beyond such sincere environmentalism is to miss the point. To be sure, we should not ask Morris to be an earth scientist or to have intuited the asymmetry of Enzensberger's laundry list. Consumption is the true cause of pollution and scarcity of resources. Bring into the picture site-specific artworks, which bear a nuanced relation to the commodity market, as many critics of contemporary art prac-

Hans Baumann, *Black Forest (29,930,000 tons)*, 2014. Photograph by Emma Rogers.

tices have elaborated since Morris gave his lecture. And of course, the early years of land art, that rather masculine and muscular form of earthmoving, exist on the other side of the climate change divide as I have described it. The most famous example of heroic spatio-temporal ambition may be James Turrell's work in progress, *Roden Crater*. The artist purchased a volcanic crater in the Arizona desert, and for decades he has been moving earth into it to create an immersive space for viewing the night sky.

Swiss-American artist Hans Baumann developed an installation, *Black Forest: 29,930,000 tons*, near Seattle. Assembled over two years, this land artwork consisted in bringing in 50,000 pounds of biochar (also known as *terra preta do Indio* or Indian Black Earth in the Amazon), equivalent to the amount of coal that was mined in the area during an earlier era.[29] The biochar looks like—it is made analogous to—the coal that was previously removed from the subsurface. But biochar, which could in fact be burned, actually serves as a carbon sink, taking up global atmospheric emissions into a local surface-based sculpture. Biochar is known to have several properties that make it especially desirable: it is stable and absorbs nutrients, making soil more fertile. In this sense, *Black Forest* is a work of reclamation. Still, the artist acknowledges that its assembly, which involved a series of heavy trucks to convey the material, aroused controversy. Some visitors to the site failed to grasp the conceptual rigor. What was the point of bringing a natural material into a natural landscape? Was he actually attempting to intervene in the process of reforestation of an area that had been depleted of both (surface) timber and (subsurface) coal for a period of about a hundred years, from the mid-nineteenth to the mid-twentieth centuries? How should one interpret the gesture of replacing a bad material (coal) with a good one?

I see this work—or rather, what we have of its assembly in photographs—as a provocation to think about history, time, and the surface. As the artist notes, "Cougar Mountain and its surrounding landscape was the site of intensive industrial operations based around the extraction of coal and timber. The forests covering the mountain were clear-cut and a vast network of mine tunnels were dug into the mountainside."[30] Over time, though, the investment in deep infrastructure failed to produce efficient sources and the project was abandoned. As it turned out, the land was too unstable for building, so it was made into a park rather than lucrative housing.

In response to a proposal for an oil pipeline, Alberta artist Peter von Tiesenhausen copyrighted the top six inches of his land by placing an installation there. Von Tiesenhausen's *Lifeline* appears, on the surface, like a banal white picket fence that has nothing particular to do with what lies below. It is a piece of sculpture that the artist intends to add to each year he is alive, which is to say that it is dynamic. It has a distinct and performative value in that, through the legal structures that protect his creative or intellectual property, he blocks oil companies from buying his land (as he forces them to pay for his time to negotiate). Notably, these same legal structures do not grant him the right to the subsurface or its resources below his land. He has literally made a shallow or superficial work that calls out the disproportion between governance of surface and subsurface. In this sense, he has granted a kind of political force

Peter von Tiesenhausen, *Lifeline*.

to the top levels of soil that hold up his fence. However limited his work might be in the grand scheme of carbon emissions or the vastness of subsurface resources that cross property and national boundaries, he opens a new way of thinking (beyond the purely salvational or soteriological). He has also created an artwork that, like Baumann's, functions through narrative.

These land artworks—let us call them surface land art, to distinguish them from other works that require a deeper penetration below—challenge the viewer to think differently about the surface in ways that parallel Peter Haff's (2014) speculations about a future for the pedosphere. Since great technological leaps are taking place in space or in the subsurface, why not speculate about a future for the surface that is different enough but not so terribly far that humans have to disappear from it? Whereas under supposedly normal or natural conditions, we might approach the soil in geological scales, Haff writes that evolution can be expected to be sped up even at the level of the soil. Acknowledging sacred beliefs surrounding the soil as homeland, as well as sacred beliefs surrounding the subsurface and how they are often different, he imagines the increasing technicization of the top layers. Why not? Why would we assume that great technological leaps could and would take place in space or in the subsurface but not at the level of humus, as if this were somehow so sacred as to be off-limits?

As Jules Verne had no real restrictions on his narration, one might expect that he would have written what he would claim as the first ever voyage undertaken down there. Instead, he chooses to make it the second. Not only that, but the first traveler got farther and must have seen all that Lidenbrock and Axel see; he must have experienced all the dangers, but he chose not to write about them and instead left the most obscure and coded map imaginable for someone else. At the same time, Verne makes sure that the reader knows, at the end, as part of the narration and in an afterword or coda, that the novel itself, in the guise of a factual account of an actual journey, was/is a huge success, translated into every language of the globe. The novel's own fate is embedded in the ending of the writing so that you, the reader, are only one of many in a long line. This requires a degree of flexible mastery that one might expect from an author like Verne. So already, when we have reached the end of the novel, we are experiencing it for the first time, drawn into it with all of the suspense and excitement that comes from such an experience, yet the novel is already a best seller and widely known.

When the reader arrives at the end, does she then feel compelled to go back and rethink or possibly reject all of the moments of suspense? And then again, recall that the first third of the novel is taken up with the preparations for the journey. In retrospect, will you feel disappointed when, after such a detailed account, the actual narrative time spent underground is so sparse? What should we make of this inconsistency with regard to space/time in the organization of the narration? One could simply imagine that the writer, in his study, fiddled with different endings and beginnings, putting them together like so many pieces of a puzzle and perhaps, having alighted on the story of Saknussemm, he was intrigued. Certainly he read other works of literature and picked elements from them. Perhaps he deliberately sought out earlier precedents, including Kircher and Agricola, as well as the more contemporary geologists, and deliberately cherry-picked elements from them. In a sense, though, no biographical information will help settle these issues. Yes, Verne borrowed from other authors (as did others before him). Whether he did so hoping not to be discovered is difficult to say.

Verne was sued for plagiarism by René de Pont-Jest, the author of an 1863 novella titled *Mimer's Head*. Perhaps this authorial dispute seems petty while the world burns, but then, one has to ask if there is any point to doing anything, to study or teach or write anything other than to address the climate crisis. So, let us imagine that we are on the side of Verne. We believe he never read this story, and in this case, the similarities are purely coincidental and can therefore only be explained by the randomness of the universe or by a series of tropes in the air at the time that both men lived. In a letter Verne, who claims he never read *Mimer's Head* before he wrote *Journey,* now reads it. As he notes, the hero does not journey to the center of the earth. He finds a head on top of a mountain in a shadow cast and then he dies. That is all. ("Il se contente de decourvrir une tête dans un cercueil au haut d'une montagne, puis, il meurt, et c'est tout." Letter printed in Dumas, Gondolo della Riva, and Dehs 2001, 1:270.) The only overlap is that the location of the skull is found through a shadow cast (by the moon, whereas for Verne it is the sun). So Pont-Jest's novella ends more or less where mine begins, Verne asserts.

Following Verne's declaration of innocence, one might attempt a forensic surface reading of *Mimer's Head* to look for formal elements it bears it common with *Journey*. I do so here, with common elements in bold: *Mimer's Head* is written in **French but set in Germany** (Frankfurt) and narrated by an omniscient, disinterested third party. A **wealthy** man, Franz, desperate for **knowledge** is drawn to the **Jewish** quarter of the city, where a group of people suffer from the disease of **bibliomania**. Franz already has so many books his study is covered in dust "as if the wrath and ashes of **Vesuvius** had passed that way" (Pont-Jest [1863] 2011, 72). In addition, one could find paraphernalia of **alchemy**, including "twisted and grimaced flasks, alembics and crucibles still full of strange substances, the sight of which made one think of poisons, the elixir of life and the philosopher's stone" (74). The author offers up a very long **list of books for sale**, a catalog of the sort that one finds in many of Verne's works (including, in *Journey to the Center of the Earth*, in the account of items to be taken on with the men). Franz **buys a book**, purely by accident, much as Professor Lidenbrock's purchase is casual. Franz becomes obsessed with the book he purchased, again, like Lidenbrock. He falls asleep and when he wakes up, he notices **figures on the parchment** that are not from any contemporary European language. Rather, as he deduces, they are **runes**. As in *Journey to the Center of the Earth*, the protagonist cannot easily decipher the characters; he relies on a sage, who translates. The runes include the names of three main **Scandinavian** deities: Freyr, Thor, and Odin. The text is an invocation asking the one who deciphers them to go "very far into the **North**" and, during the **summer solstice, climb a mountain**. "With a runic staff inscribed with the sacred formula in hand, you will stand it up, inclining it toward the pale star as it rises, in the lowest of the mysterious signs engraved in the granite, and, **following its shadow** to the place where it stops, you will lift up the rock, while invoking Vidar" (95). This detail, Pont-Jest argues, is too close for coincidence to the moment in *Journey* at the top of the volcano when the men have to wait for the sun to hit a particular shaft at a particular hour of a particular day of the year to indicate the proper place to begin their descent. The protagonist of *Mimer's Head* has a **cousin** who loves him (like Axel and like the protagonist of George Sand's novel *Laura*), but he is more interested in **absolute knowledge** than love. He sets off to climb the mountain with his servant and a guide. After he discovers the head and gains great knowledge, very suddenly, "science has lavished him with its most impenetrable secrets; his knowledge has **astonished the entire world**; his name is on everyone's lips, with admiration, but all forms of affection have deserted him" (110). After two years, though, he dies. These elements are surrounded by others that are quite dissimilar to *Journey to the Center of the Earth*.

Let us imagine, then, for the sake of argument, that Verne, because he was under pressure from his editor, or he had lost inspiration or was bored or due to other external factors, did indeed borrow elements from *Mimer's Head*. This plagiarism represents a serious lapse in judgment. He imagined he would not be caught, or he did not think through the consequences of his actions. To adjudicate the case one would have to gather evidence, engage expert witnesses with knowledge of these authors and their libraries, and engage in parallel readings of their texts as I have done. In the end, Verne did win. His rival could prove similarity but not access, to use terms of modern copyright law. But he might also be guilty of lying to his editor, his readers, and the court. Did he feel guilty? And if so, how did this manifest itself in other writings or actions? Perhaps Verne did read or hear of *Mimer's Head,* but he forgot, in his conscious mind, so that only unconscious elements of the novel bubbled up to the surface. In that case he did not lie, but a court would be forced to accept the fact that threads and ideas can be repressed and return in distorted forms, thus, in a sense, making a distinction between what happens "up there" and what such material becomes "down there." If Verne did not read the other text and the similarities are mere coincidences, as he claims, then we have to assume they are superficial or familiar tropes readily available to any particular mind or pen. They are elements of narrative or variants and thus not subject to proprietary protection.

Just before the end of *Journey to the Center of the Earth,* we come to a comment on the fate of the book itself, a comment that echoes the end of (the possibly plagiarized) *Mimer's Head.* The voyage (and the book), notes Axel (or Verne), aroused jealousy among Lidenbrock's peers:

> [He] received his share of envy, and since his theories, based on facts that were certain, contradicted the scientific doctrines of fire in the centre, he engaged in some remarkable debates with scientists of every country, both in writing and in the flesh. As for myself, I personally cannot accept the theory of the cooling of the Earth. Despite what I have seen, I believe, and always will, in heat at the centre. But I admit that circumstances which are still not properly explained can some times modify this law under the effect of certain natural phenomena. (Verne 1992, 215)

Finally, Verne remarks on the fate of the book that you are still in the process of reading, even as you feel that you have reached a point very near the end, as the pages on the left now heavily outweigh those on the right. He notes: "As a conclusion, I should perhaps say that this *Journey to the Center of the Earth* created a sensation in the whole world. It was translated and published in every language: the most important newspapers competed for the main episodes, which were reviewed, discussed, attacked, and defended with equal fervour in the camps of both believers and unbelievers. Unusually, my uncle enjoyed during his lifetime all the fame he had won, and everyone, up to and including Mr Barnum himself, offered to 'exhibit' him in the entire United States, at an exceptional price" (216).

This is certainly an odd moment, as you have reached the end of your reading but rather than feeling alone with the narrative, you are exposed to prose that informs you that the book has already been so widely read that it now boasts a history of reception in which you are included as a reader and yet you are also excluded, having read the book as it was fresh for you. But you then learn it has already been chewed up by other readers to a degree that your own readership—and perhaps your own intervention into the geological debate—matters not at all. That is Verne; that is his peculiarity as a writer, one might say, to distinguish him from E. T. A. Hoffmann or from Georges Sand. Her *Laura: A Voyage into the Crystal* is most definitely a source for Verne, and yet it does not end with any declaration of its own fame. In fact, that work has the most expected of all endings—a middle-class marriage without drama or fascination—while, as I noted, one of Sand's clear influences, "The Golden Pot" of E. T. A. Hoffmann, ends in hallucinations. We understand that at the end of *Journey* Axel will settle down with his beloved Gräuben while his uncle will remain a great man of science. But that takes place out of frame, so to speak.

That this scenario occurs between men and precisely with the feminine left at home to wait, to verify and to justify this kind of writing, should not be forgotten—the feminine is what is bracketed off so that the exploration can take place. Of course, such a structure is not unique to Verne or to this novel. Consider the dangerous voyage of Arthur Conan Doyle's *The Lost World*, which begins at least three times, first with a poem:

> I have wrought my simple plan
> If I give one hour of joy
> To the boy who's half a man,
> Or the man who's half a boy (Doyle [1912] 2002, n.p.)

But if boys as men or men as boys are the only ones reading the book, why include this poem addressed to all but then only to some? And then, before the reader begins the actual narrative, he encounters a disavowal: "Mr. E. D. Malone desires to state that both the injunction for restraint and the libel action have been withdrawn unreservedly by Professor G. E. Challenger, who, being satisfied that no criticism or comment in this book is meant in an offensive spirit, has guaranteed that he will place no impediment to its publication and circulation" (n.p.). But if there was an injunction to reading and this was then removed, why bother prefacing the narrative with it? These elements that precede the narration are followed by a framing story in which the entire narrative is put forward and then recanted, only to be alibied once again:

> And now my patient readers, I can address you directly no longer. From now onwards (if, indeed, any continuation of this narrative should ever reach you) it can only be through the paper which I represent. In the hands of the editor I leave this account of the events which have led up to one of the most remarkable expeditions of all time, so that if I never return to England there shall be some record as to how the affair came about. I am writing these last lines in the saloon of the Booth liner Francisca, and they will go back by the pilot to the keeping of Mr. McArdle. Let me draw one last picture before I close the notebook—a picture which is the last memory of the old country which I bear away with me. It is a wet, foggy morning in the late spring; a thin, cold rain is falling. Three shining mackintoshed figures are walking down the quay, making for the gangplank of the great liner from which the blue-peter is flying. (62)

This is a firsthand account by a journalist of a journey in progress (but then, we know, successfully, since it has already been enjoined and then released) originally motivated by the desire to win a woman, Gladys, who, as it will turn out at the end, marries another man during the author's absence—not an adventurer, as she claimed she wanted, but a petty solicitor. At least after the voyage Malone is welcomed back by his gentlemen friends. He might finally settle down and get married, one of his companions surmises, but Malone has now caught the adventure bug. His next voyage will never be recounted, however, at least not by Doyle or Malone. Being open to sequels is one way for the author, the narrator, and the reader to come together, beyond the pleasure principle, to repeat just one ultimate (but if one is superstitious then is it not better to say *penultimate*?) journey.

So where does Verne's journey end? Perhaps at the moment when the men are finally on the surface, having beaten all odds and avoided death? Or does *Journey* deserve a deeper reading, one, say, linked by Peter Brooks to Freud's *Beyond the Pleasure Principle*? As Brooks (1992, 50) notes, "If the motor of narrative is desire, totalizing, building ever-larger units of meaning, the ultimate determinants of meaning lie at the end, and narrative desire is ultimately, inexorably, desire for the end." One can only tell a life at the limits or margins in terms of an impending end, and the beginning of a work presupposes an end. "The very possibility of meaning plotted through sequence and through time depends on the anticipated structuring force of the ending" (9). As Brooks (107) insists, Freud discovers that any analysis is interminable since resistance and transference can always generate new beginnings, but fictional plots impose an end, which suggests a return, a rereading. Brooks, recalling an essay by Tzvetan Todorov titled "Narrative Transformations," notes that "transformation—a change in a predicate term common to beginning and end—represents a synthesis of difference and resemblance; it is, we might say, the same-but-different" (91). This is also a common definition of *metaphor*, as Brooks notes, although it is not adequate. For plot, in fact, the key figure is not metaphor but metonymy: "The description of narrative needs metonymy as the figure of linkage in the signifying chain: precedence and consequence, the movement from one detail to another, the movement toward totalization under the mandate of desire" (91).

After many days of danger and fear, after encountering hostile atmospheres, logistic nightmares, and terrifying beasts, Professor Lidenbrock, Axel, and Hans come to an absolute impasse—a piece of granite, the hardest rock. It is inscribed with the initials "A. S." so they know that they are following in the steps of the Icelandic alchemist who must have passed this way (and then returned, inscribing his parchment back up on the surface). Apparently, in the past two hundred years since Saknussemm's journey, something has changed down there. Perhaps an earthquake or other major event has shifted the granite so that the way down to the absolute center of the earth is blocked. If they want to reach their goal, the men have no choice but to make use of the dynamite they carry, to become, for the only time in the novel, "miners." By this term, Verne means not that they extract matters from the subsurface but that they prepare to perpetuate violence against the rock. To mine, in Verne's *Journey*, is to light a fuse. The result is not quite what the men had hoped. Yes, the rocks are changed, but the sea where they have taken shelter on a raft, from the site of explosion, begins to rise with the tremendous force of an earthquake. The men are propelled on their raft through the opening that Saknussemm had taken, but they have no control over their movements. Finally, after some time, they realize that they are rising through a chasm, propelled upward, still on their raft, by the water, and yet the temperature is also rising. Could they be going down and up at the same time? Lidenbrock has enough of his wits to examine the strata, so he notes that they are climbing. Following this, however, another series of catastrophic events ensues, and the compass starts going mad. While Axel imagines they are in the middle of an earthquake, Lidenbrock counters—he hopes, in any case—that it is a volcanic eruption. Axel realizes:

> We're in the middle of an eruption! Fate has placed us in the path of red-hot lava, fiery rocks, boiling water, of all the

> substances that are thrown up in eruptions! We are to be expelled, thrown out, rejected, regurgitated, spat out into the air, in a whirlwind of flame, along with huge amounts of rock and showers of ash and scoria! And that's the best thing that could happen to us! (Verne 1992, 205)

On this part of the journey there is no longer a chance to gaze at strata—only the flames that surround them.

While the most logical conclusion would be to suppose that the men are back at the Sneffels volcano where they began, the more they look around the more they realize that they are in some southern country, without snow, and, perhaps more significantly, a volcano without a very tall base, as was the case in Iceland. Rather, this one is mostly subterranean. Its crater peeks out from groves of Mediterranean vegetation, and the men soon discover that it is the island of Stromboli, in Southern Italy. While they have not totally traveled from one pole to another, they are certainly disoriented, having moved from north to south.

In *Journey to the Center of the Earth*, the men make it almost all the way to the core—close enough that the reader imagines it can be done (and indeed, the narrative is premised on the idea that it had already been done by an earlier explorer) but leaving the absolute core unnarrated, and so open as possibility, a sliver of the earth that is still to be conquered. Their failure—caused by purely natural forces and not by any fault or lack of virtuosity on their part—leaves open various theories: the earth's core may be unbearably hot (the plutonist theory) or it may be cold and, in this case, geological difference on the surface can essentially be explained by aqueous movements of flooding and recession (neptunism). Verne placates potential readers from both schools of thought. Lidenbrock's theory of water as the prime mover of geological change (which he shares with the real-life figure of Humphry Davy) may be borne out, but Axel's theory of heat may also be true.

The adventure story contains a core that panders or begs for readership, in this sense, rather than a scientific text that lays bare facts and conclusions and cares not about its reader. Verne's characters are subjected to immense and dangerous forces of nature near the center, but a more beneficent force sends them back up to the surface where they are ejected through a volcano. The science is absolute, and what the men have witnessed is unimpeachable. Yet one might be disturbed, only if one actually thinks, by the idea that the usual notion of scientific progress is not respected in this particular novel. A sixteenth-century alchemist, that is, a premodern with beliefs still wrapped in myth and falsehood, did what they are not able to do even if he did not leave a definitive statement behind. As Axel thinks to himself, at one point, given that he would have had no barometer or manometer available, how could Saknussemm even be sure he had reached the center?

Moreover, it seems likely that, equipped with Lidenbrock's knowledge, future explorers could now undertake this treacherous journey, but Verne not only makes no mention of this, he deliberately closes off the possibility (with an enormous granite boulder). If we read *Journey to the Center of the Earth* according to its own logic, no one will ever come along to repeat the experiment. Yet, Verne quite clearly drew on narrations of previous journeys to the earth's core. His deep dive, if we like, down there is clearly "his" and not "his" in the modern sense of influence. The reader is immersed in the prose at the moment of reading, and yet, as I noted above, she understands that the narration is made later, after a safe return, and that the book itself (which the reader is experiencing for the first time) has already had tremendous success in the past.

Now perhaps we should not make too much of this, but it is precisely because this book refuses to take one side, to commit to either one theory or the other, or to exist in the past or present, in its inexorable desire to please all readers, that we find something useful for thinking the subsurface. As long as this space remains fluid and open to different possible futures, as long as it is uncolonized and uncolonizable, there is hope of a rhetorical sort, of the sort that must be maintained for a certain kind of writing to go on.

5
Subterranean Futures

Kansas (near Wichita), 2008

Following the events of September 11, 2001, a former government contractor named Larry Hall purchases a site, formerly used for missile silos, where he builds an underground survivalist apartment complex. "Worldwide economic conditions, historical disaster evidence, and the obvious signs of global climate changes" are all mentioned in the sales literature.[1] The technologies to sustain life down there, while also keeping track of life on the surface, have developed exponentially since the wealthy outfitted their bomb shelters with all mod cons during the Cold War. The Kansas condos are sealed off yet still able to communicate with the outside world. The entrance to the complex has the same form we have seen before: a nondescript driveway leads to concrete doors positioned slightly below surface level. We might be entering a site for the burial of toxic materials or a mine rather than an inverted skyscraper with accommodations ranging in price from US$1.5 million to $5 million, as well as many private and shared amenities, including a swimming pool, dog park, and aquaponic farm. Naturally, there is an armory for protection against intruders and a shooting range to keep in practice. The residents are expected to form an extended family—think of Jules Verne's *grande famille* in the Scottish mine—and no doubt those who have purchased underground residences have recommended them to their friends, creating a fairly homogeneous clientele. All potential buyers are screened for criminal records. In other words, this is far from the democratic or multiethnic crew of some contemporary sci-fi survivalist fantasies. But that is their right in a free yet privatized subsurface. They can invite whomever they like to their party, and such a construction has analogs in literature, to be sure.

Survival condo, Survivalcondo.com.

Owners may visit their condos now—as vacation homes or temporary "work from bunker" sites. Depending on where the survivalist family maintains a primary residence and on the type of disaster, it may not be easy to get to the Kansas site in time. Americans of a certain age may recall that an ICBM launched from territories once known as Soviet can arrive within about ten minutes. This fact, repressed in collective memory for decades, suddenly became relevant again in 2022. An attack might occur without warning, making the condo contract moot. In comparison, in Gabriel Tarde's ([1896] 1905) narrative, humans begin to perceive the weakening of the sun over several years, granting leaders enough time to organize the subsurface. With enough notification to arrange for a private jet or helicopter flight, the Kansas condo owners might arrive at the security gates intact and hide out until things on the surface have calmed down or a new order is restored or concentrations of carbon dioxide have returned to acceptable levels (after all, nature is quite resilient), regardless of the events that have led here. Time will have passed on the surface, yes, but then one could reestablish a similar sort of condominium or, better, colony on the surface. That is a story that some may tell themselves. Many have done so in various forms.

There is no future for the subsurface (which is, after all, a record of the past of various species). The terraformed subsurface is the future.[2] These two statements are noncontradictory in a certain form of geo(il)logics. The desire to keep the subsurface as a terrain to be explored while also exploiting it for everything it is worth—this very contradiction lies at the heart of a narrative and an alibi that could also be said to constitute a way of reading as deferral. This is why it matters little how we actually define the borders of this area that is beneath us or how deep we understand it with relation to our activities on the surface. As in Verne's *Journey to the Center of the Earth*, it is a goal that we posit, but one that we tacitly agree never to reach.

The Hague, 1965

An executive of Royal Dutch Shell is assigned to think about long-term futures using scenario planning, a term that derives from the RAND Corporation's Herman Kahn, game theorist, a.k.a. one of the models for Dr. Strangelove.[3] Shell's scenario planning has had significant reverberations for the oil and gas industries more broadly.

And now, cynically, we might say, they have produced scenarios for net zero, including, as I suggested earlier, a portfolio of decarbonizing practices and technologies that allow for the core business of Shell to continue in some forms. Scenarios offer readers (stakeholders, industry leaders, consumers) a range of outcomes. Because of the tremendous investment in infrastructure, research and development, and so on, scenario lock-in can cause executives to ignore conditions in the real world. So ideally, scenarios allow for a degree of openness, but if along the way they embrace nonlinearity or uncertainty, ultimately they end up with the status quo tinged with futuristic aesthetics—skyscrapers, personal transport pods, aerodynamism, robotics, and the like. While they imagine discontinuities or obstacles driven by forces both human and nonhuman, while they move along a timeline from left to right, the scenarios flatten out difference. Scenarios are "not policy proposals" but "nor are they forecasts" (Shell Corporation 2018, 4). They offer pathways forward, and in the case of those produced by Shell beginning around the turn of the current millennium, their scenarios have incorporated climate change as one key issue, among others. It is only by reading back, retrospectively, that one can determine if a planner was right or wrong, that one can legitimize the story. Like the stabilizing wedge strategy of Stephen Pacala and Robert Socolow (2004), the Shell Sky scenario depends on various transformations all taking place in incremental ways between the time of the writing (2018) and the target of 2070.[4] For Shell, these include: a change in consumer mindset; an increase in energy efficiency, the institution of universal carbon pricing, electrification of the energy sector, a phasing out of fossil fuels, carbon capture and storage, and net-zero deforestation. If all of the above can be brought into play—and yes, all of the above is in the realm of possibility—then there will be no need for major disruptions. Warming can be kept below 2°C—what they call an ambitious and yet practical goal. Now to be truly cynical, one could say that Shell has covered itself: it has told shareholders what would have to be done and how it will contribute, but the primary actors will come from future generations, and the authors of the story will no longer be around to see how things turned out.

The form of the scenario is, for me, not just a sign of limited imagination or a quantification and hence reduction of qualitative issues; it is, above all, a story in the most stripped-down sense of this term, as when one asks colloquially, "What's your story?" Scenarios are like literature that has managed to finally rid itself of pesky ambiguity. Scenarios, like storytelling, express the desire for pure narrative without the messiness of language, but as Roland Barthes puts it, perhaps better than anyone, narrative is a putting into language of experience so that it "ceaselessly substitutes meaning for the straightforward copy of the events recounted" (quoted in White 1980, 6).

To be sure, scenario planning has become increasingly common. In the lawsuit brought by the New York Attorney General, ExxonMobil defended itself by presenting public documents, available to any potential investors, called "Outlooks for 2030 and 2040" and written around 2013–2014—that is, several decades prior to the so-called future. In these relatively near-term scenarios, the company predicts that the cost of carbon will rise in the future either in the form of carbon tax or cap and trade. They even attempt to quantify the cost by imagining various external issues that "could make our products more expensive, lengthen project implementation times, and reduce demand for hydrocarbons, as well as shift hydrocarbon demand toward relatively lower-carbon sources such as natural gas."[5] By 2040, the reports note, carbon could cost $80 per ton, affecting Exxon's bottom line in a significant way. This information was and is clearly available to anyone considering buying or selling shares of the company, and it was part of the reason the company prevailed in litigation against them. The judgment states, "Nothing in this opinion is intended to absolve ExxonMobil from responsibility for contributing to climate change," but the judge ultimately concluded that securities fraud had not been proven. Here it might be worth noting, then, that this same company anticipated in 2020 that it would have to significantly increase greenhouse gas emissions for an undefined period after the pandemic in order to survive into the future.

Speaking of Exxon, the company was disrupted in 2021 when a

hedge fund, Engine No. 1, with a (minuscule) $40 million investment (0.02 percent), pressured other institutional shareholders and demanded that that the oil giant accept new board members and address climate change. Their central argument of this "insurrection" was that the company's profits were falling and would continue to do so in the transition away from fossil fuels.[6]

In the past several years, there has been a noticeable shift in public or media discourse around climate change, with terms like *emergency, extinction,* and *Apartheid,* as if, at least among a certain slice of the population, we are experiencing a genuine collective sense of disruption, at least for brief periods, in a foundational narrative of steady-state progress, once described by sociologist Daniel Bell (1973, 1,810–11) in the following terms:

> If in the foreseeable future—say for the next hundred years—there will be neither Utopia nor Doomsday but the same state that has existed for the last hundred years—namely, the fairly steady advance of "compound interest"—the banality of this fact (how jaded we soon become of the routinization of the spectacular!) should not obscure the extraordinary achievement Keynes called attention to. For the first time in human history, he reminded us, the problem of survival in the bare sense of the word—freedom from hunger and disease—need no longer exist. The question before the human race is not subsistence but standard of living, not biology but sociology. Basic needs are satiable, and the possibility of abundance is real. To that extent, the Marx-Keynes vision of the economic meaning of industrial society is certainly true.

Bell's words refer to a bedrock of common sense of the generation that came of age after World War II, and it is what is being dislodged by the generation coming of age during a time when each year is warmer than the one before. This older model assumes that we continue to emit carbon because it costs nothing to discharge waste into the air and water. It is now more expensive to clean up than to use, so abundance does not necessarily equate to quantity but more precisely to how much things cost. This is the model from which new calculations about the cost of use and nonuse of ecosystems and resources must now deviate.

In the darkest times, one imagines that renewable resources, which appear free and endless, will be subjected to new forms of privatization, commodification, and weaponization. Andreas Malm (2016) distinguishes between water, a common good that flows across boundaries (although, he notes, sluices could be patented), and steam, which is contained and made into the property of the factory owner, who is no longer forced to build near a river but can choose a location in the town center, closer to the mass of workers. It goes without saying that such a shift reverberated in many directions. Imagine a counterfactual history in which instead of Manchester, a solar center such as Southern Spain—perhaps colonized by English industrialists, if we do not wish to deviate too far from the reality—grew as a center for manufacture. The idea is not so far-fetched as it might seem. Malm notes that the idea of harnessing the sun to power machines was in circulation at least by the late 1860s (159). The Industrial Revolution—or fossil capital, more broadly—might have proceeded in a different part of the globe. Proximity to water was necessary for waterwheels, of course. Proximity to mines was desirable but not absolutely necessary, since coal could be—and was—transported by boat through a system of canals, notably, in Britain, to various locations and then by rail. But before this, it was used widely in a more local context for home heating. "Coal in stoves contributed to the pattern of centralised settlements; water mills came into contradiction with this pattern; the conversion to steam resolved it by bringing capital and labour together. The spatial crystallisations of wage labour that played such a major role in the transition to steam rested on proto-fossil coal consumption—including, of course, the burning of coal for heat in manufacturing" (161). Certainly, though, the fossils lead more obviously to the idea of central power, whereas solar and wind fit better with microgrids and smaller communities of autonomous energy producers (who might also be consumers). But we do have to ask: is such community energy trading really "disruptive technology" or simply a gimmick?[7]

It is customary for books on climate change or the environment to end with a note of hope. Often, this hope is wound around a call to live with and embrace nonhuman forms, and in this case, hope might include some vague language of the potential of the subsurface to shelter a post-fossil-fuel society. In his (late nineteenth-century) grand history written from the far future, French sociologist Gabriel Tarde ([1896] 1905) recounts how survivors of the fading sun have electricity, hydro, wind, and ocean waves for power underground. Yes, they are less potent than "steam" (he does not say "coal"), but they are still servants ("serviteurs de l'homme" [10]). And then, they are able to capture the heat of the earth's core—a virgin force more powerful than the sun itself. Such an incursion into the far future—down there ("en bas")—might be a plausible point to stop, for now.

Instead, though, I prefer to end with another narrative to think about narrative itself. Claude Lévi-Strauss's *The Elementary Structures of Kinship* (1969) is not a novel or fiction. It is a long work of cultural anthropology that went through various editions. It is focused on locating or defining the division between nature and culture through the process of exchange between different groups of humans. It was published in 1949 and then revised and republished in 1967. Many of the rules of culture, anthropologists observe, circle around the exchange of women. The reader who devotes herself to the whole work over time comes to realize that the accounts of different rules are essential precisely because it is the importance of having rules rather than the content of them that matters most. Marcel Mauss's *Essai sur le don* (1923), translated as *The Gift*, is an important precursor, of course. It turns out that the prohibition of incest is not so much negative but, rather, positive. It leads to the formation of alliances between different groups. The principle of reciprocity (that a gift creates a need for a reciprocal gift, hence alliances) would seem to stand in all societies as a universal. But woman is a unique kind of gift. Must sexual difference be universal as well, or are there possibilities for other unique gifts? Are there traces of the elementary forms of kinship that persist in generalized exchange, or have we moved beyond the foundational principle that "woman" has a unique place? Other anthropologists reject Lévi-Strauss's theory in favor of kinship as based on descent, while still others reject both theories on the grounds that they are normative or ignore variations. But viewed in relation to narrative, one must say that yes, precisely, there can be only one ending, one choice. Each chapter furthers an argument until the end when it is revealed that the true dream of man, let us say, of Anthropos, is to keep the signs (that is, woman) for himself, to avoid having to exchange, which is to say, to stay in the state of nature. After many years of reading and returning to Lévi-Strauss, I still find this astounding: "The prohibition of incest is less a rule prohibiting marriage with the mother, sister or daughter, than a rule obliging the mother, sister or daughter to be given to others. . . . All the errors in interpreting the prohibition of incest arise from a tendency to see marriage as a discontinuous process which derives its own limits and possibilities from within itself in each individual case" (Lévi-Strauss 1969, 481). This means that a mother, daughter, or sister are not appropriate choices not because of anything particular about them but because of what the anthropologist calls "intrinsic qualities." By this he means something structural, so he can preserve their viability as women but also as something biological.

Gayle Rubin's pioneering work in the 1970s must be acknowledged here. In "The Traffic in Women," she refers to *The Elementary Structures of Kinship* as "the boldest twentieth-century project to understand human marriage. . . . It is permeated with an awareness of the importance of sexuality in human society. . . . Since Lévi-Strauss sees the essence of kinship systems to lie in an exchange of women between men, he constructs an implicit theory of sex oppression" (Rubin [1975] 2012, 42). It is well known that the gift of woman is the supreme gift that solidifies groups, in part because their offspring will be related by blood. Women are traded, but as Rubin notes, this does not mean they are "objectified" in the sense we might use the term today. For Rubin, the logical conclusion is that to enact a feminist program one must get rid of "culture," but since this is impossible, it must be the case that the exchange of women is a foundation of (any) culture.

My citation of this now canonical feminist text should not be taken as a way of saying that gender should be the defining characteristic of any approach to narrative and climate change. What I am saying is that there are moments of resistance in narrative. For some readers these moments are easily detectable, perhaps embodied, precisely, in the idea of hope: I know the planet is on the brink and yet . . . No matter how much we are willing to think differently, there will always be a part of narratives that allow for some kind of return. We have to cling to some outcome, and so I am suggesting that "woman" has the same value as "property," that which is mine, a form of control. Giving that up is not a solution, but it does allow that we might read in a different way. We no longer expect to return to a point of departure or move along a smooth timeline; instead, we cling to that form while being subjected to periodic disruptions, as with the coronavirus pandemic. The expectation remains, especially for those born and raised "before," but for those to come, this will be the norm. Could we think of the new mode of species-being in the fossil era, what Dipesh Chakrabarty (2009, 222) calls a "negative universal history," as a kind of historiographic revolution? What was called for in the relatively recent past—what did not happen then and so is now all the more unlikely to happen—is revolutionary decarbonization, radical engagement. There is perhaps no text to correspond to this in part because there is no time left to write or think. Certainly, the elegiac temporality of most ecological writing does not seem adequate.

Inasmuch as the future of the human species on the planet is geological, we are bound to find ourselves under layers that will come to supplant the Holocene. As part of a thought experiment meant, in part, to help us realize our insignificance in terms of geological time, several scientists put forward the hypothesis that there are plenty of spaces in the record for the existence of an advanced civilization.[8] They published their findings in the *International Journal of Astrobiology*. Did this now-forgotten civilization advance without fossil fuels? And is it possible that their existence was so brief or left such a small footprint that we cannot detect it in the records of the subsurface? We will find no texts or documents on the surface but perhaps in places we have not yet explored. This too seems a fantasy of a kind, not of control but of possibility from lack of control. Yet even this is a fantasy anticipated by Jules Verne when he posited different timescales in the subsurface than on the surface rather than a mirror or past history.[9]

The thought experiment is more complicated than one might think, since, as we know from nineteenth-century geology, not all of the future earth will be built up uniformly on top of the traces of our culture. There will be other places that are laid bare, scraped down, blown away as dust, or covered with water that will subside. And yet as long as we are here, we will have to reckon with our representation of geological time as a column. We might imagine another layer at the top of ours, assuming ours is even legible given our brief presence here. We do so with a consciousness of our presence that far outweighs the actual time and space we were there. This could be equated, metaphorized with our arrogant destructiveness as imagined stewards of the nature we found out there, within a narrative that we would want to posit for our past and project into our future while we lament our present actions.

Will future beings narrate our story with the simple past tense, and we can imagine this without succumbing to the worst sort of bad faith with regard to our present? Gabriel Tarde ([1896] 1905, 21) employs a conventional narrative voice to explain to readers that "it was towards the end of the twentieth century of the prehistoric era, formerly called the Christian, that took place, as is well known, the unexpected catastrophe with which the present epoch began." The fact that there is no need for him to recount the history (except for the reader who antedated it, or who now postdates it and knows that it did not come to pass) means that he can be light on details or, better, that he has given himself an alibi, but then he goes on to write a rather conventional history of the big events—wars, diplomacy, migrations, advances in medicine, linguistic unity (Greek as a nearly universal language), but also reglaciation and other geological events—leading up to the time of life in the subsurface. Tarde even glides to the present tense when he quotes from a leader's speech on the new policies for underground dwelling. Then he moves outside of the quotation marks to note: "The speaker next entered into lengthy details, which it is useless to reproduce here, on the Neo-troglodytism which he pretended to inaugurate as the acme of civilization, 'which had,' said he, 'began with caves, and was destined to return these subterranean retreats, but at a far deeper level'" (78–79).

We should, if we have the imaginative powers, allow that such stories are being told to others without us, that they are likely to fall apart at times or come to abrupt endings or fail to cohere, and that they would be illegible to our cognition. Such future storytellers might even be aware of the fracture that we saw growing in our times that is now so wide that the other shore—before climate change—is scarcely visible and that our ways, including our faith in structures like compound interest and steady states of familiar landscapes, are no longer perceptible. Perhaps they will think of us or write stories about us. Or perhaps not.

Notes

Introduction

1. I generally avoid *Anthropocene* in this book. I am specifically interested in how we should, could, or would think the subsurface in light of the increasing concentrations of greenhouse gas emissions in the atmosphere—a realm we sometimes imagine as separated off from the subsurface by the surface, the place of the Anthropos. To be clear, I do not mean to suggest that humans do not also have an effect on the subsurface. On the contrary—I certainly acknowledge that colonization, exploitation, settlements, and other human practices have changed what lies below and that these changes emerge in the discussion of the spatiotemporal golden spike of this new geological era. However, at this particular point in time, use of *Anthropocene* forces a writer to lay down yet another stratum on a rapidly growing formation of approaches or "cenes," disclaimers, or apologies, and so on. It is only to the degree that such debates are immediately pertinent to this book that I wish to devote time and energy necessary to that enterprise. Nigel Clark and Bronislaw Szerszynski (2001) cite the work of earth system scientists on relations between surface (what we know, the "thin envelope in which life mingles with air, water and rock" [28]) and subsurface (another space, whose boundaries are not as clear as we might like [29]).

2. Various scholars have explored the implicit bias of the *we* in environmentalism and of the Anthropos as the central figure of responsibility. A number of works explore the subterranean in literature and culture. One author who is almost universally cited is Lewis Mumford, whose 1934 work *Technics and Civilization* still serves as a crucial reference point. Notably, Rosalind Williams (2008) reminds us of the centrality of the descent to the underworld, including the trope of katabasis (usually followed by a return to the living, or anabasis) in ancient literature. In describing the subsurface, she invokes Fredric Jameson's notion of "world reduction"—that is, a limit to diversity (the wholesale exclusion of nature) in comparison with the surface. Robert Macfarlane (2019) refers to various literary precedents and recognizes the nineteenth century as the time of the greatest expansion of this genre of underground narratives. Some of the best-known examples are H. G. Wells's *The Time Machine* (1895), Edward Bulwer-Lytton's

The Coming Race (1871), which I address in detail in my 2016 book *Fuel*, and other works by Jules Verne.

3. A number of recent critical works address the question of how we should or do read literature differently under the cloud of climate change. See, among others, Hensley and Steer 2018 (esp. "Introduction: Ecological Formalism; or, Love among the Ruins," 1–20; "Signatures of the Carboniferous: The Literary Forms of Coal," 63–84); Taylor 2018; Ghosh 2017; Pinkus 2013; Aravamudan 2013; Baucom 2012; François 2017; Menely and Taylor 2017; Woods 2017. Adam Trexler (2015) is primarily focused on reading contemporary cli-fi in his *Anthropocene Fictions*. Patricia Yaeger's (2011) *PMLA* editor's column is foundational for suggesting how unconscious energy regimes may be read subtending literary works and, obviously, climate change is a key element of this mode of reading.

4. Of course, the use of rock oil as fuel is quite old, but we should acknowledge the attractiveness of the origin story of Drake at Titusville—a single figure and a single discovery.

5. This is the situation, of course, in H. G. Wells's *The Time Machine*, published in 1895.

6. People of the State of New York, by Letitia James, Attorney General of the State of New York, Plaintiff, v. ExxonMobil Corporation, Defendant, 65 Misc. 3d 1233 (N.Y. Sup. Ct. 2019) at 2.

7. For about a minute in 2022, the more rapid than expected cooling of the earth's core, as suggested in a scientific paper by lead author Motohiko Murakami (2022) of ETH Zurich, was the subject of breaking news, only to be quickly displaced by more pressing matters.

8. A recent study by Anne M. Hofmeister, Robert E. Criss, and Everett M. Criss (2022) explores an extraplanetary mechanism for plate tectonics. For a simplified version, see David Nield, "Wild New Paper Suggests Earth's Activity Has an Unseen Source," *ScienceAlert*, January 26, 2022, https://www.sciencealert.com/the-pull-of-the-sun-and-moon-could-be-affecting-plate-motion.

9. "Not in my backyard"—a slogan that began to pop up around 1980 (notably in white U.S. suburbs) to combat rampant development, eminent domain land grabs, and even to assure the pristine quality of neighborhoods—has now also morphed in certain contexts into "Not under my backyard," or NUMBYism.

10. For the most part, the ancient Greeks believed in the existence of immense underground caverns, but not a totally hollow earth. As late as 1692, Edmond Halley wrote that the earth was a hollow shell with different poles inside. Others sustained the idea of multiple shells. The theory of a hollow earth is considered to have been definitively disproven by the

so-called Schiehallion experiment in 1774. Funded by the British Royal Society, the experiment involved measuring the relative density of a triangular-shaped mountain (in Scotland) with a pendulum and then extrapolating density for the earth itself. Still, as Rosalind Williams (2008) details, there were hollow earthers into the nineteenth century. Perhaps there are still some floating about today. In his *Journey to the Center of the Earth*, Verne alludes to what was called the Pluto-Proserpina theory, the idea that the earth contained two central suns (Pluto and Proserpina). This was proposed by Sir John Leslie, a Scottish scientist (1766–1832). Some hollow earthers imagined an entrance to the core through a hole in the North Pole, and this becomes an important detail for Edgar Allan Poe and other writers whom Verne read.

11. In addition to Agricola's ([1556] 1950) *De re metallica*, his *De ortu et causis subterraneorum* of 1546 treats subterranean waters, air, and fires, *res fossiles*, stones, and metals in an Aristotelian key. The volume includes illustrations of the cutaway type that allow the viewer access into a subterranean realm. Agricola's *De natura eorum quae effluunt ex terra* focuses on subsurface waters, while his *De animantibus subterraneis* is about different animals that live underground, including demons. Agricola recognizes petrified animal remains for what they were. In his day, *fossil* (from the Latin *fodere*, "to dig") referred to elements taken out of the ground from the mineral realm, including plants, animals, and anything else that seemed to hold a distinctly definable form. Some of these were called "intrinsic" or native fossils. Only later the word *fossil* came to mean something organic. As for Kircher, Verne may not have read him closely or directly, but the Jesuit's influence cannot be ignored. Kircher's relationship to traditional forms of alchemy was ambivalent. He promotes a theory of panspermia rerum grounded in the idea that the earth is gendered female, a fertile womb that gives rise to all life. This theory also opened up the possibility that alchemical work repeated such engenderment in a laboratory and on a small scale. In a treatise of 1661, *Diatribe de prodigiosis crucibus*, Kircher writes of "accidental" crosses observed on the street clothing of the people of Naples. Such images, like those found in rock formations, could be simultaneously natural and willed by God. The *Mundus subterraneus* portrays the earth as a vital system, a macrocosm, in line with alchemical thinking. It is common in the alchemical tradition to refer to the earth as a womb (or a feminine sphere) into which male sperm are injected to produce underground rivers and generate the metals that grow under the surface. Kircher believed the subsurface contained cavernous spaces with flowing water that could sustain life. Although for him stones were not alive, the theory of the generation of metals is one way to explain their immense variety and lifelike

properties. In this sense, Kircher anticipates current debates about vitalism, and his fascination for these liminal forms is not far from discussions today of where to draw the boundary between life and nonlife. Geologists today might not draw a precise distinction between a fossil formed through direct petrification (e.g., a shell turned to stone) and a fossil formed when a shell is impressed on surrounding material (so-called mold versus cast types). Both are fossils and can be studied for what they tell us about the stones around them, their relative ages, and other geophysical conditions. But for Kircher there is a difference between actual organisms fossilized and rock images that look like actual organisms. He thought the latter were "not as bones, but as a true and genuine picture of the animal, impressed in this manner into the rock" (230). Interestingly, Kircher was also a code cracker. Stephen Jay Gould (2004, 209) redeems Kircher from what he calls a traditional triumphalist or Whig history in which the Jesuit would be the last medievalist, an Aristotelean encyclopedist who "denied the organic nature of fossils and attributed their origin to occult (or divine) forces acting in the mineral kingdom—in other words, as the last important obstacle to paleontology's victorious entry into the second stage, where a mechanical worldview and a rejection of final causation would potentiate the advance of this discipline into its next phase of basic understanding: the key recognition of fossils as remains of ancient organisms."

12. In "Lyric Geology: Anthropomorphosis, White Supremacy, and Genres of the Human," Devin Garofalo (forthcoming) argues that the emergence of humankind as geological event was self-reflexively white supremacist because the subject "garners its authority from its continuity with and assertion as Earth—from its positing of human and planet as processually uniformitarian, the former undifferentiable from and thus 'succeed[ing] to the discharge' of the latter," a reference to a phrase from Charles Lyell.

13. Coal is the main focus here, but even extraction of so-called good resources have consequences, of course. In 2006, engineers were drilling in Basel, Switzerland, to extract geothermal heat for district heating (via pipes). They triggered a series of earthquakes, and this led to a work stoppage and, consequently, major opposition to geothermal energy in Europe.

14. For instance, see Bruyère 2018 and Moisey 2017.

1. Cracks

1. Snæfellsjökull (Sneffels), like Vesuvius near the Bay of Naples, is a stratovolcano, meaning it is built of strata (or composite) of cooled matter.

2. Conventional technologies have confirmed tremendous energetic potential far below the surface. In the near future, perhaps, beams of en-

ergy (fusion) directed downward might be able to do what drill bits cannot: reach the basement without melting. An MIT-based startup, Quaise, intends to drill a hole up to 12.4 miles (20 km) with the help of a gyrotron (old Soviet tech). They believe they will reach temperatures of around 932°F (500°C), making this energy source highly efficient. In a few years the company hopes to begin reusing existing fossil fuel infrastructure, inserting heat rather than gas or liquid fuels to convert steam into electricity. As one of the project engineers notes, "Importantly, it'll take up almost no space on the surface, in contrast to industrial-scale solar and wind. It'll also precipitate a global geopolitical shift, since every country will have equal access to its own virtually inexhaustible energy sources, and it sure will be nice when big countries don't have to 'liberate' the populations of smaller ones to gain access to energy resources." See Loz Blaine, "Fusion Tech Is Set to Unlock Near-Limitless Ultra Deep Geothermal Energy," New Atlas, February 25, 2022, http://newatlas.com/energy/quaise-deep-geothermal-millimeter-wave-drill/.

3. The ocean—perhaps a fourth space—raises another series of issues that I address at various points. We might perceive it as being composed of a surface that we navigate and a subsurface that we sometimes enter or imagine but where we are not truly at home (think of Verne's twenty thousand leagues under the sea). This will also be important in E. T. A. Hoffmann's "Mines of Falun," since the protagonist, Elis, begins his career on the sea and then turns to the subsurface for salvation. Then, the ocean has its own floor, hence, potentially, its own subsurface, making it difficult to categorize for the purposes of this book. Obviously, the ocean raises problems with respect to national borders and other metrics that complicate our modes of calculating and knowing. And in terms of geoengineering and climate governance, it is also considered different from land. Soil scientist Peter Haff (2014) suggests we add the "pedosphere" as an acknowledgment of the global reach and importance of soil and then the "anthroposphere" and "technosphere," as these three new areas are all massive and all exercise a global influence. Recent scientific work also considers what it would mean to mine the ocean subsurface.

4. *Terrane* is a term used by some geologists to refer to a swath of land along both horizontal and vertical axes, present and past. In this regard it is ampler and more flexible than *terrain* and its indeterminacy suits this book well. Geologist and writer John McPhee (1981, 10) resisted the term earlier in his career but eventually came to use it. He writes: "Terrain is topography. Terrane is a large chunk of the Earth, in three dimensions."

5. When I came across this term in Lyell I was quite struck, and I began to research its origins. In a private correspondence, Ghosh told me that he did

not take "the great derangement" from any particular source and in fact, he probably had in mind a response to "the great acceleration," another term in circulation and the title of a book by J. R. McNeill on the Anthropocene and environmental decay beginning around the middle of the twentieth century. A search of "the great derangement" in Google Books (thanks to David Auerbach) produced a series of references, some pertaining to the movements of people, but a number, from the 1820s, pertain to geological forces, including one from a speech that Edmund Burke (1833, 278) gave on India in which he discusses geological nonlinearity: "the great derangement observable in the position of the sandstone and limestone strata, near their line of junction with the older formations." That such forces are considered "natural disasters" (echoing claims of some climate deniers) makes the title of Ghosh's work even more powerful.

6. Of course, earthquakes can also be caused by localized human activities under the surface, such as drilling for resources.

7. I doubt very much that Smithson read Deleuze and Guattari. He never cited them, and we have a good archive of his sources. But he is coming out of a similar milieu, incidentally a key term in geophilosophical thought.

8. An exhibit at the Center for Land Use Interpretation in Los Angeles, "Hollowed Earth: The World of Underground Business Parks," included a photograph taken from precisely this angle. The exhibit opens up for the public a "vast network of underground office, storage, and logistics facilities in the former limestone mines of the USA." CLUI Lay of the Land newsletter, Winter 2017, http://www.clui.org/newsletter/winter-2017/hollowed-Earth.

9. See Ialenti 2020 for this facility. The entrance to the survival condo that I discuss in chapter 5 is also quite similar. A number of recent films find the camera spelunking along with people. Among these are a stunning documentary of the rescue of a children's soccer team from Thailand, *The Rescue* (dir. Elizabeth Chai Vasarhelyi and Jimmy Chin, 2021), and *Il buco* (*The Hole*, dir. Michelangelo Frammartino, 2021), a fiction film about the exploration of a deep cave in Calabria, Italy, in 1961 and filmed in situ. In the first case, the photographers (who are also the cave divers) begin their journey without knowing the outcome.

10. See Jason Hickel, "Our Best Shot at Cooling the Planet Might Be Right Beneath Our Feet," *Guardian*, August 8, 2017, https://www.theguardian.com/global-development-professionals-network/2016/sep/10/soil-our-best-shot-at-cooling-the-planet-might-be-right-under-our-feet.

11. It is possible to think of SRM as equally removed as something in the subsurface. One only need think of both the "good science" solution and the "bad tech-bro billionaire" solution to break apart the comet in Adam McKay's 2021 *Don't Look Up*.

12. See IPCC 2018, C.1.4, 16–17: "Although SRM measures may be theoretically effective in reducing an overshoot, they face large uncertainties and knowledge gaps as well as substantial risks, institutional and social constraints to deployment related to governance, ethics, and sustainable development. They also do nothing to mitigate ocean acidification."

13. For instance, see the National Academies (2018, 14) report that discusses how "NETS [negative emission technologies] have been part of the portfolio to achieve net emissions reductions, at least since reforestation, afforestation, and soil sequestration were brought into the United Nations Framework Convention on Climate Change, albeit as mitigation options, more than two decades ago."

14. There is no international body of experts in *Don't Look Up*, only nation-states vying for solutions and power against each other and a ragtag group of policy makers and scientists from what is presented as a second-tier university.

15. The media often reports on CDR projects with either hope or despair. In any case, the future—a time when they will sequester more carbon than they emit—is often invoked in vague terms without rigorous analysis of what or when this term refers to.

16. See, for instance, a Brooklyn-based startup called Air Company that is producing artisan vodka from captured CO_2. With regard to the previous note, the company's mission statement is: "At our core we're a carbon technology company creating indisputable impact for the future." Under the rubric "future," they continue: "At scale globally, we'll commercialize our technology and products while offering equitable distribution of our systems to communities disproportionately affected by the climate crisis" (Air Company, https://aircompany.com/). See also Aether Diamonds (https://aetherdiamonds.com/): "Diamonds from thin air: Crafted using carbon extracted from the atmosphere, each carat positively impacts our climate. . . . No hazardous working conditions or unfair wages, no conflicts funded, no earth uprooted, and a negative carbon impact."

17. Robinson Meyer, "*The Weekly Planet*: Why a Political Philosopher Is Thinking about Carbon Removal," interview with Olúfẹ́mi Táíwò, *Atlantic Monthly*, March 3, 2021, https://www.theatlantic.com/science/archive/2021/03/why-political-philosopher-thinking-about-carbon-removal/618195/.

18. Axel reckons that the temperature should rise about 1°C for every 70 feet of depth. Given that he calculates the radius of the earth to be about 4,000 miles, the temperature at the core should be well over 200,000°C and it should be filled with "white-hot gasses, for even metals like gold or platinum, even the hardest rocks, cannot resist such a temperature" (Verne 1992, 52). Here he echoes Louis Figuier, who writes that the earth is about 30 miles (48 kilometers) at its deepest and that the temperature rises

1°C for every 100 feet. He based his projections on measurements taken in coal mines in France, tin mines in Cornwall, and other places. Miners had reached as far down as 2,919 feet in his time. It is now understood that the distance to the center of the earth is nearly 4,000 miles (6,371 kilometers). The deepest hole ever drilled, the Kola Superdeep Borehole, is nearly 7.5 miles (12 kilometers) deep. The metallic core of the earth is believed now to be molten and reach temperatures as hot as 6,000°C. The mantle—about half of the bulk of the planet—ranges from 1,000°C to nearly 4,000°C as it reaches near the core. The crust or surface makes up only about 1 percent of the earth. But in the novel, when prompted by Axel's concern, Lidenbrock replies that no one knows for certain for what happens down there. Perhaps the heat of the center has been diminishing over time, as suggested by Sir Humphry Davy, whom Lidenbrock claims to know and with whom he spoke, in Hamburg, in 1825 (a date that would have made Lidenbrock a child at the time, so either Verne was careless or simply did not care to be accurate). These two men of science had agreed that the core must be solid because if it were liquid, there would be internal tides subject to the moon's attraction and these would push upward, causing "regular earthquakes" (Verne 1992, 32). Lidenbrock and Davy seem to have come to the conclusion that as the earth formed, it was heated up through the combustion of metals located on the surface. Metals on the surface burned, and hot bits fell to the ground as rain, while water worked its way into cracks on the surface. Hence at the start, there were many volcanoes; as the earth cooled, there were fewer. He describes an experiment that Davy did to prove this. He made a model of the earth. "When a fine dew was dropped on its surface, it blistered, oxidized, and produced a tiny mountain. A crater opened at the summit; an eruption took place; and it transmitted so much warmth to the whole ball that it became too hot to hold" (54).

19. See Pinkus 2016a.

2. Extracting

1. Jules Verne deeply loved Scotland, which he knew primarily through reading Walter Scott and other authors. He did visit there three times. See Thompson 2011 for detailed accounts of these trips.

2. Aberfoyle was never—and could never have been—a coal mine. Verne may have been intrigued by the name. It was the location of a remote slate quarry, where stone was removed from the shallow subsurface. Slate is not a renewable resource, meaning that at some point the quarry will become fallow and exist as a landscape of ruin, and perhaps in need of some form

of (aesthetic) reclamation, by land art, such as proposed by figures like Robert Smithson or Agnes Denes in the twentieth century. Verne used the device of a mysterious letter to open *The Voyages and Adventures of Captain Hatteras*.

3. Michel Serres (1974) analyzes *Les Indes noires* from a structural point of view. He notices patterns and repetitions that are not clearly subconscious in the sense of having been repressed but that correspond to something like archnarratives in broader circulation.

4. As Thompson (2011) notes, Starr might well have a taken a train, but Verne, of course, reveled in lists and completeness, so the more forms of transportation he could fit into a work the better. He repeats this trope in another of his Scottish novels, *The Green Ray*, where he obsessively, one might say, has his protagonists take various ships and boats to find a spot of coastal horizon where they might observe a phenomenon at sunset.

5. Graeme Macdonald (2013) produces important work on the hidden energy in narratives. See also Yaeger 2011.

6. Verne also visited the mines at Anzin, but unlike Émile Zola, who researched his coal epic *Germinal* there, Verne never went down below. For a comparison of their different experiences and commitments, see Marel 1980.

7. Nitasha Tiku, "An Alternative History of Silicon Valley Disruption," *Wired Magazine*, October 22, 2018, https://www.wired.com/story/alternative-history-of-silicon-valley-disruption/.

8. For Verne's broad conception of electricity, see Chesneaux 1971, 40.

9. Actual (gold) mining, as Verne notes elsewhere, is debasing to humans. See Chesneaux 2001, 218. Catherine Gallagher (1980, 11), among other scholars, notes that early nineteenth-century reformers deployed an analogy of factory workers to slaves as a means of emphasizing the repressively long hours, lack of protection, and physical brutality of the factory system.

10. For a discussion of electricity in Verne, see Pinkus 2016a. The quasi-magical quality of electricity is prevalent in current popular discussions of electric vehicles, for instance. Electricity is assumed to be fuel-free or, at least, fueled by some clean and green force that exists "out there," beyond the sphere of our collective concerns.

11. For this relation, see Pinkus 2016b.

12. There are many studies concerning superstitions and creatures of the mine. In particular, Philip Usher (2019, 104) explores the relations of demons and illness in Georgius Agricola. "Structurally, floods, noxious air, poison, demons, collapses, and military activity are comparable members of a list of dangers, but the demons also appear . . . to emerge as presences

that stand in for and translate miners' fear regarding the more obviously material dangers."

13. Michel Butor ([1949] 1960) notes the nineteenth-century author's aversion to cold, ice, and all that could freeze, whereas Verne tends to embrace sun and warmth as having redemptive qualities.

14. Marx and Friedrich Engels might have attended lectures by John Tyndall on the greenhouse effect in London in 1859, but "when the capitalist mill owners of Malm's narrative turned to fossil-fueled steam power, neither they nor their contemporary social critics could have understood the long-term climatic repercussions" (Clark and Szerszynski 2001, 44). Marx most certainly did not read "On the Heat in the Sun's Rays," by Eunice Foote, an American scientist and suffragette, published in 1856. She details an experiment in which a cylinder containing carbon dioxide was heated by the sun at a much higher rate than one containing air. She writes: "An atmosphere of that gas would give to our earth a high temperature; and if as some suppose, at one period of its history the air had mixed with it a larger proportion than at present, an increased temperature from its own action as well as from increased weight must have necessarily resulted." See Nichola Daunton, "This Woman Discovered Climate Change 5 Years Before the Man Who Gets Credit for It," Euronews, February 18, 2022, www.euronews.com/green/2022/02/18/this-woman-discovered-climate-change-five-years-before-man-who-gets-credit-for-it.

15. See Hensley and Steer 2018, "Signatures of the Carboniferous: The Literary Forms of Coal."

16. See Sieferle 2001, 181. This 1693 treatise discusses the potential of coal in place of wood, which was becoming scarce.

3. Burial

1. There are many variants of the tale. Johann Peter Hebel's version, cited by Walter Benjamin (1968), was published in 1811 as "Unverhofftes Wiedersehen" ("Unexpected Reunion").

2. Hoffmann's sources include a five-volume account of travel in Sweden by J. F. L. Hausmann and Ernst Moritz Arndt. He was also certainly influenced by a version of the tale by Gotthilf Heinrich von Schubert that stressed the importance of fossils and fossilized plants in the mine. Jon Neubauer (1980) describes the tale in terms of the Romantic image of descent into mines or caves, the withdrawal of the self, and the search for a purer self (as in Novalis and Friedrich Wilhelm Joseph von Schelling) or the return to the inorganic realm (death). He sees most variants of the miner's tale as an interplay between these two broader themes. For another fundamental work of criticism that treats the tale, see Ziolkowski 1990.

3. The figure of the underworld queen also stems from and results in many variants. She may be associated with Persephone or Cybele (a goddess linked not only with the surface of mountains but also with what lies beneath), the Phrygian "Mother of the Gods" or "Mountain Mother," goddess of nature, assimilated in Greece to other figures such as Gaia, Rhea, and Demeter (mother of the harvest, of Persephone). In Rome she was called "Magna Mater" and was a patron of the Roman people.

4. This is also the subject of his treatise *De Animatibus subterraneis* (1549), which deals with the creatures that inhabit the mine.

5. Sand and Verne shared an editor, Louis-Jules Hetzel. The two writers corresponded, and scholars have established the influence of *Laura* on Verne's *Journey to the Center of the Earth,* published later the same year. See Vaclavik 2004. Sand was also influenced by Novalis, Gérard de Nerval, and perhaps by Edgar Allan Poe's *The Narrative of Arthur Gordon Pym.*

6. Currently, anthropogenic activity accounts for about 50 gigatons of CO_2 equivalent (carbon and other greenhouse gases). Since the Industrial Revolution, humans have emitted around 2,200 gigatons, and another 1,000, which we are on target to reach before midcentury, might be expected to raise global average temperatures by 2°C.

7. Terms like *exotic* or *bizarre* or *niche* are used in describing geoengineering schemes around the time of this writing, usually with the assumption that they will become more mainstream.

8. Christopher Helman, "Billionaire Harold Hamm Plans to Reverse Course and Pump Millions of Tons of Carbon into the Earth," Forbes, March 2, 2022, www.forbes.com/sites/christopherhelman/2022/03/02/fracking-billionaire-harold-hamm-reverses-course-and-starts-pumping-carbon-into-the-earth/?sh=51283ab02a6b. The plan is to capture fourteen million tons per year, but five billion is emitted per year in United States. The initiative is tied to the Summit Agricultural Group, owner of corn ethanol plants.

9. Bruyère (2018), Ialenti (2020), and Moisey (2017) all discuss the WIPP surface markers in detail.

10. See Buck (2019) for an overview of current proposals to market CO_2 as a commodity for the oil industry to transmute it into a fuel or into other useful products. These proposals appeal to different markets and may require different definitions of the substance.

11. There would be much to say about the ongoing discussions of a price/tax, but I do not cite the vast literature here since much of it concerns the surface and assumes that the subsurface (or rocks) will take care of the carbon.

12. See "Turning CO_2 into Products," XPRIZE, https://carbon.xprize.org/prizes/carbon.

13. Keynes worked on the *General Theory* beginning in 1934, and it was

published in 1936. After I had begun working on the burial passage, I read Timothy Mitchell (2011) and found that he, too, cited it, in the context of thinking about the very notion of economy as it develops in the early twentieth century, intertwined with oil.

14. John Schwarz (photos by Brandon Thibodeaux), "They Grew Up around Fossil Fuels. Now, Their Jobs Are in Renewables," *New York Times Magazine*, March 26, 2019, https://www.nytimes.com/interactive/2019/03/26/climate/wind-solar-energy-workers.html.

15. Gold mining is, in fact, a highly toxic activity. In the cultural imagination, it has been thought of as an activity of degradation, as opposed to coal mining, which yields energy for fruitful purposes. Gold-mining countries are not rich but poor. Gold mining is painted as corrupting, bringing dismal conditions to people, and creating boom-to-bust towns. As Chesneaux (2001, 218) notes, Jules Verne found gold mining degrading.

4. Surface Depth

1. The novel was first published in 1864. I cite the translation by William Butcher, based on the 1867 second edition with two added chapters (37–39) containing more material derived from the work of French naturalist Louis Figuier and including illustrations by Édouard Riou, who also provided illustrations for Figuier. *Journey* came out just before Verne's long-time editor, Pierre-Jules Hetzel, began his *Magasin d'Education et de Récréation*, so it was not serialized, unlike most of the later novels. There is little archival material detailing the process of the composition or editing of the novel. As Butcher notes in his introduction (1992, xxvii), Verne's choice of names may have been playful (but not necessarily portent). *Otto* is a palindrome, for what it is worth, a word that circles back on itself perhaps like the voyage itself. *Lidenbrock* may be a combination of *eyelid* and *brocken*, a crumb or lump of coal or scrap. *Axel*, the narrator, might refer to an axe or it might be *lexa*, "words," written backward. Axel's beloved, Gräuben, is from Virland. In French, the adjective to describe her, *Virlandaise*, (almost) contains Verne's name, a calembour in French, a type of wordplay.

2. The novel was not without controversy. Verne was accused of plagiarizing portions of it. He was sued by Léon Delmas (René de Pont-Jest) for taking at least one element from the latter's novella *La tête de Mimer* (*Mimer's Head*) of 1863, published in the magazine *Revue contemporaine*, which Verne claimed never to have read. The suit dragged on for years and caused Verne no small degree of personal consternation. Verne also drew heavily on material in other writings, including George Sand's *Laura*

and perhaps E. T. A. Hoffmann's "The Mines of Falun." See Unwin 2005 for various influences. Verne was well-read in the geography of his time. As mentioned, Louis Figuier's *Terre avant le deluge* (*Earth Before the Deluge*) was especially important, and Verne copies passages from it nearly verbatim.

3. The parchment falls out of a book that Lidenbrock purchases from a Jew named Hevelius in his hometown of Hamburg. Johannes Hevelius was a (Christian) Polish astronomer of the seventeenth century and the author of an important treatise on the moon, *Selenographia* (1647), that Verne might well have read. Perhaps he associated the name with science, broadly speaking. In his story of the acquisition of the book, Verne could be making a subtle reference to the French alchemist/bookseller Nicolas Flamel, who purchases a book of alchemy (by one "Abraham the Jew") in a market stall. Scholars dispute if Flamel was a real person (presumed to have lived from c. 1340 to c. 1418) or the invention of seventeenth-century editors who published his texts. According to the *Book of Hieroglyphical Figures* ascribed to him, Flamel travels to Spain to find a converted Jew who can tell him about the first matter of the philosopher's stone. He returns to Paris to perform the great work multiple times. In a sense, his is the story of a journey to wisdom. The book that Lidenbrock purchases is the *Heimskringla*, the chronicle of Norwegian princes in Iceland, by Snorri Sturluson, from the twelfth century. Axel assumes it must be a German translation. The professor replies: "What! A translation! what would I be doing with your translation? Who's bothered about your translation? This is the original work, in Icelandic [it is actually Old Norse]: that magnificent language, both simple and rich, containing the most diverse grammatical combinations as well as numerous variations in the words." The nephew then asks, "Like German?" (Verne 1992, 36). This exchange may mean nothing to the reader, who is only anxious to move beyond. It is interesting, though, that the book purchased by Lidenbrock is a rather dry chronicle, and not the *Prose Edda*, a work with a significant component about the underworld and a dragon that guards a treasure. Incidentally, Sturluson's nephew wrote a mean-spirited biography of his uncle.

4. Arne Saknussemm is probably loosely based on a real figure, Professor Árni Magnússon (1663–1730), an Icelandic scholar descended from Snorri Sturluson who traveled on behalf of the King of Denmark to collect the manuscripts of the Sagas—and who always wrote in Latin. Why make Saknussemm an alchemist? It might seem like Verne simply using *alchemist* to refer to something like "equivocation," since there is no necessarily rigorous connection between a Jewish bookseller, geological exploration, runic writing, and the kind of transmutational activities classified under

the theory or practice that was early modern alchemy. This is not the first or last time that Verne (probably following Edgar Allan Poe in "The Gold-Bug") reverts to the device of a code to spur his plot. In his 1881 novel *La Jangada: Huit cent Lieues sur l'Amazone*, a piece of paper bearing coded text gives rise to a treasure hunt, for instance.

5. For a more developed reading of *Topsy Turvy* in relation to geo-engineering, see Karen Pinkus, "The Arctic Upside Down," *Technosphere Magazine*, November 6, 2018, https://technosphere-magazine.hkw.de/p/The-Arctic-Upside-Down-5nGCrN1bD6HpK7XKQ4kDPt.

6. Some variants of *The Aeneid* use *averno*. As Butcher (1992) notes in his introduction to the novel, *Averni* is another (near) anagram, or, better, a calembour, of *Verne*. The compass, it will turn out at the end of the novel, is reversed, "à l'envers," another calembour, and there is a cavern in the center of the earth.

7. Volcanoes open up the semihollowed earth to men who dare to explore the core. Other authors who Verne read, and who subscribed to the hollow earth theory, believed there were openings at the poles. Through his device of the runes, Verne does not discount this other theory, but his men have their own path to follow. Verne was influenced by geologists including Élie de Beaumont, Charles Sainte-Claire Deville (on volcanoes), Louis Agassiz (for fossil fish), and Pierre Boitard, author of the speculative *Paris avant les hommes* (1863).

8. See Oliensis 2001 and Starobinski 1987 for two different views of Freud's relation to Virgil.

9. Letter to Wilhelm Fliess, August 6, 1899, quoted in Freud 1954, 290.

10. There were strong cultural links between alchemy and the figure of the Jew that Verne might have drawn upon, and this is another area where the novella *Mimer's Head* comes into the picture. In *Journey*, Lidenbrock is apparently well-known in Hamburg. Verne (1992, 5) wants to grant him a certain degree of authority, but he also mocks him, gently, as when he writes in the passive voice that "a work had appeared in 1853 in Leipzig, Treatise upon Transcendental Crystallography by Professor O. Lidenbrock, printed in large-folio pages with plates—but without covering its costs."

11. Indeed, the choice between two (think of the trope of Hercules at the crossroads) or three (doors/caskets, as in the *Gesta Romanorum*, Apuleius, and Shakespeare) are classic figures of dilemma.

12. *Prehistoric* is the term used by Gabriel Tarde ([1896] 1905) in his history of the present written from the future to refer to what we readers know as "our times."

13. This is the phrase used by Martin Rudwick (2008, 310–11).

14. The French reads: "Je me bornerai donc à reproduire ici ces notes

quotidiennes, écrits pour ainsi dire sous la dicté des evénéments" (Verne 1864, 151).

15. Poe wrote a lengthy review of a speech made to Congress by Jeremiah Reynolds, a disciple of John Cleves Symmes Jr., asking for funds to visit the pole in 1834. *The Narrative of Arthur Gordon Pym of Nantucket* bears clear influences of Symmes's fiction. In Jules Verne's 1879 novel *The Sphinx of the Ice Realm*, the protagonist finds Pym's corpse underground.

16. Verne's *Adventures of Captain Hatteras* (1864) also borrows various elements from Poe.

17. It is interesting to note that in Tarde's ([1896] 1905) deep future, all paper has disappeared (along with all nature, except for humans), so the author interrupts his narrative to mention that he is writing it in chalk on schist in the year 596 (of the new era)!

18. See Jason Hickel, "Our Best Shot at Cooling the Planet Might Be Right Beneath Our Feet," *Guardian*, August 8, 2017, https://www.theguardian.com/global-development-professionals-network/2016/sep/10/soil-our-best-shot-at-cooling-the-planet-might-be-right-under-our-feet.

19. Perhaps the largest experiment right now in this area is the (controversial) Archer-Daniels-Midland plant in Illinois. BECCS has close connections to my work in *Fuel* (2016a), as it involves drawing energy from plants to produce electricity, liquid fuels, or heat and then sequestering unused carbon dioxide produced by this process. BECCS includes carbon dioxide both captured at the flue stack and produced through pyrolysis (liquid fuels). The National Academies (2018) report does not consider the capture and reuse of carbon dioxide as fuel to be a negative emissions technology as it is (or would be) rereleased into the atmosphere, in contrast, say, to CO_2 used in building materials. Conservation agriculture includes processes that might be classified as adaptation and mitigation, depending on context and emphasis. It is a set of practices that includes "minimizing tillage, maintaining vegetation cover year-round, diversifying crop rotations, re-incorporating crop residues, and use of composts, manures or other organic amendments" (Wolfe 2001, 24). Such practices generally make farmers more resilient while also increasing the capacity for carbon sequestration and reducing the needs for nitrogen fertilizers. In general, farmers can get behind conservation agriculture because it makes economic common sense.

20. See Velasquez-Manoff 2018.

21. Japanese botanist Akira Miyawaki developed a system for rapid afforestation in areas of degraded soil, drawing on the extraordinary power of mychorrhizae, or fungi.

22. Anna Tsing's influential book *The Mushroom at the End of the World*

has brought mycology and climate change into proximity for various thinkers in the humanities.

23. HiveMind has contracts with two of the world's top ten emitters: Cummins and Shell. This is not the place to dive into the complex economics of carbon trading. Right now, it is primarily facilitated through ERPA (Emissions Reduction Purchase Agreements). "The agreement privatizes and discursively abstracts carbon, so that it can be traded as pieces of information (tCO$_2$e) that are essentially its commodity form" (Bumpus and Liverman 2008, 136). The ERPAs separate carbon from its context, abstracting it, decontextualizing it for a network of different actors. VCUs are usually governed by smaller organizations and NGOs, so they are less supranatural and more like a form of "horizontal linking" (141).

24. I am grateful to Ziggy Snow, who alerted me to the fact that the project and its principal promotor, Joseph Kelly, were unveiled as scams. As investigative journalist Zahra Hirji notes in the May 6, 2021, *Buzzfeed* article "Magic Mushrooms: This Scammer Is Twisting Science in a Scheme to Save the World," various pieces of the puzzle as I have briefly outlined them have fallen apart. It was simply too good to be true.

25. The group's website, https://www.spun.earth/, lists as key principles scientific rigor, open data, and inclusive action.

26. In geological terms, this is different from the weathering as a form of erosion undergone by various works built by humans, say.

27. A recent study estimated a cost of between $60 trillion and $600 trillion to remove 50 parts per million of carbon dioxide from the planet's atmosphere in this manner. The HiveMind mycelium network also impedes the release of N$_2$O (nitrous oxide), a short-lived but very potent greenhouse gas, and it increases the fertility of the soil, allowing the plants to release more oxygen.

28. See Eklund 2017, esp. introduction, 13.

29. There are different forms of black earth. It is believed that terra preta is not natural but a product of deliberate (or accidental) soil management practices of Indigenous people in the Amazon.

30. See "Black Forest [29,930,000 tons]," Hans Baumann, http://hbaumann.com/Black-Forest.

5. Subterranean Futures

1. See "Welcome to Survival Condo," Survival Condo, https://survivalcondo.com/overview/.

2. Nigel Clark and Bronislaw Szerszynski (2020) speculate on the nature of planets. They do so not because they are in favor of terraforming

or colonizing other planets but in order to think differently about Earth, as an "astronomical body with the inherent capacity to become otherwise; to reorganize its constituent parts—at multiple scales—into new arrangements" (78). Different planets have different subsurfaces. As they mature over deep time, they become "closed" but they "typically remain energetically open, which is to say that they are subjected to flows of energy over long timescales from their parent star and their own interior" (79). Not all planets are quite like Earth. Some are rogues, meaning they do not rely on energy from a star but "could nevertheless receive enough energy from residual heat, radioactive decay and tidal forces to prolong their passage to equilibrium and allow them to realize some of their own potentialities—perhaps even biological life" (81). Life on such planets might exist below the surface! Perhaps visiting subsurface alien life forms would not bother looking around the surface of Earth but might bore underground, as theorized in an animated sequence in Peter Galison and Robb Moss's film *Containment*, potentially disturbing buried waste.

3. Incidentally, several years early, Kahn authored a study of the feasibility of nuclear fallout shelters for residents of Manhattan in the rock some eight hundred feet below the surface. See Rose 2001, 30.

4. Stephen Pacala and Robert H. Socolow, two Princeton researchers, did an influential study to see how carbon could be stabilized below 500 ppm in fifty years using currently available technologies and practices. They created a series of stabilization wedges that cannot but strike us as entirely commonsense. Their research, carried out beginning around the turn of the millennium, was funded by Ford (and later by BP) and was published in *Science*. The wedges and stabilization triangles have been widely used as a teaching and business tool, including in school curricula. The logic of their wedges is, for me, the following: look what we could do with little disruption to any given sector or way of life, but we did not do it when we could have, so now we can only look back into the very recent past and lament that we lacked the political will to do what was so easy then.

5. People of the State of New York, by Letitia James, Attorney General of the State of New York, Plaintiff, v. Exxon Mobil Corporation, Defendant, 65 Misc. 3d 1233 (N.Y. Sup. Ct. 2019) at 17.

6. In fact, Exxon has lost so much value that it was recently delisted from the Dow-Jones Industrial Average (in favor of a tech company). For proxy activism as "insurrection," see Jessica Camille Aguirre, "The Little Hedge Fund Taking Down Big Oil," *New York Times*, June 23, 2021, https://www.nytimes.com/2021/06/23/magazine/exxon-mobil-engine-no-1-board.html.

7. A small Brooklyn collective is using blockchain (a highly energetic

monetary form, to be sure) to trade credits and create a peer-to-peer local solar microgrid. A representative of Sonnen, a German energy service, calls peer-to-peer a "disruptive technology" because "the customers are also the owners—they are the producers of the energy." See Diane Cardwell, "Solar Experiment Lets Neighbors Trade Energy among Themselves," *New York Times,* March 13, 2017, https://www.nytimes.com/2017/03/13/business/energy-environment/brooklyn-solar-grid-energy-trading.html.

8. For an account of the study, see Adam Frank, "Was There a Civilization on Earth Before Humans?," *Atlantic,* April 13, 2018, https://www.theatlantic.com/science/archive/2018/04/are-we-earths-only-civilization/557180/.

9. In *Journey to the Center of the Earth,* the men encounter a preserved corpse of what appears to be a man. At another point, when Axel has been separated from his uncle and their guide, Axel fears death and somehow "strangely enough—it came into my mind that if one day my fossilized body was found again, encountering it 70 miles into the bowels of the Earth would raise serious scientific questions" (Verne 1992, 127). Axel's remark underscores, however, that a single (heroic) individual, whether preserved mostly intact or as bones set into rock, would precisely not disrupt chronology or science because a fossil must be unrecognizable, unnamable, and part of a species to be of value. As a singular body, it is illegible in the rock record.

Bibliography

Agamben, Giorgio. 2017. *The Fire and the Tale*. Translated by Lorenzo Chiesa. Palo Alto, Calif.: Stanford University Press.
Agricola, Georgius. (1556) 1950. *De re metallica*. Translated by Herbert Clark Hoover and Lou Henry Hoover. New York: Dover.
Albrecht, Glenn. 2006. "Solastalgia." *Alternatives Journal* 32 (4/5): 34–36.
Althusser, Louis. 2015. *Reading Capital*. Translated by Ben Brewster and David Fernbach. New York: Verso.
Aravamudan, Srinivas. 2013. "The Catachronism of Climate Change." *Diacritics* 41 (3): 6–30.
Arendt, Hannah. 1968. "Walter Benjamin: 1892–1940." In *Illuminations*, by Walter Benjamin, translated by Harry Zohn, 1–55. New York: Schocken Books.
Augé, Marc. 1995. *Non-places: An Introduction to Supermodernity*. Translated by John Howe. New York: Verso.
Barthes, Roland. 1970. "Par où commencer?" *Poétique* 1:3–9.
Baucom, Ian. 2012. "History 4°: Postcolonial Method and Anthropocene Time." *Cambridge Journal of Postcolonial Literary Inquiry* 1:123–42.
Bell, Daniel. 1973. *The Coming of Post-Industrial Society: A Venture in Social Forecasting*. New York: Basic Books.
Benjamin, Walter. 1968. "The Storyteller." In *Illuminations*, translated by Harry Zohn, 83–109. New York: Schocken Books.
Best, Stephen, and Sharon Marcus, eds. 2009. "The Way We Read Now." Special issue, *Representations* 108:1–148.
Bonta, Mark, and John Protevi. 2004. *Deleuze and Geophilosophy: A Guide and Glossary*. Edinburgh: Edinburgh University Press.
Brooks, Peter. 1992. *Reading for the Plot: Design and Intention in Narrative*. Rev. ed. Cambridge, Mass.: Harvard University Press.
Bruyère, Vincent. 2018. *Perishability Fatigue: Forays into Environmental Loss and Decay*. New York: Columbia University Press.
Buck, Holly Jean. 2019. *After Geoengineering: Climate Tragedy, Repair, and Restoration*. New York: Verso.
Bumpus, A. G., and D. M. Liverman. 2008. "Accumulation by Decarbonization and the Governance of Carbon Offsets." *Economic Geography* 84:127–55.

Butcher, William. 1992. Introduction to *Journey to the Center of the Earth*, by Jules Verne, xvii–xxix. Oxford: Oxford University Press.

Burke, Edmund. 1833. "The Valley of Oodipoor." *Edinburg New Philosophical Journal: Exhibiting a View of the Progressive Discoveries and Improvements in the Sciences and the Arts* 14.

Butor, Michel. (1949) 1960. "La point suprême et l'âge d'or à travers quelques oeuvres de Jules Verne." In *Répertoire*. Paris: Éditions de Minuit.

Calvino, Italo. 1995. "The Petrol Pump." In *Numbers in the Dark and Other Stories*. Translated by Tim Park, 170–75. New York: Pantheon.

Chakrabarty, Dipesh. 2009. "The Climate of History: Four Theses." *Critical Inquiry* 35 (Winter): 197–222.

Chesneaux, Jean. 1971. *Une Lecture politique de Jules Verne*. Paris: François Maspero.

Chesneaux, Jean. 2001. *Jules Verne. Un regard sur le monde*. Paris: Bayard Editions.

Chisholm, Dianne. 2007. "Rhizome, Ecology, Geophilosophy (A Map to This Issue)." *Rhizomes: Cultural Studies in Emerging Knowledge* 15 (Winter): http://www.rhizomes.net/issue15/chisholm.html.

Clark, Nigel. 2018. "Bare Life on Molten Rock." *SubStance* 47 (2): 8–22.

Clark, Nigel, and Bronislaw Szerszynski. 2020. *Planetary Social Thought: The Anthropocene Challenge to the Social Sciences*. Cambridge: Polity Press.

De Landa, Manuel. 2005. *A Thousand Years of Non-linear History*. Cambridge, Mass.: MIT Press.

Deleuze, Gilles, and Félix Guattari. 1987. *A Thousand Plateaus: Capitalism and Schizophrenia*. Translated by Brian Massumi. Minneapolis: University of Minnesota Press.

Derrida, Jacques. 1974. "White Mythology: Metaphor in the Text of Philosophy." Translated by F. C. T. Moore. *New Literary History* 6 (1): 5–74.

Doyle, Arthur Conan. (1928) 1969. "When the World Screamed." In *The Professor Challenger Stories*, 547–77. London: John Murray.

Doyle, Arthur Conan. (1912) 2002. *The Lost World*. Edited by Philip Gooden. New York: Penguin.

Dumas, Olivier, Piero Gondolo della Riva, and Volker Dehs, eds. 2001. *Correspondance inédite de Jules Verne et de Pierre-Jules Hetzel (1863–1886)*. Vol. 1 (1863–1874), Vol. 2 (1875–1878). Geneva: Slatkine.

Eklund, Hillary, ed. 2017. *Ground-work: English Renaissance Literature and Soil Science*. Pittsburgh: Duquesne University Press.

Figuier, Louis. (1863) 1871. *La terre avant le deluge*. Paris: Hachette.

François, Anne-Lise. 2017. "Ungiving Time: Reading Lyric by the Light of the Anthropocene." In *Anthropocene Reading: Literary History in Geologic Times*, edited by Tobias Menely and Jesse Oak Taylor, 239–58. University Park: Penn State University Press.

Freud, Sigmund. 1954. *The Origins of Psychoanalysis: Letters to Wilhelm Fleiss, Drafts, and Notes, 1887–1902*, edited by Marie Bonaparte, Anna Freud, and Ernst Kris, translated by James Strachey. Garden City, N.Y.: Doubleday.

Freud, Sigmund. 1955. "The Uncanny." In *The Standard Edition of the Complete Psychological Works*, vol. 17, edited and translated by James Strachey, 217–56. London: Hogarth Press.

Freud, Sigmund. 1965. *The Interpretation of Dreams*. Edited and translated by James Strachey. New York: Avon Books.

Gallagher, Catherine. 1980. *Industrial Reformation of English Fiction, 1832–1867*. Chicago: University of Chicago Press.

Garofalo, Devin. Forthcoming. "Lyric Geology: Anthropomorphosis, White Supremacy, and Genres of the Human." *Diacritics*.

Ghosh, Amitav. 2017. *The Great Derangement: Climate Change and the Unthinkable*. Chicago: University of Chicago Press.

Gould, Stephen Jay. 2004. "Father Athanasius on the Isthmus of a Middle State." In *Athanasius Kircher: The Last Man Who Knew Everything*, edited by Paula Findlen, 207–38. New York: Routledge.

Günel, Gökçe. 2016. "What Is Carbon Dioxide? When Is Carbon Dioxide?" *Political and Legal Anthropology Review* 39 (1): 33–45.

Haff, Peter. 2014. "The Far Future of Soil." In *The Soil Underfoot: Infinite Possibilities for a Finite Resource*, edited by G. Jock Churchman and Edward R. Landa, 61–72. Boca Raton, Fla.: CRC Press.

Hensley, Nathan, and Philip Steer, eds. 2018. *Ecological Form: System and Aesthetics in the Age of Empire*. New York: Fordham University Press.

Hoffmann, E. T. A. 1969. *Tales of E. T. A. Hoffmann*. Edited and translated by Leonard J. Kent and Elizabeth C. Knight. Chicago: University of Chicago Press.

Hoffmann, E. T. A. 1992. *The Golden Pot and Other Stories*. Translated by Ritchie Robertson. Oxford: Oxford University Press.

Hoffmann, E. T. A. 2021. *Die Bergwerke zu Falun: Der Artushof*. Stuttgart, Germany: Reclam.

Hofmeister, Anne M., Robert E. Criss, and Everett M. Criss. 2022. "Links of Planetary Energetics to Moon Size, Orbit, and Planet Spin: A New Mechanism for Plate Tectonics." "In the Footsteps of Warren B. Hamilton: New Ideas in Earth Science." *GSA Special Papers* 553: https://doi.org/10.1130/SPE553.

Hutton, James. 1795. *Theory of the Earth, with Proofs and Illustrations: In Four Parts.* London: Messrs Cadell, Junior, and Davies.

Ialenti, Vincent. 2020. *Deep Time Reckoning: How Future Thinking Can Help Earth Now.* Cambridge, Mass.: MIT Press.

IPCC. 2018. "Summary for Policymakers." In *Global Warming of 1.5°C*. https://www.ipcc.ch/sr15/.

Keynes, John Maynard. 1936. *The General Theory of Employment, Interest, and Money.* London: Macmillan.

Kircher, Athanasius. 1664–1665. *Mundus subterraneus in xii libros digestus: Quo divinum subterrestris mundi opificium, mira ergasteriorum naturæ in eo distributio, verbo Protei regnum, vniversæ denique naturæ majestas & divitiæ summa rerum varietate exponuntur: Abditorum effectuum causæ acri indagine inquisitæ demonstrantur: Cognitæ per artis & naturæ conjugium ad humanæ vitæ necessarium usum vario experimentorum apparatu, necnon novo modo, & ratione applicantur.* Amsterdam: Joannem Janssonium and Elizeum Weyerstratenm.

Leifchild, J. R. (1856) 1968. *Our Coal and Our Coal-Pits: The People in Them and the Scenes Around Them by a Traveller Underground.* New York: Augustus Kelley.

Lekachman, Robert. 1966. *The Age of Keynes.* New York: Random House.

Lévi-Strauss, Claude. 1969. *The Elementary Structures of Kinship.* Translated by James Harle Bell, John Richard von Sturmer, and Rodney Needham. Edited by Rodney Needham. Boston: Beacon Press.

Lyell, Charles. 1830. *Principles of Geology, Being an Attempt to Explain the Former Changes of the Earth's Surface by Reference to Causes Now in Operation.* Vol. 1. London: John Murray.

Macdonald, Graeme. 2013. "Research Notes: The Resources of Fiction." *Reviews in Cultural Theory* 4 (2): 1–24.

Macfarlane, Robert. 2019. *Underland: A Deep Time Journey.* New York: W. W. Norton.

Malm, Andreas. 2016. *Fossil Capital: The Rise of Steam Power and the Roots of Global Warming.* New York: Verso Books.

Marel, Henri. 1980. "Jules Verne, Zola et la mine." *Les cahiers naturalistes* 54:197–200.

Marx, Karl. 1967. *Capital.* Vol. 1. Edited by Frederick Engels. Translated by Samuel Moore and Edward Aveling. Moscow: Progress Publishers.

Massumi, Brian. 1987. Translator's foreword to *A Thousand Plateaus*, by Gilles Deleuze and Félix Guattari, ix–xv. Minneapolis: University of Minnesota Press.

McPhee, John. 1981. *Annals of the Former World.* New York: Farrar, Straus and Giroux.

Menely, Tobias, and Jesse Oak Taylor, eds. 2017. *Anthropocene Reading: Literary History in Geologic Times*. University Park: Penn State University Press.

Mitchell, Timothy. 2011. *Carbon Democracy: Political Power in the Age of Oil*. New York: Verso.

Moisey, Andrew. 2017. "Permanent Negative Value: The Waste Isolation Pilot Plant." *Critical Inquiry* 43:861–92.

Morris, Robert. 1980. "Notes on Art as/and Land Reclamation." *October* 12:87–102.

Murakami M., A. Goncharov, N. Miyajima, D. Yamazaki, and N. Holtgrewe. 2022. "Radiative Thermal Conductivity of Single-Crystal Bridgmanite at the Core-Mantle Boundary with Implications for Thermal Evolution of the Earth." *Earth and Planetary Science Letters* 578 (January 15, 2022): https://doi.org/10.1016/j.epsl.2021.117329.

National Academies of Sciences, Engineering, and Medicine. 2018. *Negative Emissions Technologies and Reliable Sequestration: A Research Agenda*. Washington, D.C.: National Academies Press. https://doi.org/10.17226/25259.

Negri, Antonio. 1994. "Keynes and the Capitalist Theory of the State." In *Labor of Dionysus*, by Michael Hardt and Antonio Negri, 22–50. Minneapolis: University of Minnesota Press.

Neubauer, John. 1980. "The Mines of Falun: Temporal Fortunes of a Romantic Myth of Time." *Studies in Romanticism* 19:475–95.

Neyrat, Frédéric. 2018. *The Unconstructable Earth: An Ecology of Separation*. Translated by Drew Burk. New York: Fordham University Press.

Oliensis, Ellen. 2001. "Freud's 'Aeneid.'" *Vergilius* 47:39–63.

Pacala, Stephen, and Robert H. Socolow. 2004. "Stabilization Wedges: Solving the Climate Problem for the Next 50 Years with Current Technologies." *Science* 305 (5683): 968–72.

Parcell, William. 2009. "Signs and Symbols in Kircher's Mundus Subterraneus." In *The Revolution in Geology from the Renaissance to the Enlightenment*, edited by Gary Rosenberg. Boulder, Colo.: Geological Society of America.

Parikka, Jussi. 2015. *A Geology of Media*. Minneapolis: University of Minnesota Press.

Pinkus, Karen, ed. 2013. "Climate Change Criticism." Special issue, *Diacritics* 41 (3).

Pinkus, Karen. 2016a. *Fuel: A Speculative Dictionary*. Minneapolis: University of Minnesota Press.

Pinkus, Karen. 2016b. "Humans and Fuels, Bíos and Zōe." In *A Cultural*

History of Climate Change, edited by Tom Ford and Tom Bristow, 128–37. London: Routledge.

Playfair, John. 1822. *The Works of John Playfair*. Edinburgh: A. Constable.

Poe, Edgar Allan. (1838) 1999. *The Narrative of Arthur Gordon Pym of Nantucket*. New York: Penguin Books.

Pont-Jest, René de. (1863) 2011. *Mimer's Head (La tête de Mimer)*, edited and translated by Brian Stableford. In *The World Above the World and Other French Scientific Romances*, 70–111. Encino, Calif.: Black Coat Press Books.

Remane, Jürgen. 2003. "Chronostratigraphic Correlations: Their Importance for the Definition of Geochronologic Units." *Palaeogeography, Palaeoclimatology, Palaeoecology* 196:7–18.

Rose, Kenneth D. 2001. *One Nation Underground: The Fallout Shelter in American Culture*. New York: New York University Press.

Rubin, Gayle. (1975) 2012. "The Traffic in Women: Notes on the Political Economy of Sex." In *Deviations: A Gayle Rubin Reader*. Durham, N.C.: Duke University Press.

Rudwick, Martin J. S. 2008. *Worlds Before Adam: The Reconstruction of Geohistory in the Age of Reform*. Chicago: University of Chicago Press.

Sand, George (Aurore Dupin). (1864) 1977. *Laura: Voyage dans le cristal*. Paris: Librarie A.-G. Nizet.

Sand, George. 1992. *Journey Within the Crystal: A Study and Translation of George Sand's "Laura: Voyage dans le cristal."* Translated by Pauline Pearson-Stamps. New York: Peter Lang.

Serres, Michel. 1974. *Jouvences: Sur Jules Verne*. Paris: Éditions de Minuit.

Shell Corporation. 2018. *Shell Scenarios: Sky—Meeting the Goals of the Paris Agreement*. Pamphlet available at "Sky Scenario," Shell, https://www.shell.com/energy-and-innovation/the-energy-future/scenarios/shell-scenario-sky.html.

Sieferle, Rolf. 2001. *The Subterranean Forest*. Translated by Michael P. Osman. Cambridge: White Horse Press.

Smithson, Robert. 1970–1971. "Strata: A Geophotographic Fiction." *Aspen* 8 (Fall–Winter): sec. 12.

Stapledon, Olaf. (1930) 2008. *Last and First Men*. Mineola, N.Y.: Dover Publications.

Starobinski, Jean. 1987. "Acheronta Movebo." Translated by Françoise Meltzer. *Critical Inquiry* 13 (2): 394–407.

Tarde, Gabriel. (1896) 1905. *Underground Man*. Translated by Brereton Cloudesley. London: Duckworth & Co.

Taylor, Jesse Oak. 2018. "Mourning Species: In Memoriam in an Age of Extinction." In *Ecological Form: System and Aesthetics in the Age of Empire*,

edited by Nathan Hensley and Philip Steer, 42–62. New York: Fordham University Press.
Thompson, Ian. 2011. *Jules Verne's Scotland in Fact and Fiction*. Edinburgh: Luath Press.
Trexler, Adam. 2015. *Anthropocene Fictions: The Novel in the Time of Climate Change*. Charlottesville: University of Virginia Press.
Unwin, Timothy. 2005. *Jules Verne: Journeys in Writing*. Liverpool: Liverpool University Press.
Usher, Philip. 2019. *Exterranean: Extraction in the Humanist Anthropocene*. New York: Fordham University Press.
Vaclavik, Kiera. 2004. "George Sand & Jules Verne: A Missing Link." *French Studies Bulletin* 25 (90): 8–10.
Verne, Jules. 1864. *Voyage au centre de la terre*. Paris: J. Hetzel.
Verne, Jules. (1877) 1883a. *The Underground City*. Translated by W. H. G. Kingston. Philadelphia: Porter and Coates.
Verne, Jules. 1883b. *The Green Ray (Le Rayon Vert)*. Translated by Mary De Hauteville. London: Samson Low, Marston, Searle & Rivington.
Verne, Jules. 1890. *Topsy Turvy, or The Purchase of the North Pole (Sans dessus dessous)*. New York: J. G. Ogilvie Seaside Publishing Company.
Verne, Jules. (1877) 1967. *Les Indes noires*. Paris: Hachette.
Verne, Jules. 1992. *Journey to the Centre of the Earth*. Translated by William Butcher. Oxford: Oxford University Press.
Verne, Jules. (1875) 2001. *The Mysterious Island*. Translated by Jordan Stump. New York: Random House.
Wenzel, Jennifer. 2016. "Afterword: Improvement and Overburden." *Postmodern Culture* 26 (2): https://doi.org/10.1353/pmc.2016.0003.
White, Hayden. 1980. "The Value of Narrativity in the Representation of Reality." *Critical Inquiry* 7 (1): 5–27.
Williams, Rosalind. 2008. *Notes on the Underground: An Essay on Technology, Society, and the Imagination*. Cambridge, Mass.: MIT Press.
Wolfe, David Walter. 2001. *Tales from the Underground: A Natural History of Subterranean Life*. Cambridge, Mass.: Perseus Publications.
Woods, Derek. 2017. "Accelerated Reading: Fossil Fuels, Infowhelm, and Archival Life." In *Anthropocene Reading: Literary History in Geologic Times*, edited by Tobias Menely and Jesse Oak Taylor, 202–19. University Park: Penn State University Press.
Woods, Derek. 2020. "The Fungal Kingdom." *Alienocene: Journal of the First Outernational*, https://alienocene.com/2020/12/04/the-fungal-kingdom/.
Yaeger, Patricia, ed. 2011. "Editor's Column: Literature in the Ages of Wood, Tallow, Coal, Whale Oil, Gasoline, Atomic Power, and Other Energy Sources." *PMLA* 126 (2): 305–26.

Yusoff, Kathryn. 2018. *A Billion Black Anthropocenes or None*. Minneapolis: University of Minnesota Press.

Ziolkowski, Theodore. 1990. *German Romanticism and Its Institutions*. Princeton, N. J.: Princeton University Press.

Ziser, Michael. 2011. "Oil Spills." In "Editor's Column," edited by Patricia Yaeger. *PMLA* 126 (2): 321–23.

Index

Page numbers in italic refer to illustrations.

Aeneae descensus ad inferos cum
 Sybilla Cumaea, 143
Agamben, Giorgio: on alchemy, 79;
 The Fire and the Tale, 78–80; on
 Rimbaud, 79
Agricola, Georgius, 11, 32, 55,
 82–83, 120, 166; *De re metallica*,
 26, 44, 76, 91, 96
Albrecht, Glenn, 14–15
alchemy, 25, 32, 55, 76–77, 79–85, 102,
 120, 122, 126, 161, 167, 173, 175
Alighieri, Dante, 11, 133; *Divina
 Commedia*, 93–94
Althusser, Louis, 73
analogy, 36, 40–42, 48, 65, 71–72,
 77, 79–81, 84, 93–94, 118–19,
 121–22, 127, 155, 161
Annals of Saint Gall. *See* White,
 Hayden
Anning, Mary, 14
Arendt, Hannah: on Walter
 Benjamin, 81–82
Aristotle, *Poetics*, 41
Arrhenius, Svante, 70
Augé, Marc, 7

Barthes, Roland, 77, 181; "Par où
 commencer?," 77; on Verne's *The
 Mysterious Island*, 77–78
Bateson, Gregory, 39
Baucom, Ian: and Claude Lévi-
 Strauss, 100

Baumann, Hans, *Black Forest*,
 163–65
Bell, Daniel, 182
Benjamin, Walter: on Johann Peter
 Hebel, 80–81, 98; "The Story-
 teller," 80–81. *See also* Arendt,
 Hannah
Benoit, France, *Guardians of Eter-
 nity*, 111–12
Best, Stephen, and Sharon Marcus,
 136
Bill and Melinda Gates Foundation,
 112
biochar, 157, 163–64
bioenergy with carbon seques-
 tration and storage (BECSS),
 50–51, 53, 106, 157
Bretton Woods, 116
Brooks, Peter, 12–13; on Freud,
 172–73
Bruyère, Vincent, 96
Buck, Holly Jean, 50, 156–57
Butor, Michel, 141
Buy Clean (nonprofit), 108
Byrd Polar and Climate Research
 Center, 47–48

Calvino, Italo, "The Petrol Pump,"
 31–32
carbon capture and sequestration
 (CCS), 16, 50, 52, 108, 110–12,
 116, 158, 160

Index

carbon dioxide removal (CDR), 16, 50–52
Chakrabarty, Dipesh: "The Climate of History," 100; negative universal history, 186
Chesneaux, Jean, 77
Chisholm, Diane, 42–43
Clark, Nigel, 1
Climeworks, 52, 112
Cold War, 177
Conan Doyle, Arthur, 39, 87; *The Lost World*, 9, 59, 171–72; "When the World Screamed," 9, 43, 129
coronavirus pandemic, 18, 106, 115, 118, 181, 186

Davy, Humphry, 29, 137–38, 174, 196
Defoe, Daniel, *Robinson Crusoe*, 149
Dehs, Volker. *See* Dumas, Oliver, Piero Gondolo della Riva, and Volker Dehs
De La Beche, Henry Thomas, *Duria Antiquior*, 13–14
De Landa, Manuel, 40; *A Thousand Years of Nonlinear History*, 36, 41–42
Deleuze, Gilles, and Félix Guattari, 7–8, 42–43, 159; *Anti-Oedipus*, 39; *A Thousand Plateaus*, 39–41
Derrida, Jacques, "White Mythology," 41
Descartes, René, 54, 138
Devonian era, 145, 147
Dumas, Oliver, Piero Gondolo della Riva, and Volker Dehs, 75, 167

Emerald Table, 83
Emmerich, Roland, *The Day after Tomorrow*, 3
enhanced weathering, 160

European Emissions Trading System, 110
ExxonMobil, 6–7, 181–82; and Engine No. 1, 182; "Outlooks for 2030 and 2040," 181

Férat, Jules, *The Black Indies*, 10, 23, 45
Figuier, Louis, 11, 13, 29, 74, 145, 148; *La terre avant le deluge*, 30
Freud, Sigmund, 136, 140; *Beyond the Pleasure Principle*, 172; and Dante, 133; *The Interpretation of Dreams*, 133; and the *unheimlich*, 94; and Virgil, 134
fungi, 158–60

Galison, Peter, and Robb Moss, *Containment*, 107–8, 112
Garofalo, Devin, 13
geoengineering, 8, 17, 49–51, 53–54, 63–64, 157
Ghosh, Amitav, 3, 32
Gondolo della Riva, Piero. *See* Dumas, Oliver, Piero Gondolo della Riva, and Volker Dehs
Green New Deal, 111, 114–15
Guattari, Félix. *See* Deleuze, Gilles, and Félix Guattari
Günel, Gökçe, 109, 110–11

Haff, Peter, 157–58, 160, 165
Hamm, Harold, 106–7
Harper and Brothers (publisher), 152
Hebel, Johann Peter: and Franz Kafka, 98; "An Unexpected Reunion," 80–81, 98. *See also* Benjamin, Walter
Heidegger, Martin, rape of the land, 63

Index

Hensley, Nathan, and Philip Steer, 73
Hetzel, Pierre-Jules, 55, 60, 75
Hickel, Jason, 156–58
HiveMind (start-up): and Sacred Rivers Climate Project, 158–60
Hoffmann, E. T. A., 17, 98, 170; "The Golden Pot," 102–3, 170; "The Miner of Falun," 89–96, 100, 102, 104, 124; "The Sandman," 102
Holocene, 157, 186
Humboldt, Alexander von, 36
Hutton, James, 1, 33–35; *Theory of the Earth*, 27–28, 38–39, 84

Intergovernmental Panel on Climate Change (IPCC), 49–50, 51

Jameson, Fredric, on symptomatic reading, 136
Jevons, William Stanley, 115, 116, 121

Kansas survival condos, 177–79; and Larry Hall, 177
katabasis, 93, 123, 131, 133
Keeling Curve, 52
Keynes, John Maynard: and analogy, 118–19, 121–22; *General Theory of Employment, Interest, and Money*, 113–19
Keynesianism, 113, 116–17, 120, 122
Kircher, Athanasius, 37, 55, 120, 154, 166; *Diatribe de prodigiosis crucibus*, 154; *Mundus subterraneus*, 11, 25–27, 82–83, 96–97
Klein, Naomi, and shock doctrine, 117
Kola Superdeep Borehole, 24
Kubrick, Stanley, *Dr. Strangelove*, 179

Lackner, Klaus, 52
Lawrence, D. H., 64
Leifchild, J. R., 68
Lekachman, Robert, and John Maynard Keynes, 114–15, 119
Lévi-Strauss, Claude: *The Elementary Structures of Kinship*, 184–85; *The Savage Mind*, 100. See also Baucom, Ian
Locke, John, 76
Lyell, Charles, 32–33, 35, 146; *Principles of Geology*, 22, 32

Macfarlane, Robert, 11
Madsen, Michael, *Into Eternity*, 46, 107, 112
Malm, Andreas, 67–68, 111, 183
Mantell, Gideon, 13
Marx, Karl, 136; *Capital*, 36, 70–72
Massumi, Brian, 39
Mauss, Marcel, *The Gift*, 184
McPhee, John, 39; and Benjamin Silliman, 121
metaphor, 172
metonymy, 172
Mitchell, Timothy, 3; and John Maynard Keynes, 115–16, 121
Morris, Robert, 161–63
Moss, Robb. *See* Galison, Peter and Robb Moss
Mundus subterraneus, 154–55. *See also* Kircher, Athanasius

National Academies, and NETs, 105–6
Negri, Antonio, 119
neptunism, 98
Neyrat, Frédéric, 54; on geoengineering, 63; on Marx, 54
Nixon, Rob, 63

Olúfẹ́mi, Táíwò, 53–54
Ovid, 76

Pacala, Stephen, and Robert Socolow, 180
pandemic. *See* coronavirus pandemic
Parcell, William, 83
Parikka, Jussi, 24
Paris Conference of the Parties (COP), 52, 155
phylogenic history, 91
Pinkus, Karen: *Alchemical Mercury*, 79; *Fuel*, 70–71
Playfair, John, 28–29
plutonism, 97–98, 104
Poe, Edgar Allan, *The Narrative of Arthur Gordon Pym of Nantucket*, 149–54
Pont-Jest, René de, *Mimer's Head*, 167–69

Remane, Jürgen, 37–38
Rimbaud, Arthur, *A Season in Hell*, 79. *See also* Agamben, Giorgio
Riou, Édouard: and Louis Figuier, 13; *Journey to the Center of the Earth*, 132, 142, 144; and Jules Verne, 13, 143
Royal Dutch Shell. *See* Shell Corporation
Rubin, Gayle: and Lévi-Strauss, 185; "The Traffic in Women," 185–86
Rudwick, Martin, 33, 35

Sand, George, 100; *Laura*, 101–5, 135, 170; *La ville noire*, 61–62
scenario planning, 179–81; and Herman Kahn, 179
Scott, Walter, 62, 85
Scrope, George Julius Poulett, 35

Serres, Michel, on *The Black Indies*, 77
sexual difference, 184–85
Shell Corporation, 179–80
Shubert, Gotthilf Heinrich von, 97
Silliman, Benjamin, 121
Smith, Adam, 76
Smith, William, *A Stratigraphical System of Organized Fossils*, 35
Smithson, Robert, 161–62; and Hans Magnus Enzensberger, 162; on psychic pollution, 162; *Strata*, 40, 43
Society for the Protection of Underground Networks (SPUN), 160
Socolow, Robert. *See* Pacala, Stephen, and Robert Socolow
soil enhancement, 155–57
Solar Radiation Management (SRM), 49–50
Splendor Solis, 84
Stamets, Paul, 158
Stapledon, Olaf, *Last and First Men*, 48
Steer, Philip. *See* Hensley, Nathan, and Philip Steer
Survival condo, 178
Sylva subterranean, 73

Tarde, Gabriel, 184, 187–88
Thatcher, Margaret, 120
Thompson, Lonnie, 47, 64
Tiesenhausen, Peter von, *Lifeline*, 164–65
Todorov, Tzvetan, "Narrative Transformations," 172–73
Trump era, 115, 118
Turrell, James, *Roden Crater*, 163

Velasquez-Manoff, Moises, "Can Dirt Save the Earth?," 157

Index

Verified Carbon Units (VCUs), 159
Verne, Jules, 13, 79, 121, 123, 151, 177, 187; and *antediluvian era*, 145; *Around the World in Eighty Days*, 59; *The Black Indies*, 9–10, 16, 21, 44–45, 57–63, 64–70, 72–73, 75–78, 82, 85–87, 127, 129; *The Green Ray*, 57, 58, 60, 129; *Journey to the Center of the Earth*, 4–5, 9, 14, 18, 21, 25, 54–56, 60, 62, 82, 98, 101, 102, 125–35, 137–49, 152, 155, 166–70, 172–75, 179; *The Mysterious Island*, 9, 70, 77, 141; *Topsy Turvy*, 74, 127–28, 129; *Twenty Thousand Leagues under the Sea*, 9
Virgil, *The Aeneid*, 130–31, 133

Waste Isolation Pilot Plant (WIPP), 107
Wenzel, Jennifer, 61
Werner, Abraham Gottlob, 97
White, Hayden, 98–99; and *Annals of Saint Gall*, 99–100; and Roland Barthes, 181
Williams, Rosalind, 63
Woods, Derek, 159
World War II, 182

Yusoff, Kathryn, *A Billion Black Anthropocenes or None*, 38, 62

Ziser, Michael, 3–4
Zola, Émile, *Germinal*, 69

(continued from page ii)

50 *Anthropocene Poetics: Deep Time, Sacrifice Zones, and Extinction*
   David Farrier

49 *Metaphysical Experiments: Physics and the Invention of the Universe*
   Bjørn Ekeberg

48 *Dialogues on the Human Ape*
   Laurent Dubreuil and Sue Savage-Rumbaugh

47 *Elements of a Philosophy of Technology: On the Evolutionary History of Culture*
   Ernst Kapp

46 *Biology in the Grid: Graphic Design and the Envisioning of Life*
   Phillip Thurtle

45 *Neurotechnology and the End of Finitude*
   Michael Haworth

44 *Life: A Modern Invention*
   Davide Tarizzo

43 *Bioaesthetics: Making Sense of Life in Science and the Arts*
   Carsten Strathausen

42 *Creaturely Love: How Desire Makes Us More and Less Than Human*
   Dominic Pettman

41 *Matters of Care: Speculative Ethics in More Than Human Worlds*
   María Puig de la Bellacasa

40 *Of Sheep, Oranges, and Yeast: A Multispecies Impression*
   Julian Yates

39 *Fuel: A Speculative Dictionary*
   Karen Pinkus

38 *What Would Animals Say If We Asked the Right Questions?*
   Vinciane Despret

37 *Manifestly Haraway*
   Donna J. Haraway

36 *Neofinalism*
   Raymond Ruyer

35 *Inanimation: Theories of Inorganic Life*
   David Wills

34 *All Thoughts Are Equal: Laruelle and Nonhuman Philosophy*
   John Ó Maoilearca

33 *Necromedia*
   Marcel O'Gorman

32 *The Intellective Space: Thinking beyond Cognition*
   Laurent Dubreuil

31 *Laruelle: Against the Digital*
   Alexander R. Galloway

30 *The Universe of Things: On Speculative Realism*
   Steven Shaviro

29 *Neocybernetics and Narrative*
   Bruce Clarke
28 *Cinders*
   Jacques Derrida
27 *Hyperobjects: Philosophy and Ecology after the End of the World*
   Timothy Morton
26 *Humanesis: Sound and Technological Posthumanism*
   David Cecchetto
25 *Artist Animal*
   Steve Baker
24 *Without Offending Humans: A Critique of Animal Rights*
   Élisabeth de Fontenay
23 *Vampyroteuthis Infernalis: A Treatise, with a Report by the Institut Scientifique de Recherche Paranaturaliste*
   Vilém Flusser and Louis Bec
22 *Body Drift: Butler, Hayles, Haraway*
   Arthur Kroker
21 *HumAnimal: Race, Law, Language*
   Kalpana Rahita Seshadri
20 *Alien Phenomenology, or What It's Like to Be a Thing*
   Ian Bogost
19 *CIFERAE: A Bestiary in Five Fingers*
   Tom Tyler
18 *Improper Life: Technology and Biopolitics from Heidegger to Agamben*
   Timothy C. Campbell
17 *Surface Encounters: Thinking with Animals and Art*
   Ron Broglio
16 *Against Ecological Sovereignty: Ethics, Biopolitics, and Saving the Natural World*
   Mick Smith
15 *Animal Stories: Narrating across Species Lines*
   Susan McHugh
14 *Human Error: Species-Being and Media Machines*
   Dominic Pettman
13 *Junkware*
   Thierry Bardini
12 *A Foray into the Worlds of Animals and Humans*, with *A Theory of Meaning*
   Jakob von Uexküll
11 *Insect Media: An Archaeology of Animals and Technology*
   Jussi Parikka
10 *Cosmopolitics II*
   Isabelle Stengers
 9 *Cosmopolitics I*
   Isabelle Stengers

8 *What Is Posthumanism?*
  Cary Wolfe
7 *Political Affect: Connecting the Social and the Somatic*
  John Protevi
6 *Animal Capital: Rendering Life in Biopolitical Times*
  Nicole Shukin
5 *Dorsality: Thinking Back through Technology and Politics*
  David Wills
4 *Bíos: Biopolitics and Philosophy*
  Roberto Esposito
3 *When Species Meet*
  Donna J. Haraway
2 *The Poetics of DNA*
  Judith Roof
1 *The Parasite*
  Michel Serres

Karen Pinkus is professor of Romance studies and comparative literature at Cornell University. She is author of *Fuel: A Speculative Dictionary* (Minnesota, 2016).

Ingram Content Group UK Ltd.
Milton Keynes UK
UKHW022315090423
419890UK00003B/7